BALZAC ᴛᴏ BECKETT

BALZAC to BECKETT

Center and Circumference
in French Fiction

LEO BERSANI

New York

OXFORD UNIVERSITY PRESS

1970

for Ulysse Dutoit

ACKNOWLEDGMENTS

I am grateful to the John Simon Guggenheim Memorial Foundation for awarding me in 1967–68 a Fellowship which allowed me to complete a substantial part of this book. I would also like to thank Rutgers University for granting me a leave of absence during that time.

I am greatly indebted to Eléonore M. Zimmermann for her suggestions concerning the revisions for several chapters. I am also thankful to Marcelle Gindre for help in translating passages from the writers I quote.

Parts of my sections on Flaubert, Camus, and Robbe-Grillet have appeared, in somewhat modified form, in *Partisan Review*, *The Massachusetts Review*, *Novel: A Forum on Fiction*, and *The Yale Review*.

L. B.

New York, N. Y.
June, 1970

CONTENTS

BALZAC to BECKETT

INTRODUCTION

Who is Honoré de Balzac? Who is Marcel Proust? Who is Samuel Beckett? Names expose but also encourage the deceit of designation. They are philosophically harmless tokens of differentiation in human communities as long as we think of them as corresponding to merely partial or contingent attributes of particular lives. The name Miller posits no ontological mysteries if it refers to nothing more than a man's trade; and the title of Duc de Borgogne, however full of historical associations it may become, designates an accident of birth rather than an essence of being. But it requires an effort for us to think so modestly of names. We are like the young Marcel in *A la Recherche du temps perdu*: the names of people and of places contain and promise fixed, coherent personalities. To say a name is to totalize an existence. Even empty of content, the name comforts us with the prospect of a conceptual unity behind a world of bewilderingly fragmented phenomena.

With other people, that unity is what we call personality or self. More generally, we live in a culture where it has been

assumed for more than two thousand years that the world is a
sign of truth. Significance precedes experience, which is both
expressive and deceptive and which therefore needs to be de-
coded or interpreted. No one has ever perceived an identity; it is
behind phenomena, and the latter are self-effacing signs which
point to their invisible source. Experience is a mystery story in a
world where the truth is always a hidden referent. The proto-
type of Western civilization is *Oedipus Rex*: all things are puzzling enigmas, but behind the enigmas lie the perfectly designed
plans of human destinies.

In recent years, Michel Foucault and Jacques Derrida have
provided the most brilliant analyses of the history and consequences of those habits of thought of which I have just given
the barest outline.[1] My own concern in this study will be the
much more limited one of discussing some major examples of
French fiction from Balzac to Beckett. But even a partial survey
of one literary form in Western culture can obviously not be
detached from our culture's fundamental assumptions about the
organization of experience. It is, after all, easy enough to recognize how pervasive those assumptions are in all areas of human
discourse. Nothing is more commonplace, for example, than the
generally invidious distinction between an apparent self and a
real self. We can, to be sure, often make valid distinctions between what someone says and what he means, between a detect-
able lie and an indisputable truth. But to be indirect or even
devious is not to be unreal, although we tend to deduce from
deceitful behavior a self more authentic than its manifestations.
We encourage people "to be themselves"—an injunction which
dismisses large chunks of their lives and which, it seems to me,
proceeds from a prejudicially normative view of what it means
simply "to be." The apparently benevolent call for spontaneity
is, on the surface, also an appeal for more varied responses to

1. In Foucault, *Les Mots et les choses/Une Archéologie des sciences humaines*, in Bibliothèque des sciences humaines (Paris, 1966); and Derrida, *De la Grammatologie* (Paris, 1967).

the world. But spontaneity is of course impossible to verify, and the word is often a moral reward for behavior conforming to an already established ideal of behavior. Our supposedly suppressed real self is the moral component of the neatly unified identity evoked by a name. If names create a neutral space ready to be filled with totalizing notions of identity, much of our everyday psychological language impoverishes life even more effectively by defining the content of authentic identity. Supposedly descriptive psychology ("you're not being yourself now") is, to say the least, moral exhortation, and—to say the worst—moral tyranny.

Professional psychological theory can, unfortunately, be a dignified version of the widespread and unreflective banalities I have just referred to. What, for example, is meant by the statement that emotionally "sick" persons lack a sense of self? The peculiarity of this notion can be felt if we ask someone we judge *not* to be sick to define the self he presumably has a sense of. We should, I think, at least consider the possibility that emotional sickness consists in the very need to have fixed, stable self-definitions, instead of inferring from the disturbed person's complaint of having no sense of self a securely fixed notion of identity in comparatively undisturbed individuals. In literature, Proust is particularly instructive in this respect. Marcel's anguish derives from his inability to immobilize a permanently recognizable image of himself, but, as we shall see, the "literary cure" of this anguish consists in an ability to renounce the very need for such images. Marcel the writer is able to enact the self along such a variety of surfaces that it tends to disappear in its own enriching diffusions. The healthy self may be a superficial self—one relatively unconstrained in its acts by a "profound" identity which would make each act dully similar to all the others.

But we hunger for fixed identities, and, since great literature tends to dissolve personalities (that of the author and, as far as easy definitions go, even that of its most memorable characters), we may prefer biography to literature. If biography is more popular than criticism, it is not simply because criticism tends to be more difficult to read than the reconstruction of a man's life. Criticism is a bastard exercise, a halfway stop on the road to identity. The critic reformulates the work's sense, but even when he serves meaning up in the most satisfactorily reductive and definitive way (the whale in *Moby Dick* symbolizes evil, a Faulkner character is Christ), he has really not given us the source and the key to the very creation of the work. Only the biographer gives us the Hemingway or the Balzac behind those enigmatic performances called *The Sun Also Rises* and *La Comédie humaine*. What could be more puzzling than the cover of a novel? "*Le Cousin Pons*, by Honoré de Balzac": where is Honoré de Balzac in *Le Cousin Pons*? Is he in the narrator, the heroes, the villains—or elusively and perversely spread out among all of them? The biographer has a comforting answer to such questions: Balzac is in the biography of Balzac. The work is the phenomenological enigma which becomes negligible once we possess the identity which the work expresses in ways so exasperatingly difficult to conceptualize. But would we now be willing to conclude that when we say: "I like Balzac" or "I like Proust," we mean that we like the biographies of André Maurois and of George D. Painter? Obviously not; and since we will naturally continue to use such expressions, biography is no help at all to us in our efforts to know that mysterious figure somehow different both from the stories of his novels and from the man who once lived and for whom the novels were only a part of his existence.

To what extent can the self be discussed nonreferentially in criticism? More generally, can literary criticism offer a model for discussions of experience which elucidate sense from and within the visible gestures of behavior (literary and nonliterary) rather than from the supposed antecedents or sources of those gestures? The attempt to answer these questions is complicated from the very start by the hardly surprising fact that writers share the assumptions about reality characteristic of their culture. If people prefer a biography of Balzac or a history of the French Restoration to *La Comédie humaine,* it is partly the fault of Balzac himself. In his *Avant-propos,* he presents his fiction as a trustworthy document of social reality; why, then, should we not prefer the reality to the fiction? The *Avant-propos* does provide an answer: *La Comédie humaine* extracts the hidden meanings of the life it imitates. But do the novels really profit from such a claim? Balzac refers us to a reality outside his work as a criterion for judging his work; at the same time, the reality is subordinated to a novelistic distillation of its significance. We seesaw from one to the other. Society is behind the novel, and the novel tells us what is behind society, but to look at either one is to feel its deficiency. The value of *La Comédie humaine* depends on a world whose value is expressed only in *La Comédie humaine* . . .

In Proust, the validity of novelistic creation (and of self-creation) is subverted by the narrator's interest in universal laws of human behavior. The aphorisms of *A la Recherche du temps perdu* introduce the psychological fatality behind the work into the work itself. They are a way of announcing the purely illustrative nature of fiction, and the happily unrealized aspiration they reveal is that of dissolving time, particularity, and self-renewal in the adequate formulation of the laws determining the monotonous phenomena which merely reflect them. Even Beckett, who seems anxious to break with the dualisms of realistic art when he proclaims his dream of an art expressive of nothing at all, is haunted in his work by the fantasy of a self hidden far behind a language whose inventiveness he acknowledges only with despair. Beckett is as much a realist as Balzac—with the difference that he is constantly reminding us that he is *not* telling us "how it is." But somewhere outside the work lies the work's subject (a perfectly Balzacian proposition). The change in consciousness from Balzac to Beckett involves a change in the writer's confidence about bringing that subject into the work. For Balzac, fiction is the infinitely expandable container for the reality of the universe. For Beckett, fiction is a progressively impoverished speech, a movement toward blather, incoherence, and finally silence, designed to remind us of the supreme value of a permanently inexpressible reality.

The loss of confidence in the expressiveness of language which Beckett illustrates most spectacularly today is, of course, not a sudden phenomenon in the history of fiction. I think that the most interesting continuities and revolts in major French novelists since Balzac can be discussed in terms of the ways these writers have dramatized their questions or assumptions about the correspondences between language and reality in fiction. And by "interesting" I mean that the history of those assumptions may help us to define the extent to which we want to revise or dispense with them *now*—revise or dispense with them in adopting styles of life, in the writing of literature, and even (as I will presently explain) in the more modest activity of choosing a method of literary criticism.

Balzacian and Stendhalian fiction is obviously not closer to "reality" than the work of Virginia Woolf or of Djuna Barnes. Every human act expresses someone's sense of reality, and, in that sense, is realistic. What we call realism in the novel refers to certain kinds of novelistic subjects, to a certain mode of narrative presentation, and, most fundamentally, to assumptions *about* the "place" of reality in words. The narrator of a realistic novel reports on the lives of his principal characters in the context of social images which we are expected to recognize as accurate reflections of life in society at a particular moment and in a particular place. In the ideal realistic novel, there would be no confusion of identity between the narrator and his story. Realistic fiction thrives on secure dualisms: there is reality and the copy (or interpretation) of reality, and there is the observer and the world he is observing. It is easy enough, as we shall see, to find in Balzacian society a massive metaphor for private fantasies about the dangerous power of will and desire, but the fantasy-like quality of social life in *La Comédie humaine* has no effect on the *narrator's* sense of documenting a reality external to himself. His constant digressive intrusions into his story only confirm the security with which he feels removed from the story: his involvements are judgmental rather than ontological. He gives us information, he condemns and praises, but his entire work is supported by the confident assumptions that words "carry" nonverbal realities, and that they can be used to describe accurately realities distinct from the author's self.

Stendhal's image of the novel as a mirror reflects a similar confidence, although his curious remark, in the first preface to *Lucien Leuwen*, that "the hero's passion" is an exception to that law creates a new problem. Stendhal likes to present his realism as a painful obligation: he would be unfaithful to the life of his times if he didn't continue to bore us with the petty details of political intrigue. But we will see that the relation of politics to passion in *La Chartreuse de Parme* undermines Stendhal's use of the mirror as a metaphor for the derivative nature of his social images. The happiness-politics polarity in Stendhal's fiction suggests that the nature of political life in Stendhal is part of an *imaginary* structure created within the novel itself rather than a reflection of life outside the novel. Stendhal's report on society may, of course, include shrewd observations about European politics, but in *La Chartreuse* it operates most profoundly as a function of the hero's passion—that is, within the thematic scheme of Stendhal's self-dramatization. And politics reduced, or rather promoted, to the status of fantasy helps Stendhal to make of his novel an exercise in self-creation. If political life, like the dream of passion, has only a minimal responsibility to what is already on the road of life before the novelist walks along it with his mirror, then the novelist has a greater chance of changing it by his imaginative responses to it. Our ability to transform the world, and the self, perhaps depends on what may seem like a naïvely unrealistic aptitude for seeing and expressing the world as a metaphor for the self.

The crisis in realistic fiction generally associated with Flaubert proceeds from a simple but unsettling question about the effects of fiction: what, Flaubert asks in *Madame Bovary*, do people respond to in art? Emma Bovary provides a nice critique of Marshall McLuhan's notion of how cultural products are received in an age dominated by the printed word. She (undoubtedly like the vast majority of people) is anything but a slave to the consequences of linearity in literature. The messages she receives from books are neither verbal nor conceptual; instead, they are images of sensory gratifications which language inspires but to which the quality of particular uses of language is irrelevant. Nothing is more natural; but we can understand that for the writer nothing may appear more bizarre than this peculiar metamorphosis of the words he plays with into the material settings for real passions. Emma is the most serious realist imaginable. Art is the vehicle for experiences which already exist and which, somewhere in the world, must be waiting for the superior provincial housewife to come and enjoy them.

The banal story of this rather banal woman is the occasion for a major crisis in the history of literature, for, however silly she may be, Emma raises the question for Flaubert of how *any* use of language can correspond to the exact nature of realities richer than or at least different from language. If Emma is ridiculous, does that mean that art is not a mirror of reality? If that is the case, what *are* the inspirations of art, and what is the bizarre nature of an imagination capable of endlessly producing, but whose productions are perhaps determined and structured by nothing external to itself? But perhaps Emma has simply read the wrong books. In that case, the superior writer would be the man capable of fitting his words to the way things really are. But is there a way of knowing which perceptions or which intuitions are more real than others? And, if he should happen to have the right perceptions, how can the writer know which words are apt to express them most accurately? Flaubert's tortured interrogation of art proceeds from his need to know what and where its subjects are. The questions he asks are perhaps unnecessary ones, but to realize and accept even that will be a difficult victory—still not entirely won—for modern literature.

Proust's hero-narrator continues this meditation on (and potentially against) literature within the structure of an ambiguous autobiography. If the subject of a literary work is the writer's self, is the self remembered or invented? In memory itself, what is the relation between history and self-creation, as well as between the self and the external world? In a work intended as a kind of definitive memorial of the writer's essential self, the self-portrait is blurred by a mass of images apparently distinct from those reflecting Marcel's personality. On the other hand, there are continuities of nature among all the images of *A la Recherche* which suggest a continuity of being between the narrator and the world he is presumably remembering from his past. The self is documented as pictures of the world, and the very transparency of Marcel's self-projections points to what I shall be discussing as his techniques of self-expansion through an abundance of self-diffusing metaphors. Poised between a Balzacian or Flaubertian commitment to the use of literature as a medium which translates the real into language, and, on the other hand, the discovery that each compositional choice can help to create an unpredictable future for the self as well as for the work, Proust's narrator gives the most impressive performance we shall encounter of a self learning to be identified with projects irreducible to their supposed sources. In Proust, a proposed esthetic of incompleteness is equivalent to an ethic of incompleteness for a self too open to be defined—and confined—by the fixed design of a permanent identity.

The examples from more recent French fiction which I will be discussing could be thought of as enthusiastic or anguished responses to Proust's experiment in a literature willing to risk being deprecated, even dismissed as a result of the energy with which it contests and renews itself. I have suggested that the very notion that phenomena reflect or correspond to a reality behind them prejudices both our sense of what is possible and our reading of what we see. The understandable if not entirely logical assumption implicit in the belief in realities deeper than appearances is that if behavior is derivative, it is also intelligible. A personality explains an individual's acts; an artist's life provides the key to his work's coherence; or the obsessive themes of his imagination organize the artist's work into a unified design. The pursuit of *in*coherence in modern art can therefore be thought of as the most dramatic aspect of an attack against art's complicity with cultural myths about hidden realities as the designers of experience. The offbeat heroes of modern literature are not just symptomatic of a moral skepticism about the value or possibility of heroic behavior in modern society. They are experiments in psychological dislocation. If the novelist can prevent us from associating figures in his work with accepted notions of personality, he can perhaps also force us to participate with him in demolishing some of the supposed boundaries of personality. What is bizarre, trivial, and irresponsible in behavior thus assumes a function far more important than the content of such behavior. If inconsistent or eccentric gestures cannot be fitted into a unified psychological portrait, personality has the chance of appearing admirably insignificant—by which we can mean that particular performances will continuously disrupt general definitions. Each moment will revise significance rather than confirm an already fixed significance.

This sort of experimentation in fiction has, of course, taken various forms, from the psychologically uninteresting ingenuities which plot the remarkable fictions of Raymond Roussel to the (theoretically) indeterminate characters of Sartre's *Les Chemins de la liberté*, to the (again theoretically) neutral "describers" in the novels of Robbe-Grillet. Even a writer as essentially conventional as Camus provided a source of inspiration for the "floating" characters of more radical novelists by allowing Meursault's fairly intelligible personality, in *L'Etranger,* to be partly subverted by a liberating superficiality of motive. As we shall see in

Robbe-Grillet, superficiality is a perhaps ideal if inaccessible goal in the struggle I'm speaking of to free both characters in fiction from established schemes of identity, and fiction itself from being tested against realities supposedly more authoritative than literature and which literature is expected to copy. While Proust indicates the possibility of a freedom (for the self and for the novel) which would deny neither history nor even a certain kind of psychological depth, the most extreme versions of freedom proposed in contemporary fiction involve such radical self-contestations that literature may tend to disappear along its suicidally inventive surfaces. With Borges, Robert Pinget, and Robbe-Grillet, we have become accustomed to a kind of writing which constantly denies its own affirmations. Or, in Thomas Pynchon's *V.*, we have the best example since Roussel of a work so "occupied" by the ingenuities of structural or anecdotal play that it seems entirely unpressured by any obsessional themes, that is, by anything we might ordinarily think of as the writer's self.

How can we talk about such fiction? The works I have just referred to are both aggressively self-destructive and aggressively self-protective. The apparent frivolity of the games they play with their own unimportant meanings could also be thought of as a defiant *noli me tangere*. The critic hungry for significance is reduced to paraphrasing plot or to unraveling puzzles of spatial design; but will he be able to resist the temptation to interpret the design? If not, he falls into the well-set trap of inferring meaning from a carefully plotted construction. The work has perversely encouraged the pleasure of interpretation as a reward for the labor of rearranging surfaces. Many modern works, as Robbe-Grillet has suggested, seem to be proposing an esthetic of disappointment.[2] They are enigmatic, but their enigmas are false or impenetrable ones. Roussel's explanations of the miraculous machines in his novels explain the functioning of the machines rather than their possibility (which is the only real mystery);

2. See Alain Robbe-Grillet, "Temps et description dans le récit d'aujourd'hui," *Pour un nouveau roman*, in Collection Idées (Paris, 1963), p. 160.

nothing in *La Jalousie* guarantees the *truth* of the events and feelings which we can reconstruct from the novel's descriptions.

Now in a sense art depends on criticism, if we understand "criticism" in the broadest sense: even the most hermetic, least widely distributed work of art is a public act, and its existence *as* a work is confirmed only by someone's response to it. (In the most restricted confrontation imaginable, the artist himself becomes his own critical public as soon as the work has "left" him and he begins to look at it—to formulate it in other terms, to appreciate and judge it—as an object external to himself. Criticism begins with *reenactment.*) To assault the reader and to frustrate his expectations can never be attempts to do away with the reader. Rather, the aggressive tactics of modern art reveal perhaps more clearly than ever before the vulnerability of art to the ways in which it is talked about. Such tactics are efforts to change the nature of art by changing the nature of critical participation in art. By disappointing traditional expectations of more or less reliable meanings, modern works are first of all undermining their own prestige—a prestige conferred on art by the critical habit of treating it as a privileged conveyor of the significance of experience. The inconclusive critic will define and, in a way, even create the inconclusive work. Criticism, it goes without saying, also depends on art, and both its categories of analysis and its criteria of judgment are, originally, *descriptive* of the assumptions about art's nature and value implicit in art itself. The modern work, by making a mockery of secure interpretations, redefines itself as a tentative, self-contesting, even self-effacing process of proposing equally tentative and self-contesting ways of describing it.

That process is, it seems to me, an immensely exciting exercise in freedom. The kind of self-dismissal I'm speaking of is an experiment in diminishing the constraints of past behavior on present and future behavior. It is a way of proclaiming that art is not the servant of realities already constituted, and that criticism itself can perhaps best participate in art by a certain disrespect for the established object of art as well as for its own established readings. At the extreme, art would be the sacrificial model for critical reinventions of art; and criticism would ultimately inspire the critic out of criticism—into the testing of art's self-revising inventiveness in the multiple contexts of his own life. Art would then no longer have the permanent value of definitive statements *about* life; rather, it would turn us away from itself and toward the use of its freedoms for the invention of new realities in our lives.

It may seem perverse to preface a book of criticism by promising the disappearance of criticism. But of course it is only the practice of criticism which reveals when particular critical acts are sufficiently generous and creative to "deserve" to disappear. Furthermore, we could say that an esthetic of disappointment and disappearance promises the *universalizing* of art and criticism rather than their end. "Art is life," Robbe-Grillet says simply[3]— which is a way of encouraging us to transform life into an art of self-renewal. Extraordinarily optimistic, such statements confer on art the power to promote revolutions in the self and in the world. And they do this by the very same stroke with which they demolish the freakishly exceptional or sacred quality astutely attributed to art by a conservative Platonic esthetic. But it would obviously be foolish to think that we already live in a culture structured by a kind of continuous dialectic among mutually contesting experiments in expanding and renewing the forms of our experience. When we must pay a fee in order to *contemplate* an Oldenberg soft hamburger on display in the New York Museum of Modern Art, when objects mildly satiric of the objects we consume (objects ideally suited for advertising: they would promote sales by gracing an economic coercion with humor) are placed as if they were the *David,* we quickly enough realize how many interests are vested in the effort to prevent the secularization of art.

3. "Du réalisme à la réalité," *Pour un nouveau roman,* p. 173.

Finally, it would be a tyrannical denial of the very freedom
we are, hopefully, anxious to promote if we were to equate new
ways of thinking about art with a refusal to think about anything
but new art. To throw the Rembrandts out of a museum and to
hang hammered car parts in their place is to prefer bad art to
good art, and not at all to redefine our relation to art. For the
study of fiction, is there a critical method which (if this is necessary) will soothe our conscience about continuing to enjoy
Balzac, which will approach him in ways reflecting our interest
in assumptions about art essentially alien to Balzac, but which
will also make evident why we have chosen now to read and
discuss Balzac?

Works of art tend to repeat, in their structure, the tension I
have discussed between referential or derivative art and "superficial," projective art. In each of the novels I will be considering,
there is a thematic structure which criticism can articulate and
which we might be inclined to designate as the writer's self *in*
that novel. Now the self has been the most referential concept in
criticism, a concept analogous to the premise in realistic art that
its material derives from and is responsible to realities anterior to
art. Even when the self has been defined as an imaginary structure wholly contained within the artist's work (so that biographical data would be unnecessary and perhaps even misleading),
criticism has tended to go behind the work even while staying
within the work by implicitly setting up a dualism between narrative surface and psychological depth. This seems to me true of
the best French thematic criticism (as it is practiced by Jean-
Pierre Richard, Georges Poulet, Jean Starobinski, and Roland
Barthes in his book on Racine and in some of the pieces in *Essais
critiques*). This criticism has been a brilliantly executed experiment in separating the notion of self from biography in literary
studies. Starobinski's "Rousseau" and Richard's "Flaubert" are
not the biographer's Rousseau or Flaubert; they are profound
and secret thematic selves which inform the writer's work but
which the language of the work does not explicitly express. The

critic uncovers a particular psychological unity which Richard has defined as "a concrete organizing principle, a fixed pattern or object, around which a universe would tend to crystallize and unfold itself." [4] But even in the subtlest working out of the history of these hidden projects, the X-raying of contexts in particular works leads the critic to equate (and reduce) the writer's self to its principal theme. The latter is a recurrent pattern to which local choices of composition can not only be referred but in the light of which they can be reinterpreted—or perhaps simply ignored.

Thematic criticism does, it seems to me, liberate possibilities within the work in a way which diversifies our responses to the work. I have read few essays on literary figures more exciting than those written by the men I have just mentioned. And I certainly prefer such criticism to structuralist analyses of supposed narrative laws which belong to no writer in particular but which presumably govern every narrative before it is begun. But we can easily see a certain complicity between thematic and structuralist (or myth-oriented) approaches to literature. What these approaches have in common is an emphasis on what I will call *centers* in art—personal obsessions or formal laws or archetypal behavior—from which particular performances "radiate" and *back to which* the critic draws the work. Individual books are satellites which create circumferences around centers of personality (or of literary forms or mythic modes of thought and feeling). The critic, on the other hand, collaborates with the centripetal movement in each work which would "return" it to its original design. The center focuses the work—but it also makes it appear somewhat unnecessary.

The esthetic ideal—which is also a psychological and a moral ideal—proposed by Robbe-Grillet in *Pour un nouveau roman* would involve the elimination of such centers both in art and in the rest of life. The only reference in the present to the past (and

4. *L'Univers imaginaire de Mallarmé* (Paris, 1961), p. 24.

therefore the only continuity with the past) would be one of contestation. But however vitalizing our reaction against a psychology and a literature of sources may be, it seems to me impossible, now at any rate, to confront a work of art or indeed any experience at all without feeling the constraints of the *already given* on human behavior. The strength of the realistic premise as I have been defining it undoubtedly derives from our perhaps invincible sense of reality not only as something which we create but also as something which in part determines what we create. At the very least, particular acts are performed by bodies, and the chemistry and mere mass of our bodies preclude any definition of freedom as pure, unconstrained invention. Similarly, as long as we cannot conceive of not dying, the fact of time which, whatever else it may lead to, must also lead to death, provides a permanent theme for every life to which every act, however evasively, remains responsible. The body and mortality are thus the centers in life which create the magnetic field from which no human project has as yet escaped.

In literary criticism, the search for more or less determining themes is not necessarily reductive. In the same way that a man's choices in life do reflect or refer to the impossibility of living forever, the writer's fictive selves appear never to profit from the total freedom they might enjoy in their purely verbal existence. Necessity exists even in the weightless universe of words. In part, that necessity can be accounted for by the linguistic systems to which words belong. I think it can also be accounted for in more personal terms. Some fantasy or obsessional structure persists throughout the work, and while it may be arbitrary to identify the content of that fantasy as a key to the writer's life, it operates within his work as a sign of those psychological continuities in an individual's history which probably define the limits of his power to ignore history. The thematic center in a novel becomes, in the course of the novel, an analogue for those realities in life which partially chart an unpredictable future according to the designs of some permanent constraints.

But none of the novels we will be looking at can be adequately accounted for in terms of their thematic centers. My commitment to the kind of open-ended, projective, and self-contesting art I spoke of a moment ago will be expressed by a critical emphasis on those occasions in fiction which tend to disintegrate theme. If we can speak metaphorically of certain repeated designs in a novel as revealing a centripetal movement toward its center, we can also indicate a centrifugal pull which opens up the novel by multiplying the rays of interest *away* from the center. Of course, thematic criticism has not limited itself to disengaging fixed structures. It emphasizes "points of departure" and proposes a kind of itinerary for the writer's most fundamental obsessions or projects. The very organization of Poulet's essays on Proust and Richard's study of Flaubert is a hypothesis about psychic dynamics. Criticism gives a linear version (in temporal metaphors) of the writer's continuous attempt to imagine "solutions," of his experiments in both realizing and transforming the hidden projects which inform all his behavior. But even the solutions remain within the orbit of the "concrete organizing principle"; indeed, they seem to be contained within the logic of the problem itself, and thematic criticism, having defined the problem, could perhaps unfold its history without ever referring again to the writer's own words . . . But the centrifugal movement I just referred to is most authentically liberating when it creates a *dis-*continuity between its own satellites and a center to which the satellites seem no longer attracted. Each satellite, as it were, throws off other satellites further and further away from the orbit of the original planet. The extensions and diversity of circumferential points would not only subvert the meaning at the center; at the extreme, it would silence all interpretation and make the critic continue the novel by inventing his own life.

I have suggested a provisional definition of freedom: the ability to respond to particular occasions in ways too elusive or diversified to be covered by any interpretation of them. That is, we act freely when specific performances are more interesting than the themes which can perhaps be detected in all of them, when what can be said about only *this* passage in our lives successfully competes with what can be said about the text of an entire life. The justification of close, contextual reading in literary criticism (as a complement to the reading of thematic structures) is that the artist's range of inventiveness, like our range of freedom in life, can perhaps best be measured by the number of ways in which, at any moment, he can be different from himself.

In literature, the ways are of course always verbal. Much has been said recently—I will return to this in my chapters on Flaubert and on Beckett—about the impersonality of language. Language is a system constituted before I use it; therefore, the argument goes, it is not I who am speaking but rather language which speaks through me. But while this is obviously true in a general sense, it seems to me significant that the defenders of this really not so new dogma have an aversion to examining particular uses of language. The use of language does involve a certain depersonalizing of the personal; my words inevitably generalize my biological and psychological specificity. But the study of literature shows that the very generality of language can serve the cause of self-invention. As we shall see most clearly in Stendhal and in Proust, particular verbal occasions can *divert* the writer away from the monotony of thematic depth in his work. Stendhal's irony and Proust's humor are created by their willingness to play, even superficially, with what language gives them. And that play creates their style, that is, what is most intensely personal in their writing. Language provides therapeutic distractions from the self as theme. While it of course also expresses the laws of its own grammar and lends itself to the activity of structuring (and making rigid) psychological laws, language has such a fantastic potential for local variety that it also lends itself to the creation of countless individual styles. The self in a literary work is a tension between a minimally diversified use of language for the repetition of obsessional themes, and a maximally diversified use of language which dissolves theme in the succession of richly superficial, mutually contesting selves. Language will always violate an ineffable, "essential" self which I ask words merely to translate; but, because of this happy inexpressiveness, language allows me to ventilate and re-create the self as multiple stylistic textures, textures which seem, almost miraculously, to detach themselves from the psychological fabric on which they have been woven.

But the literary history I will be tracing is marked by reactions against such self-creative uses of language—or, to put it more brutally (and somewhat unjustly), by reactionary nostalgias for centers of reality before all expression. To locate this nostalgia in Flaubert and in Beckett is not to say—and hopefully my discussions of their work will confirm this—that Stendhal and Robbe-Grillet are better or greater writers that Flaubert and Beckett. If it is still necessary to point out that a biased criticism (is there any other?) can include the appreciation of enterprises working against its own biases, then I gladly say it most emphatically. My point about Flaubert and Beckett can be briefly introduced here through a distinction between two views of the mode of art's disappearance. For Robbe-Grillet, the self-negating nature of art is a function of its revolutionary nature. It contests itself and silences criticism in order to leave the field open for further inventions, for versions of reality unimagined in the work itself. But, opposed to this, there is an ideal of silence inspired by the yearning for a center of being behind *all* centers. Flaubert and Beckett help to kill the realistic novel by the very profundity of their commitment to realism. They recognize with anguish what Balzac could not believe in: the *inventive* power of words. The protagonists of Balzac's *Le Lys dans la vallée* experiment unsuccessfully with that power, and their failure confirms Balzac's faith in language as a reflector rather than an inventor of reality. Flaubert, on the other hand, writes what looks like realistic fiction in a constant state of anxiety about the very possibility of what he is presumably doing. The centripetal movement in *Madame Bovary* is toward an obsession with the very notion of centers or sources themselves. Language is *dangerously* centrifugal, and in Beckett we see the ultimate consequence of this attitude: the effort to mutilate language until it becomes so insignificant and so boring that it will no longer distract us from a self which all expression violates.

Flaubert and Beckett raise questions for literature which are by no means pertinent only to literature.[5] If language does not accurately designate preexistent truths about the self and the world, are we then condemned to a mindless asceticism designed to draw us back to the nothingness of "pure," inexpressed reality? Or, as another alternative, should we agree to obey, just as mindlessly and passively, impersonal laws (of language, of a universal unconscious) which represent more "scientific" versions of realities determining human behavior? A retreat into pure selfhood, or the servitude of a depersonalized mind programmed according to laws it did not invent: are these the only alternatives to a faith in our ability to know truths which Western civilization had trained us to think of as secretly designing the vicissitudes of personal and social histories? Oriental mysticism, or the loss of self in the structures of language, myth, and, of course, contemporary media. Silence, or a new ethic in which structural coherence is accorded the moral prestige of the old myths of truth. The face of necessity changes, but its appeal is apparently immeasurable. If we can no longer have the designs of Providence, we seem only too anxious, say, to settle for those of electronic engineering as a way of eliminating the margin of freedom in human choices.

Does the margin really exist? How can it be recognized? And can an individual's local acts of inventiveness compete for our interest with a pattern (a structure or a central source) which

5. For a good discussion of "the result of our mistrust of symbols, language and consequently, the mind itself," from a psychologist's point of view, see John H. Gagnon in "Insight and Outlook," *Partisan Review*, XXXIV (Summer, 1967), 400–414.

can find a place for everything (except, of course, the fullness of our responses at particular moments of our history)? From the point of view of these questions, the novelists we are about to look at illustrate poignantly the conflicting appeals of coherence and of freedom, of the use of history to fill out designs or to expand designs by continuously shattering and reinventing them. Art may be the best argument we have for the pleasures of centrifugal play.

I

THE TAMING OF TIGERS
[Balzac and *Le Lys dans la vallée*]

Balzac makes us uneasy. *Le Père Goriot* and *Eugénie Grandet* continue to find their way into undergraduate survey courses on the novel, but how many American and English readers would put Balzac in the same class as Stendhal, Flaubert, and Proust? The Balzacian types (Goriot, "the Christ of Paternity" [1]; Lucien de Rubempré, the beautiful, will-less poet; Valérie Marneffe, the wily, irresistible courtesan) certainly seem like rather crude inventions if we measure them against Julien Sorel, Emma Bovary, and Charles Swann. The case against Balzac is an easy one to make: his psychology is abstract and reductive, his thought is childish, he often writes sloppily and incoherently, and he has a garish, melodramatic view of social life. Martin Turnell, who finds Balzac inferior not only to Stendhal but also to Benjamin Constant, would probably subscribe to this indictment of a novel-

1. Honoré de Balzac, *Le Père Goriot*, in *La Comédie humaine*, ed. Marcel Bouteron and (for vol. XI) Roger Pierrot, 11 vols. (Paris, 1935–59), II, p. 1026. Subsequent references to *La Comédie humaine* will be to this edition. All translations in this chapter are my own.

ist whose interests, he tells us, "are by no means always those of an adult." [2] For most of us, Balzac is such a massive presence in the history of French fiction that we would probably admit his importance provided we do not have to defend it. Is Balzac, in fact, any good? What are the grounds for his greatness?

Balzac's writing both undermines and reinforces an extraordinarily schematic view of fiction. There is, to begin with, the familiar Balzacian exposition. In its purest form, Balzac's method involves an almost comical closing in on the subject of his story. As in countless films from the '30's and the '40's (where, say, we move from an air view of Manhattan to a particular district and street to a particular building to a floor in that building and, finally, to an office on that floor where the actors are "waiting" for us), Balzac proceeds from the largest to the smallest enclosures, settling at last in that human mind which, we discover, is the real center of its *milieu*. The method expresses, first of all, a view of the correspondences between people and their environments which may strike us now as a sociological cliché, but which Balzac was the first novelist to use systematically in the portrayal of character. Since, as he writes in the *Avant-propos*, ". . . man . . . tends to represent his customs, his thought and his life in everything which he appropriates to his needs," [3] the description of those things which serve his needs—his clothing, his furniture, his home—is a way of entering a character's mind. Conversely, every *milieu* has its physical and psychological effects: the *quartier* of the rue Neuve-Sainte-Geneviève—"that illustrious valley of crumbling plaster and of gutters black with mud" [4]— "explains" Madame Vauquer, in the same way as the world of finance explains Nucingen and the bad air of Parisian court-rooms has affected Popinot's complexion.

Now the schematic intelligibility of Balzac's work would be

2. *The Novel in France* (New York, 1951), p. 213.
3. I, *Avant-propos*, 5.
4. II, *Le Père Goriot*, 647.

much less interesting if we were not always aware of how seriously it is threatened. The outline and progress of his expositions suggest his concern for completeness and detail, and this appearance of orderly thoroughness may obscure the vagueness, the occasional incoherence, and the lack of detail in a Balzacian description. The introduction to the *quartier* of the Maison Vauquer in *Le Père Goriot* immediately creates that level of abstraction where much of the story will take place. The social scene is first of all a scene of moral allegory. Balzac describes

> a valley filled with real sufferings, with often false joys, and so dreadfully agitated that only something exorbitant can create a sensation which will last for a while. However, here and there one finds sorrows which the agglomeration of vices and virtues makes grand and solemn: at the sight of them, all the forms of egoism and self-interest stop and take pity; but the impression given by these sorrows is like a tasty fruit promptly devoured. The chariot of civilization, like that of the idol of Jaggernat, hardly delayed by a heart less easily pulverized than others and which jams its wheels, soon enough breaks that heart and continues on its glorious way.[5]

Balzac can certainly write better than this,[6] but it is perhaps just as well to face this sort of confusion and melodramatic vagueness from the start. He is, like Musset, a writer often more interesting than the rhetoric he uses. While Balzac proceeds in ways that tend to draw our attention to apparently autonomous passages (a character's portrait, a digression on bankruptcy or on the life of courtesans), the interest of such passages depends on the latent and explosive action which they seem to be indefinitely postponing. The action, we come to realize, is *there* like a delayed

5. II, 847–48.
6. His stylistic range is astonishing. There is, for example, in contrast to the passage just quoted, the Proustian density and humor of the portraits of Madame de Bargeton and Monsieur de Châtelet in the first part of *Illusions perdues,* or the acidly comic writing we find in *Le Cousin Pons,* where the style often has a Stendhalian abruptness or shock quality.

charge of dynamite. Balzac's descriptions, for all their superficial self-containment, have just as much impatient projectiveness as Stendhal's, although the question in Balzac seems to be less *what* the future will be than *when* it will take place as events rather than as narrative prescience. And, given his narrative organizations, Balzac does run the risk of arresting our attention over passages which make for rather embarrassed *explications de texte*. The best—and most generous—way of dealing with the passage I have quoted is to suspend our undoubtedly immediate condemnation of its silly, pompous style and merely to note the kind of impatience it suggests on Balzac's part with the structure in which it appears. The meticulous description of a Parisian *quartier* has no sooner begun than it becomes an excited evocation of moral phantoms.

Albert Béguin, among others, has spoken of how readily Balzac gives in to the suggestiveness of words.[7] Within the framework of a rigidly outlined exposition, the narrator allows himself to be diverted—amused and detoured—by local occasions for verbal excess. A weird rhythmical excitement replaces precision of detail. To describe the *odeur de pension* in Madame Vauquer's *salon*, Balzac writes: "It is a close, musty, rancid smell; it makes one cold, feels humid to the nose, penetrates one's clothes; it has the taste of a room where people have been dining; it stinks of meals, of the pantry, of the poorhouse." ("Elle sent le renfermé, le moisi, le rance; elle donne froid, elle est humide au nez, elle pénètre les vêtements; elle a le goût d'une salle où l'on a dîné; elle pue le service, l'office, l'hospice.")[8] By the end of the sentence, rhyme has obviously become more important than sense. Compared with the extraordinary distinctness and precision of descriptive language in Proust, Balzac's descriptions seem designed to substitute the dizzying effect of a scene for the visualization of that scene. This intention is comically explicit in the

7. *Balzac visionnaire* (1946), in *Balzac lu et relu*, preface by Gaëtan Picon (Paris, 1965), p. 129.
8. II, 851.

way Balzac cuts short his inventory of the furniture in Madame
Vauquer's dining room. His sentence is both precautionary and
extravagant: "To explain how old, cracked, rotten, trembling,
worm-eaten, one-armed, one-eyed, invalid, and expiring this furniture is, one would have to do a description of it which would
delay the interest of this story for too long, and which those who
are in a hurry would not forgive." ⁹ "One-armed," "one-eyed"
furniture: the words will bear very little attention, and we are
struck by the grossness of an attempt to dim our perception of a
scene for which the most elaborate descriptive apparatus has
been set up—largely, it seems, in order to be dismissed.

Balzac is impatient of details, and although his method obliges
him to give us a large number of them, his descriptions are far
less detailed than those of Flaubert, in whom detail often does
serve the function it is theoretically meant to serve in Balzac. The
object in Balzac is often simply skipped, and in its place we have
an impression of the object. The many references to what some
"observer" might have felt in looking at a person or a place in
La Comédie humaine is not just an obvious way of adding dramatic interest to long analytical passages. More interestingly, this
turning away from things at the very moment of elaborately
focusing on them suggests the immediacy with which Balzac's
imagination transforms objects and events into tokens of psychic
energy. In the following passage from *L'Interdiction*, the house
Popinot lives in does not merely reflect or help to explain life in
this part of Paris; instead of providing only the setting for a scene,
it actually becomes another character in that scene:

> Its solidity seems attested by an external configuration which it
> is not uncommon to see in some Parisian houses. If we may risk
> this expression, it has something like a belly produced by the
> swelling of its first story, sagging under the weight of the second
> and third stories, but supported by the strong wall of the ground
> floor. At first glance, it seems that the spaces between the win-

9. II, 851–52.

dows, although reinforced by their cut stone borders, are going to burst; but the observer soon notices that this house resembles the tower of Bologna in that its old bricks and corroded old stones invincibly preserve their center of gravity. In all seasons, the solid rows of the ground floor present the yellowish tint and the imperceptible oozing which dampness gives to stone. The passer-by feels cold as he walks along this wall whose notched protruding stones protect it poorly against the wheels of the cabriolets.[10]

The building is a sinister beast rather than an agglomeration of stones. It exercises its will (it keeps its center of gravity in spite of its grotesque belly, of the massive weight under which certain parts seem bound to burst); it has a sickly, yellowish complexion; and the passer-by, far from considering the house as a neutral object, feels its moral influence in his own chill and thoughts of prison.

The peculiar result of this typical animation of the external world in Balzac is to make the existence of that world somewhat uncertain. Balzac so rapidly invests the world with meaning that its independent existence is almost destroyed. Balzac's hallucinated vision of things breaks down that distinction between character and environment without which environment, having *become* character, no longer mediates it. Objects in *La Comédie humaine* are so fully, so literally alive that they participate in the drama in almost the same way as the human characters do. The correspondences between the self and the world which Balzac's expositions are meant to reveal turn out to be an equivalence in ontological status, and that equivalence often makes Balzac's world seem as abstract and as internal as Madame de La Fayette's.

This is of course somewhat excessive: the mere enumeration of things in Balzac, the obvious intention to describe environment in detail do make for an important difference. However rapidly Balzac allegorizes places and things, the very space given

10. III, *L'Interdiction,* 17–18.

to their ambiguous appearance suggests an immense effort to preserve their concrete distinctness. It is as if the explanatory virtue
of environment would be lost if its physical shapes were lost, that
is, if it were entirely transformed into impressions and acts of
will. The interest of Balzac's style, which is seldom in the quality
of individual images, lies in the tension between an extraordinarily neat scheme for preserving an order of differences (as we
proceed from large to small, from things to people, from external
to internal), and a tendency to disrupt the order by blurring the
distinctions among its various terms. If everything in a Balzacian
description from the *quartier* to a particular character's desires
were, so to speak, to have the same psychic charge, the very act of
disposing and containing psychic energy in things of the world
would be pointless. And Balzac's clear intention of massively
diversifying things and people in *La Comédie humaine* suggests
how important the processes of differentiation were to him. The
irreducible variety of forms in Balzac is just as much a creative
achievement as the unity which he sought to establish and which
he often spoke of in mystical terms. Unity is that "concordance
of things among themselves" which Balzac defined as "the simplest expression of order;" [11] but, to the extent that it blurs individual presences and identities, complete unity could also be
thought of as a threat to order and to composition.

We are beginning to see the interplay, the trying out of various
types of order in *La Comédie humaine*. The exposition is designed as an exhaustive view of everything which surrounds and
explains a human act; it is meant both to establish correspondences between character and *milieu* and also to preserve the distinctness of detail in a tableau whose very diversity would make
its harmonies all the more impressive. The allegorization of environment is the dangerous short-cut to those harmonies. It de-
materializes the world of things and in so doing subverts the
possibility of proceeding *from* things *to* people. The very rigidity
of the Balzacian outline suggests a somewhat frantic defense

11. V, *La Duchesse de Langeais,* 145.

against the vagueness, the incoherence, the prompt allegories which threaten to substitute a mere manifestation of energy for its containment and visualization in an ordered tableau. Balzac's world runs the risk of disappearing in order to serve the narrator's appetite for possession. The writing of fiction provides ideal occasions for indulging that appetite, but Balzac's novelistic experiments are also attempts to imagine ways of saving the world from his own voraciousness.

The nature of this threat is particularly clear in Balzac's analogies between the human and the animal worlds. It is typical of his naïveté as a theoretician that he considered his animalization of human behavior as a scientific approach to social relations. *Le Père Goriot* is dedicated to Geoffroy Saint-Hilaire, and in the *Avant-propos* Balzac adopts the zoologist's theory of a "unity of composition" at the origin of animal species for his own portrait of society. There is, he writes, a single model or pattern for all organized beings; differences are the results of adaptation to different environments. There are Zoological and Social Species; as the naturalist's task is to classify the former group, the novelist will study and classify the more complex and diversified social species.[12] This analogy is immensely important for Balzac's work, but it certainly does not provide a model for scientific procedure. Balzac spontaneously imagines the assimilation of human life to animal life. In the *Avant-propos* he tries, after the fact, to justify that assimilation as the choice of one of his favorite characters: that is, of Balzac the man of science.

It would be pointless to attempt a list of all the animal metaphors in even one of Balzac's novels. They are, of course, a way of accentuating the main lines of a character's portrait. Bette's ferocious envy turns her into a tigress, a pythoness; Goriot's devotion to his ungrateful daughters raises him "to the sublimity of the canine nature";[13] the Comte de Mortsauf's persecution of his

12. I, 4–5.
13. II, 944.

wife in *Le Lys dans la vallée* is that of a wolf clawing at the body
of an ensnared swallow. These metaphors are most striking in
Balzac when they are linked to physical descriptions, when a
character actually begins to look like the animal he resembles
morally. The animal profile fixes his face in an unequivocal expressiveness. Such metamorphoses are often comically caricatural,
as when Madame Vauquer, intent on seducing the prosperous
looking Goriot, goes to bed, the night of his arrival at her board-
ing house, "roasting, like a partridge enveloped in lard, over the
fire of her sudden desire to shed the shroud of Vauquer and be
born again as Goriot." [14] There is, in *Le Père Goriot*, a scene at
the dinner table in which Vautrin, "like an orchestra leader,"
guides the drunken boarders in an hysterically competitive concert of animal sounds; what starts as a deliberate parody of Parisian vendors' cries becomes a grotesque but authentic rendering
of the junglelike atmosphere of Parisian life.[15] And, at the moment of Vautrin's capture, when the chief of police brutally
knocks the wig off the ex-convict's head and reveals the short,
brick-red hair which gives to his face "a frightful look of strength
mixed with cunning," Vautrin's rage transforms him almost literally into a terrifyingly powerful beast: "His face flushed, and
his eyes glistened like those of a wildcat. He sprang up in a movement stamped with such ferocious energy, he roared in such a
way that he drew cries of terror from all the boarders. At this
leonine gesture, and relying on the general outcry, the policemen
took out their pistols." [16]

Far from merely providing analogies for social classification,
these animal metaphors accurately express the dominant psychology of *La Comédie humaine*. Society, as Vautrin instructs
Rastignac, *is* a jungle where the strong devour the weak, and its
"species" are essentially the hunters and the hunted. Balzac's
appeals to science give a thinly rational disguise to an halluci-

14. II, 862.
15. II, 997.
16. II, 1013.

nated vision of human society as a struggle among wild animals, between beasts of prey and their victims. The images from nature thus provide the key to Balzac's view of the nature of society. And they draw attention to those aspects of his psychological vision most likely to lead us to dismiss him as superficial and melodramatic: his emphasis on types and his obsession with violence.

Now the question of types in literature is, at the very least, an ambiguous one. Depending on what one looks for in books, almost every memorable literary character can be praised for his generality or for his particularity. The easiest and least interesting approach to character in literature is to look for an ideal combination of the two: Molière portrayed a timeless, universal hypocrite in Tartuffe, but he managed to individualize him by giving him an uncontrollably sensual nature which finally exposes his hypocrisy. But why isn't Tartuffe's *sensuality* what is universal? From this point of view, the particularizing element would be his use of religious hypocrisy as both a disguise of his appetites and a strategy for satisfying them. Molière, like other classical writers, invites us to look at his characters abstractly; the interpretive hints provided in his titles—*Tartuffe ou l'imposteur, L'Avare, Le Misanthrope*—encourage a discussion of types. But the most "typical" characters in literature often illustrate the most extreme, even improbable, psychology. What exactly is universal in the incredible one-sidedness of Molière's Harpagon or Balzac's Grandet? Their avarice is so absolute, their behavior so unmotivated by anything but their love of money, that they are really psychological freaks, pathologically *un*recognizable as human beings. Of course, if we insist on clinging to the vocabulary of universalist criticism, we could say that they dramatize something like a universal impulse of avarice, an impulse isolated from normal psychological contexts, intensified and incarnated in a fictional creation. But where is the literary character about whom that banality could *not* be said? It has been argued that many characters in contemporary fiction are atypical, such extreme cases of social and psychological alienation that they have

no relevance to ordinary human life. But it is difficult to see why
we should find it easier to identify with an hysterically hypo-
chondriacal Argan, an incestuous Phèdre, or a mother-dominated,
voyeuristic, sadistic Néron than, say, with the watch-salesman of
Le Voyeur or even the hallucinatory "characters" of *Naked
Lunch*. Actually, any literary character can be spoken of as a
universal type *or* as a highly particularized creation, and this for
the unexciting reason that all literary characters are the creations
of particular men and women who, because they are human, will
presumably dramatize at least potentially general human traits.
In short, to call a character universal is to say nothing in particular about him. Universality is not a distinctive attribute of
"great" literature, but a category of criticism, one derived from
philosophical fictions of a permanent, global, and rational human
nature.

Certainly, as far as the future of criticism goes, no harm can
be done if we simply drop that category, if we refrain from asking the tired question of what or how much a literary character
"represents." For the criterion of universality is, finally, a prej-
udicial one, used mostly as a bludgeon to attack contemporary
art. We readily grant universality and timeless relevance to works
from the past which are in fact less accessible than we like to
think. But the remoteness of past literature, as well as pyramids
of reassuring criticism about it, cushions its shock, and we
covertly bless the monuments of the past for being innocuous by
praising them as ceaselessly relevant. The assertion of complicities
between their own perversities and those of their readers is
actually no more shocking in Norman Mailer and William Bur-
roughs than it is in Baudelaire, but we prefer to recognize ourselves in *Les Fleurs du mal* probably because we know (or think
we know) that it was not written for us. Nothing works better than the shadow of a dead audience to make a work dully
and harmlessly alive. And universality, especially when applied
to such radically peculiar writers as Baudelaire and Racine, conveniently dismisses the present and entombs the past; it protects

us not only from the assaults of our contemporaries but also from the probably violent or at least disruptive nature of all imaginative originality.

In the case of Balzac, the notion of types is primarily a narrative obsession. If we forget for a moment how often Balzac invites us to consider his characters as universal types, they will probably strike us as no more typical than those of other novelists. Esther Gobseck, la Torpille, is the type of the redeemed courtesan; the Duchesse de Langeais personifies the frivolous restlessness of an idle aristocracy; Rastignac embodies the ambitious energy of the young man from the provinces intent on making it in Parisian society. But isn't Julien Sorel the type of the sensitive, angrily rebellious proletarian; Emma Bovary, that of the bored, sentimental provincial housewife corrupted by a literature of glamorous romance; Legrandin, the portrait of the snob, Norpois, that of the diplomat? None of these characters, including those from Balzac, can in fact be reduced to his mere representativeness. What we find peculiar in Balzac in his apparent *intention* of bringing about such a reduction. Almost every character in *La Cousine Bette*, for example, falls victim to the narrator's generalizing mania: Valérie represents the hypocritically virtuous siren, Bette the dangerous energy of virginity, Adeline the saintliness of betrayed but faithful conjugal love, Steinbock the laziness of Slavs, Montes the ferocity of Brazilians . . . Few things are more recognizably Balzacian than those "stops" in the progress of the action when the narrator, with obvious satisfaction and often at exasperating length, plays dangerously with a character's individual presence by forcibly identifying him with a moral, social, or national class.

The Balzacian exposition reinforces this generalizing tendency. The narrator "gives us" his characters before they even appear. The analytical portraits which introduce characters partially solidify them in certain psychological and moral patterns, and it often seems as if the action in a Balzacian novel merely illustrates an exposition which already contains the whole story.

Whereas Proust gives us a character piece by piece, as he appears, in a succession of partial views, to different people at different moments, Balzac unhesitatingly tells us almost everything he knows about a character from the very start. He seems willing to fix his characters in the reader's mind, before they appear, as clearly defined social and moral personalities. His introductions, furthermore, partially control his novel's future: psychological patterns have been set which undoubtedly exert a certain pressure on the course of the story, and, to some extent, the Balzacian novel has an obligation to conform to the way in which it has been introduced. And since the typicality of character is more easily brought out in narrative analysis than in individual scenes, Balzac's expositions give him a large space in which to take that generalizing perspective on the particular which most often characterizes his interpretive responses to his own story.

Now when the characters themselves begin to behave exactly like the abstraction the narrator identifies them with, we have some of Balzac's least interesting characters, of whom the best known is Goriot. Most of what Goriot says consists of extravagant, uninventive variations on the theme of his degrading but somehow sublimely slavish love for his daughters. There is, as we shall see in a moment, a special kind of profundity even in Balzac's sloppiest psychological portraits, but, in Le Père Goriot, it is almost buried by the awful rhetoric of the Father, whose allegorical nature also clashes with a much more complex story of social temptations. Generally, however, Balzac's supposed types are much richer than we might expect types to be. First of all, very few of his characters lend themselves to the kind of easy identification we make of Goriot and of Grandet (for whose avarice, incidentally, Balzac finds a language much more interesting, more economically self-revealing than that of Goriot). Bette is the old-maid virgin but also the poor cousin, and her sexual envy of Adeline complicates her social envy in ways that make her singularly obscure and elusive. In the same novel, if Steinbock represents Slavs, he is also the artist who doesn't create, the sculptor who dreams of his works instead of executing them. And what exactly does Vautrin represent? Does Balzac do justice to this extraordinary creation by presenting him as the type of criminal in revolt against society? Furthermore, the supposed typicality of Balzac's characters leaves a surprisingly large margin for the unpredictable. Rastignac's openness in *Le Père Goriot* to pressures coming from sources as different as Vautrin and Victorine Taillefer makes for a genuinely suspenseful drama of indecision; his final response to Paris will have to accommodate much more than his ambitious nature. And the gloriously improbable events which make of the last part of *Splendeurs et misères des courtisanes* a masterpiece of cops-and-robbers fiction are a tribute to the always startling inventiveness of Vautrin. His criminality reaches a resourcefulness so great that he finally invents himself out of the role in which Balzac had fixed him. The maker of plots against society will now unravel them; from arch-criminal to chief of police, from the act to the divination of the act, Vautrin embodies the Balzacian parable of energy transformed from an agent of destruction to a guardian of order.

Furthermore, Balzac's emphasis on types leads us to expect a kind of psychological intelligibility usually absent from his work. Even in Goriot, we find an obscurity of motive which makes of "paternal love" an inadequate description of his behavior. His frantic declarations of love for Delphine and Anastasie occasionally suggest a carnal identification with his daughters, a profound sense of an identity of being between him and them. This is not the same thing as carnal desire, and, interestingly enough, Balzac suggests (rather weakly, I grant) that the latter may merely derive from Goriot's passionate self-love. Fatherly devotion does not simply screen incestuous feelings; incest itself both obscures and satisfies a fascination with the powers of his own body. "Well, I'm the one who made that darling woman," Goriot proudly reminds Rastignac as he details Delphine's beauty to the young man.[17] "*My* life," he tells Rastignac in another passage,

17. II, 1027.

"is in my two daughters," and his words suggest how artificial it would be, in speaking of Goriot's love, to separate his total selflessness from a total self-absorption: "I am not cold if they are warm, I am never bored if they are laughing. The only troubles I have are their troubles. When you are a father, when you say to yourself, hearing your children prattling on: That came from me!, when you feel those little creatures attached to every drop of your blood—and they were the flower of your blood!—you will think you are tied to their skin, you will think you yourself are moving when they walk." Fatherhood is the human version of divine creation: ". . . when I became a father, I understood God. He is, in his entirety, everywhere, since creation came from him." [18] To be everywhere: Goriot's love for his daughters expresses the more fundamental Balzacian theme of demiurgic power, of fantastic self-projection into the world. The Christ of Paternity sacrifices himself in the name of a self-creation.

Balzac is of course sentimentally attached to a more conventional idea of fatherhood. It is the combination of his attempt to do justice to that idea (largely through Rastignac's admiration for Goriot) and his instinctive distaste for any ethic of mildness or self-immolation which makes his portrait of Goriot so confused. The shrillness of that portrait may be the result of Balzac's uneasiness about it; Goriot's melodramatic, insane eloquence allows Balzac to obscure what really interests him in the phenomenon of paternity. Verbal excess conceals a more frightening excess, and in our impatience with the absurd language imagined for Goriot, we may overlook the more original aspects of his character which Balzac often seems determined to stifle. Goriot is easily as much a criminal as Vautrin: he quite seriously proposes to steal or kill for his daughters, and he proclaims himself ready to sell "the Father, the Son and the Holy Ghost to spare both of them a tear." [19] What undoubtedly both fascinates and terrifies

18. II, 957.
19. II, 1046 and 973.

Balzac is the possibility that familial devotion may be as destructive of the social order as the frankly antisocial designs of Vautrin. The distinction between "the father" and "the rebel" covers a more profound similarity, although the notion of types provides Balzac with a means of submitting the fantastic energy epitomized by Vautrin to psychological and moral discriminations. But the quality of character in *La Comédie humaine* depends more on the energy of desire than on its specific contents. Virtue and vice are, so to speak, secondary attributes, and a virtuous passion can be as destructive as a criminal one. It could, for example, be argued that the threat to family life in *La Cousine Bette* comes as much from the saintly Adeline as it does from Bette or Valérie. In her madly selfless devotion to Hulot, her inability to utter a single word of reproach about her husband's succession of mistresses, Adeline helps the baron to ruin his family, almost sacrifices her children for him. Because conjugal or paternal love can, in Balzac, have the same *force* as envy or rebellion, it may also have the same consequences. The fragile piety of the Balzacian narrator consists in his introducing moral categories largely irrelevant to a psychology of desire.

The idea of types does, however, correspond to a profound tendency toward psychological simplification in Balzac. And his animal metaphors help us to locate that simplification. On the one hand, those metaphors reinforce easy moral distinctions: the docility of a dog or a swan is opposed to the ferocity of tigers and lions. But, as we have begun to see, such abstractions account rather poorly for the behavior of Balzac's characters. More significantly, the images from nature suggest an inability to sacrifice or even postpone the satisfaction of desire. Both the nature and the strategies of desire are often complex in *La Comédie humaine;* what gives Balzac's characters their deceptive simplicity is the animal-like directness with which they pursue their prey, and the prey can of course be power, another person, even knowledge. The jungle metaphor provides a system of classification for social anarchy as well as an appropriate image for anarchy. Analogies meant to facilitate an ordered view of society also express the violent *dis*order which Balzac usually imagines in social life. At best, how effective would these analogies be as models of order? Moral types and social species are epistemological inventions rather than social structures. They create a kind of abstract, analytical order which Balzac imposes on his portrait of a chaotic and violently competitive humanity. And there are, unexpectedly, affinities between the order and the chaos: the classifying abstraction formalizes the rule of uncontrollable appetites. A reductive psychology supports a view of personality as ravaged by the *idée fixe*. Balzac's order thus serves the violence which subverts it.

"Is there a strong, poisonous life which feeds on gentle and tender creatures? My God! did I, then, belong to the race of tigers?" [20] These questions, which Félix de Vandenesse desperately asks himself toward the end of *Le Lys dans la vallée*, constitute the perfect *examen de conscience* in *La Comédie humaine*. Balzac's work investigates the taming, civilizing possibilities of various kinds of order. Can desire be contained? Do energy and will inevitably destroy the self and others? To what extent do systems elaborated as strategies of control actually serve the very impulses they are meant to discipline? How can the logic of an imaginary order work against the apparent purpose of that order? *La Comédie humaine* is an immense speculation—a reflection and a gamble—on the ordering powers of different fictions. There are those fragile procedural orders familiar to all Balzac's readers: techniques of exposition, the moralizing narrator, the organization of a story as a conflict of moral abstractions. But, as I have been suggesting, such orders are perhaps too easily come by; they seem to be parodies of some other, richer order which might more effectively contain and control fantasies of violence. Indeed, Balzac has a far more interesting sense of order than either his political conservatism or the mechanical, mock order of his narrative technique might suggest. We can perhaps best approach his most successful experiments in organization and dis-

20. VIII, *Le Lys dans la vallée*, 996.

cipline by looking more closely at the nature of that violent energy appropriately but inadequately expressed in the images drawn from nature. *La Comédie humaine* is a dialectic of violence and containment; each side, in its most detailed and profound manifestations, implies and inspires the other.

Desire, thought, and will are generally synonymous in Balzac. They represent different aspects of a fantastically aggressive power over the world. Thought for Louis Lambert is "the quintessential product of Will";[21] and the androgynous Séraphîta-Séraphîtus defines desire as the "torrent of your will." [22] Balzac's energetic version of mental life indicates a primitive identification of desire and effective power. Certain magic practices naturally depend on this naïve confusion (characteristic also of children) between a wish and an act, and the "magical" appeal of certain leaders (what we call their charismatic quality) perhaps consists of nothing more than their contagious confidence in the world as a nonresistant medium for their desires. What we admire as "self-confidence" may be an illusion so powerfully felt and communicated that the world actually collaborates with it and transforms it into a truth. Balzac philosophically dignifies that illusion with a theory of the materiality of will. His interest in Mesmer, for example, is neither an intellectual quirk nor does it merely reflect a fashion of the times; magnetism allows him to explain the contagion of desire as a physical phenomenon. Louis Lambert, "first of all a pure spiritualist," is "irresistibly led to recognize the materiality of thought." [23] "Feeling imprints itself in all things," Balzac writes in *Le Père Goriot*, "and crosses spaces." [24] Similar statements constantly recur in *La Comédie humaine*, and we are obviously expected to take them literally. Foedora in *La Peau de chagrin* is intrigued to learn from Raphaël "that human

21. X, *Louis Lambert*, 389.
22. X, *Séraphîta*, 575.
23. X, *Louis Lambert*, 401.
24. II, 944.

will was a material, vaporlike force; that, in the moral world, nothing could resist a man accustomed to concentrating this power, to manipulating it fully, to constantly directing toward other people's souls the projecting force of this fluid mass; that this man could, at will, modify everything concerning humanity, even the absolute laws of nature." [25] The Swedenborgian Séraphîta-Séraphîtus assures the stunned Wilfred and Minna that God "likes to be taken with force." "Know this!" she—or he— adds, "desire . . . is so strong in man, that a single ray powerfully emitted can obtain anything for you. . . ." [26] Finally, the logistics of will is studied by Lambert in the Treatise summed up by the narrator: "A logical and simple deduction from his principles had led him to recognize that Will could be concentrated in a single mass by a complete contraction of our inner being; then, by a different movement, it could be projected outside, and even be consigned to material objects. Thus a man's entire strength might be able to have an effect on other men, to penetrate them with an essence foreign to their own being, if they did not defend themselves against this aggression." [27]

Such aggression is far from theoretical in Balzac, and the theories expounded at length in the philosophical novels are interesting as an accurate commentary on human relationships in the more realistic scenes of La Comédie humaine. They can, of course, be used as a substitute for characterization. One of several weaknesses in La Femme de trente ans is that we know almost nothing about the mysterious Victor (apparently a hero in the struggle of a South American country for independence from Spain) except that he has merely to look at the Aiglemont family in order to paralyze their wills and make Hélène decide that she will run off with him a minute or so after seeing him for the first time. One accepts the incident only if one already believes in magnetism; such quick-dealing on Balzac's part is

25. IX, 103.
26. X, Séraphîta, 575.
27. X, Louis Lambert, 395.

like proving the existence of miracles by asserting that a miracle has taken place. Vautrin's domination over Rastignac and especially over Lucien is another matter. Balzac's images of Vautrin shooting bulletlike particles of his fantastic will through the air and into the soft soil of the young men's more passive minds[28] appropriately describe psychological invasions also made plausible in other ways. Rastignac's ambitious, impressionable nature, Lucien's failures in society, his softness and taste for luxury, make them perfect targets for the kind of attack Vautrin skillfully conducts. His attack dramatizes the possibility of a sexual seduction without the benefit of physical appeal. Vautrin's principal weapon is talk: he seduces Rastignac and Lucien with lengthy discourses on the nature of society. They would be much less tempted to believe his promises if they were not so dazzled by his intellect; for their naïve and generous minds, Vautrin's knowledge of society is a guarantee of his power. His talk is a subtle sexual strategy, for he plays on the pleasures of passivity: Rastignac and Lucien give in more easily to the strength of his ideas since the very display of strength comes as a flattering tribute to *them*.

We find something similar in that contemporary American Balzacian, Norman Mailer. Barney Kelley momentarily subdues Rojack in *An American Dream* with an energy not unlike Vautrin's, although it is more specifically sexual. In a brutal, simultaneous appeal to impulses of anality, homosexuality, necrophilia, and cannibalism, the magic of Kelley's power is made marvelously concrete by the energy of his indulgence in bodily fantasies, an energy so great that Rojack begins to share the fantasies, to feel "unfamiliar desire." [29] The fact that Vautrin's strategies are sexual only by implication gives Balzac a greater range of material with which to demonstrate the flexibility of desire: we see *ideas* as an instrument of seduction. Balzac's own success with women illustrates the connection more explicitly.

28. See II, Le Père Goriot, 928–29.
29. (New York, 1965), p. 254.

The first view of him was, as many of them noted, anything but appetizing: squat, plump, flabby-faced, almost toothless, Balzac could nevertheless transform a faintly disgusted lady into a passionately erotic, jealous mistress; she would "catch," it seems, the intensity of his own desires. Laure de Berny, *La Dilecta*, was, at well over fifty, writing to him: " 'I still think of myself as your darling and I send you all our usual caresses. I kiss you everywhere. . . .' " As soon as that unprepossessing presence was set into motion, there was, as André Maurois says in his biography, an "electric storm," [30] and the number of people literally floored by the lightning gives an unsettling credibility to Balzac's extravagant notions about the materiality of thought and desire, about the ability of certain men to control other people's desires by bombarding them with the rays of an overpowering will.

But, more profoundly, the very strength of sexual energy in Balzac makes sexual identities unstable and problematic. *La Comédie humaine* is full of couples where masculinity and femininity are functions of energy rather than of sex. Roland Barthes has said of Racine that sexes do not create the conflicts in his plays, but rather that conflicts create sexes. Sex is subordinate to a relation of force; Racine's characters derive their being from their place in a general constellation of strengths and weaknesses. [31] The remark is relevant to many Balzacian couples. Lucien dominates David Séchard, who loves him "with idolatry," like a "woman who knows she is loved." The steady, reliable David patiently corrects the errors of his friend's brilliantly volatile mind; he obeys and protects Lucien as if David himself were the strong, effacing lover of some superior courtesan. And, as always in Balzac, Lucien's femininity—like those feelings "which cross spaces"—has imprinted itself in the lines of his body, is materialized in his special type of beauty: "To look at his feet, a man would have been all the more tempted to

30. *Prométhée ou la vie de Balzac* (Paris, 1965), pp. 201 and 165.
31. *Sur Racine* (Paris, 1963), pp. 13–14.

take him for a young girl in disguise, since, like most subtle
(I might even say shrewd) men, his hips were shaped like a
woman's." [32] Bette, on the other hand, is the iron-willed master
of a feminized Steinbock; and if Parisians, "always too witty,"
gossip about her passionate friendship for Valérie, there are
some grounds for slander in "the contrast between the virile,
harsh nature of the woman from Lorraine and Valérie's prettily
Creole nature." [33] Finally, Balzac's artillery metaphors for the
invasion of one mind by another reinforce our sense of sex as
dependent on the projective power of will. Balzac explains Vautrin's influence over Rastignac with images of military topog-
raphy which also sexualize human relationships strictly on the
basis of offensive and defensive postures:

> Ideas are probably projected in direct proportion to the force with
> which they are conceived, and they strike wherever the brain
> sends them, according to a mathematical law comparable to the
> one which guides canon-balls once they are shot from the mor-
> tar. The effects are varied. If there are tender characters which
> ideas ravage and settle in, there are also vigorously equipped
> characters, skulls with brass ramparts on which other people's
> wills collapse and fall like bullets in front of a wall; then there
> are also flaccid, cottony characters where someone else's ideas die
> out as a bullet's impact is deadened in a redoubt's soft soil. Ras-
> tignac had one of those heads full of gunpowder which explode
> at the slightest shock.[34]

Psychologically, strength of will determines sexual identity
in Balzac. The strong, whatever their physical sex, shoot their
"will bullets" into the minds of the weak. Now if the most
obvious danger of a strong will is to the world which it brutally
—and materially—invades, Balzac is also obsessed by the danger
to the *self* in the very act of spending energy. In a curious
passage toward the end of *Splendeurs et misères des courtisanes*,

32. IV, *Illusions perdues*, 486–87.
33. VI, *La Cousine Bette*, 272–73.
34. II, *Le Père Goriot*, 928–29.

Balzac explains why most criminals "are not as dangerous as people think." "Since their faculties are constantly strained towards stealing, and since the execution of a job demands the use of all life's powers, a mental agility equal to their physical fitness, an attention which over-exerts their minds, they become witless once this violent exercise of their will is over, for the same reason that a singer or a dancer falls from fatigue after an exhausting step or after one of those formidable duets which modern composers inflict on the public." The rhythm of will is one of violent activity followed by total prostration; after their crimes, murderers and thieves "become absolutely like children." [35]

The usury of energy is treated most explicitly in *La Peau de chagrin.* I find the novel unsuccessful, mainly because Balzac's fantasy of desire as equivalent to power is dramatized in a magical object rather than in a convincingly magnetic personality such as Vautrin's or Gobseck's. The possession of the ass-skein guarantees the immediate satisfaction of each of Raphaël's desires, but with each desire both the ass-skein and Raphaël's life grow shorter. Desire *is* power, and both destroy. Raphaël attempts to escape the curse "by castrating his imagination": ". . . he was abdicating life in order to live, and was stripping his soul of all the poetry of desire." [36] This strategy of an emotional castration seems like an effort to control a fate of castration: the smaller, voluntary mutilation of desire is designed to protect Raphaël from a more massive destruction *by* desire. Balzac takes very little trouble to obscure the masturbatory fantasy recognizable in this fable. Each time Raphaël uses that magically powerful object to satisfy his desires, the object shrinks, and, exhausted by both his spent and his suppressed desires, Raphaël comes to resemble a woman: "A kind of effeminate grace and the peculiarities particular to the rich when they are ill marked his appearance. His hands, like those of a pretty woman, had a soft and

35. V, *La Peau de chagrin*, 1061.
36. IX, 171.

delicate whiteness. His blond hair, which had become thin, was curled around his temples with an effect of deliberate coquetry." [37] Thus, in *La Peau de chagrin* the aggression of an energetic will against a weaker, more passive mind is internalized in a sequence of strength and mutilation, of energy and exhaustion, within a single mind. Raphaël's tragedy helps us to see the "floating" of sexual identities in *La Comédie humaine* as a consequence of the Balzacian psychology of desire. Androgyny in Balzac is a result of the will's violent energies, energies so explosive that to spend them is to be spent, to become the object of one's own aggressions. Hermaphrodites therefore incarnate the vicissitudes of volitional bombardments; once again, every mental act in Balzac's world makes its physical imprint.

Finally, homosexuality in *La Comédie humaine* can be seen as a function of these same fantasies. On the one hand, Balzac, like Proust, seems intuitively to have interpreted homosexual tendencies both as a complex scenario of sexual imitations and parodies, and as a confusion of the desire to have and the desire to be. Bette's jealousy as a child of the beautiful and spoiled Adeline explains her lifelong hatred of the Hulot family. What Bette wants in Valérie she detests in Adeline: "that beauty which she adored, as one adores everything one doesn't possess." [38] Her attachment to Valérie could even be thought of as her way of possessing (as well as destroying) Adeline. Bette's rage goes to the real Adeline, while what seems to be a dream of *being* her adored and beautiful cousin becomes an idolatry of her cousin's demonic double. The unscrupulous Valérie combines Adeline's seductiveness with a mockery of Adeline's virtues, thus allowing Bette simultaneously to worship and profane inaccessible beauty. Vautrin's ambitions for Lucien de Rubempré seem to involve equally complex emotional projects. Lucien is of course Jacques Collin's revenge against society. Hunted by the police, the great criminal has to hide in the wings and send

37. IX, 170.
38. VI, *La Cousine Bette*, 278.

the young man whose life he has bought to represent him on
the social scene. But Vautrin also loves and is dominated by
Lucien: "With all his strength, he was so weak against his
creature's whims that he had finally confided his secrets to him."
But who exactly is Lucien? Balzac writes that Vautrin "lived
again in the elegant body of Lucien, whose soul had become his
own." [39] The poet is the criminal's "double," his "visible soul":
"Trompe-la-Mort dined at the Grandlieus', slipped into great
ladies' boudoirs, loved Esther by proxy." [40] Now there is nothing
effeminate in Vautrin's homosexuality. And it seems to me that
Balzac at least implies that his love for Lucien involves an
identification with a feminized image of himself, as well as with
an image of successful masculinity (women adore Lucien). The
reticence which undoubtedly prevents Balzac from mentioning
homosexual desires explicitly serves the most profound aspect of
his portrait of homosexuality. For sexual desire would perhaps
be simply the sign of a desire for far more than a sexual union;
Vautrin's inversion consists essentially in his "imitation" and enjoyment of the feminine sensibility he cultivates and dominates.
In his beautiful and weak creature, Vautrin has, so to speak,
internalized an image of passivity at a distance.

Inversion in Balzac is a psychic parallel to androgyny, to the
physical blurring of sexual distinctions. And, like androgyny,
homosexuality is a natural consequence of Balzac's view of the
violently and dangerously energetic self. Essentially, it has very
little to do with sexual preferences; both homosexuality and
androgyny are "moments" in the Balzacian dialectic of energy,
the sexual manifestations of energy powerfully spent. It is perfectly appropriate that the most notorious homosexual in *La
Comédie humaine* should also have the most powerful virility.
In Vautrin, and in his remarks on criminals in *Splendeurs et
misères des courtisanes,* Balzac interestingly suggests that a childlike passivity and even sexual inversion are perhaps consequences,

39. V, *Splendeurs et misères des courtisanes,* 725.
40. V, 1030.

or risks, of great strength, functions of the most extravagantly aggressive activity.

The risk can, however, be turned into a gain. The energetic will can become the victim of its own bombardments, but this internalization of its effects on the world suggests a possibility of saving the will from debilitating dissipation. Balzac curiously and brilliantly associates homosexuality with virginity: both Vautrin and Bette practice a sexual asceticism which increases their power over others. As Balzac writes in *La Cousine Bette*, in a passage which, characteristically, leads him to congratulate the Church for honoring the Virgin Mary, will and intelligence profit from an excess of unspent sexual energy: "Virginity, like all unnatural phenomena, has special riches, an engrossing majesty. Since he has economized life's forces, the individual virgin's life has a quality of incalculable resistance and duration. His brain has been enriched in the cohesion of faculties held in reserve. When chaste people need their body or their soul, when they have recourse to action or thought, they then find steel in their muscles or knowledge instilled into their intelligence, a diabolical strength or the black magic of Will." [41] Virginity provides the paradoxical and ideal solution of omnipotence and inactivity, of domination and noninvolvement. And homosexuality could, then, be thought of not only as the sign or consequence of extravagant energy, but also as a strategy to gain autonomy. Both sexes are incorporated into the self in order to spare desire the exhaustion and waste of spending itself on the world. Balzac significantly insists on Bette's sense of economy and on her self-sufficiency. Both financially and emotionally, she takes care of herself, having even refused marriage offers because ". . . she was satisfied, she would say laughingly, with being admired by herself." [42]

Thus Balzac develops, in response to the destructiveness of desire both for the self and the world, what almost amounts to

41. VI, 230.
42. VI, 163.

a mystique of emotional hoarding. The security derived from this conservation of energy—Ernst Robert Curtius speaks of a Balzacian "hygiene of passivity" [43]—is enjoyed not only by Vautrin and Bette, but by characters as different as the Duchesse de Langeais, Félix de Vandenesse, Gobseck, and Raphaël de Valentin before he accepts the deceptive power of the ass-skein. Gobseck the usurer exploits the inability of a whole society to economize passion; he and his associates, on the other hand, "have tasted and enjoyed everything, have sated themselves on everything, and have come to love power and money only for power and money themselves." [44] Certainly Vautrin spends extraordinary amounts of energy, but, significantly, he exercises power at a distance, through his "creatures," and it is Lucien and not his mentor who is destroyed at the end of *Splendeurs et misères des courtisanes*. Finally, and principally, these economies take the form of a preference for what Balzac calls "knowledge" over action. "*Will* burns us up and *Power* destroys us," warns the antique dealer of *La Peau de chagrin*, "but KNOWLEDGE leaves our weak faculties in a perpetual state of calm." And, by a curious return of what has apparently been sacrificed, knowledge turns out to satisfy the appetite for possession. "Oh! young man, isn't knowing equivalent to enjoying intuitively?" the antique dealer asks Raphaël, "isn't it the same as discovering the very substance of a fact and possessing it in its essence? What remains from a material possession? an idea." [45] And the idea is power. Raphaël sees—too late—the advantage of those solitary years when, unknown, poor, and isolated from society, he gained, through study and meditation, a power he will never have again: ". . . wasn't my sensibility concentrated in order to become the perfected organ of a will higher than the power of passion?" [46] Raphaël's lost chance is, it would appear, the choice of his creator. Surveyor

43. *Balzac*, tr. Henri Jourdan (Paris, 1933), p. 82.
44. II, *Gobseck*, 637.
45. IX, 40.
46. IX, 85.

THE TAMING OF TIGERS

of "the vast field of human knowledge," [47] Balzac can enjoy the pleasures of imaginary possession enumerated by the antique dealer: "What men call sorrows, loves, ambitions, setbacks, sadness, are for me ideas which I can change into reveries; instead of feeling them, I express them, I translate them; instead of letting them devour my life, I dramatize them, I develop them, I enjoy them like novels which I might be reading by means of an inner vision." [48] The novelist, as Béguin writes, dominates the world by limiting himself to deciphering its signs.[49] He is an exemplary miser of energy, the hoarder of images.

But the distinction between passion and a "higher will" is unconvincing. The threat to the world and to the self had originally been in the act of will itself, or, in other but synonymous terms, "the ravages of thought," and it is difficult to see how a renunciation of sex or of social life could diminish the danger. Why is Gobseck's love for power and money more self-preserving than a love for those things which power and money can buy? Is he really "satiated," a man without desires? When we think of what "pure thought" does to Louis Lambert and to Balthazar Claës (in *La Recherche de l'absolu*), can we believe that the antique dealer's passion for "seeing," for possessing worlds and even listening to God, has, as he says, left his "organs" intact? Since Balzac spontaneously associates mental power with material power (mere thought brings havoc to the world and to the self), playing the social game seems, if anything, *superfluous* rather than the crucial factor in both the exercise and the dissipation of an energetic will. In fact, there is no real difference between "the power of passion" and some "higher will" in *La Comédie humaine*. The materiality of will precludes any spiritual chastity in Balzac, and thought always acts both on the body and on the world.

Certainly Balzac made no such distinction in his life. He did not give up his social or commercial adventures when he wrote

47. IX, 84.
48. IX, 40.
49. *Balzac visionnaire*, p. 135.

his novels, and, as André Wurmser has made abundantly clear, he quite rightly thought of his "knowledge," of his talent for fiction, as his best asset in the serious business of gaining fame and making money.[50] And Balzac died from the exhaustion of "knowledge": "imaginary" possessions were no less a usury of the self than "real" ones. In Balzac's novels, the contradictory notion of a nondesiring will or thought is the sleight-of-hand designed not to assure "a perpetual state of calm," but rather to make the artillery of desire invulnerable. The fantasy of partial castration—sacrificing "the power of passion" to some "higher" will—is therefore meant not only to protect the self from greater ravages, but also to guarantee omnipotence. The shift from action to knowledge, however, is an illusory one, and the safe omnipotence is more hoped for than realized or even imagined in any convincing detail. Balzac includes in his fiction both a critique of that illusion and an attempt to replace it with a more satisfactory, less magical version of contained desire.

Nowhere does Balzac dramatize more successfully both the threats of desire and the possibilities of order than in *Le Lys dans la vallée* (1836). It is, I think, his most impressive and, in a sense, his most representative work: nowhere else in *La Comédie humaine* is violence studied more carefully than in this leisurely, often bucolic novel of contained, delayed violence. *Le Lys* is the flawless Balzacian drama of containment, and Henriette de Mortsauf dies from a failure to find the proper *form* for desire.

Le Lys, which Balzac placed in the *Scènes de la vie de campagne*—the last scene of the *Etudes de mœurs,* "the evening of that long day"[51]—could easily be thought of as a primarily private drama. The novel is in the form of a long letter sent by Félix de Vandenesse to his mistress, Natalie de Manerville, who had demanded the story of his past. In order to explain the frequent silences which anger Natalie, to account for "the

50. *La Comédie inhumaine* (Paris, 1964).
51. I, *Avant-propos,* 14.

sudden and long reveries which sometimes take hold of me at my happiest moments," Félix reluctantly agrees to tell her about the "phantom" which dominates his life.[52] He had loved Henriette de Mortsauf, married to the tyranically weak, complaining Comte de Mortsauf, whose physical and emotional health had been ruined by the hardships of the Emigration. Unable to betray her husband and, more important, unwilling to face the risk of losing her children to the hysterically self-absorbed count, Henriette persuades Félix to help her invent strategies designed to spiritualize desire, to reconcile happy love with the sacrifice of sex in love. For a while the experiment almost works. Occasionally rebellious, Félix nevertheless manages to sublimate his desires into a kind of worshipful adoration; Henriette is the "lily" of the richly sensuous valley of the Indre, a chaste, angelic sister. But finally, in Paris, Félix betrays her with the violent Lady Dudley, a sexual spitfire who glorifies in precisely that betrayal of husband and children which terrifies Madame de Mortsauf. Henriette dies of that betrayal, and in a letter Félix reads after her death, she reveals the powerful sensuality of her own nature, the heroic dimensions of the finally unsuccessful struggle against her sexual "thirst" for Félix. The novel ends with Natalie de Manerville's elegantly brutal answer to Félix. She accuses him of murdering Madame de Mortsauf and, revolted at the prospect of having to compete with both the angelic phantom of Henriette and the demonic phantom of Lady Dudley, she grandly offers Félix her friendship as she announces the end of their love.

But this secret drama, lived for the most part far from the agitations of Paris, has its general social significance. As we might expect, Félix sees Henriette's story as typical, rather than exceptional; it is a "veritable domestic epic," and Natalie will recognize "its similarity to a large number of feminine destinies" (799). Her marriage reminds Felix of other cruelly mismatched couples:

52. VIII, Le Lys dans la vallée, 770. Page references for subsequent quotations from Le Lys will be given in the text.

54

BALZAC TO BECKETT

"What is the peculiar and caustic power which perpetually throws to the madman an angel, to the man who loves sincerely and poetically an evil woman, to the insignificant man a great woman, to this ugly ape a beautiful and sublime creature; to the noble Juana captain Diard, whose story you learned in Bordeaux; to madame de Beauséant a d'Ajuda, to madame d'Aiglemont her husband, to the marquis d'Espard his wife" (880)? And, returning to Clochegourde to see Henriette die, Félix thinks of all the "unpunished murders" in society, of "those crimes for which there is no court of justice." Terrified (and perhaps consoled) at the idea of "some law" which abandons the weak to the strong and allows "a strong poisonous life" to feed on "mild and tender creatures," Félix evokes some of La Comédie humaine's most illustrious victims: Madame de Beauséant, the Duchesse de Langeais, Lady Brandon, Madame d'Aiglemont (996). Within Le Lys itself, society provides only parodies of social order. The novel is important for an understanding of Balzac's complex political feelings, and I cannot agree with Gaston Bachelard's engaging remark that the portrait of Louis XVIII's court brings too much *animus* into a work otherwise beautifully conceived under the sign of *anima*.[53] Le Lys dans la vallée is an extraordinarily pessimistic critique of Balzac's conservative principles; it dramatizes both the need for those principles and the bankruptcy of the institutions which embody them.

For Balzac, only a hierarchical organization of society corresponds to the natural fact of inequality. There is no natural benevolence to balance the excitement of possessing the godlike omniscience and omnipotence with which Vautrin and the usurer Gobseck dream of enslaving society. The secret fraternities of La Comédie humaine bring together these aristocrats of nature: Gobseck's "silent and unknown kings" who rule Paris with their knowledge of every family's financial secrets;[54] "les Treize,"

53. *La Poétique de la rêverie* (Paris, 1960), p. 64.
54. II, *Gobseck*, 636–37.

whose "religion of pleasure and egoism" leads them to form a "society apart from but within society, hostile to society, accepting none of society's ideas, recognizing none of its laws";[55] and Vautrin's confederates of the Grands Fanandels, a kind of nobility of the underworld. The secret society inverts the ordinary relation between the individual and the group: instead of subordinating individual wills to a social design, it uses its collective strength to satisfy its members' desires, to give to each of them "the diabolical power" of all of them.[56] It is a mock society which institutionalizes social rebellion.

Post-revolutionary France gave a certain historical credibility to Balzac's image of society as a fiercely competitive jungle. The race for wealth, the struggles among savagely antagonistic political and financial interests, the idolatry of commerce under Louis-Philippe, at least partly authenticated Balzac's hallucinatory vision of the power of Money. "Gold," in Gobseck's phrase, "is the spiritualism of your present societies." [57] But if there is a realism in Balzac's study of society, it is more psychic than economic in that it involves the reduction of economic affairs to the symbolic pleasures of making and handling money. Balzac's society provided a recognizable field of action for his fantasies about money's power. The July Monarchy made the fantasies intelligible in public terms, and thus helped Balzac to show, for example, the continuity between dreams and interest rates. But his images of social power work best when he dramatizes the exhilaration of exercising power, and almost not at all when he attempts to detail the social machinery which presumably makes a Vautrin or a Gobseck possible. *César Birotteau* is perhaps the most extreme example of the compulsive documentation of an obsession ruining the life of the novel: the boring, interminable brochure on bankruptcy so absorbs Balzac's attention that the characters

55. V, Preface to *Histoire des treize*, 15.
56. V, Preface to *Histoire des treize*, 15.
57. II, *Gobseck*, 636.

are brushed aside—and brushed off—with a few strokes of moral allegory. Bianchon's formula for finance—"solidified egoism" [58] —is both psychologically profound and socially superficial. Balzac convincingly dramatizes the way in which money can come to "carry" the energy of unbridled self-assertion, but he rarely shows what we might call the deflection of such symbol-making activities in complex social contexts, or the specifically political and economic events which those contexts generate.

Because of this psychological pessimism which largely determines his view of society, Balzac naturally considers democratic governments as threats to social stability. Again, recent history seemed to corroborate this view, which Vautrin succinctly expresses in *Illusions perdues*: "The French invented in 1793 a popular sovereignty which ended with an absolute emperor. There," he announces to Lucien, "is your national history." [59] A legitimate monarchy is Balzac's alternative to these extremes. Only social aristocracy can discipline the aristocrats of nature. Balzac's conservative ideology is both a consequence of and a protection against a fantastic imagination for chaos. As Béguin has said, private property and royal authority guide and moderate the spending of energy, thereby assuring social longevity. [60] Balzac's politics thus parallels the narrative tensions I discussed earlier: an inherited hierarchy disciplines the natural anarchy of social life in much the same way as Balzac's naïvely systematic narration contains and organizes his stylistic incoherence and exuberance. But the monarch also legitimizes a dream of omnipotence; he provides a myth of boundless energy achieving order with no sacrifice of power. Only the monarch can exercise power safely—and nothing could be more appealing to Balzac. His own life appears to have been characterized by an anxious squandering of energy in order to reach a fame and power so great that energy would no longer have to be spent. The monarch

58. VI, *La Cousine Bette*, 501.
59. IV, 1024.
60. *Balzac visionnaire*, p. 96.

is born into that ideal security of omnipotence without self-dissi-
pation.

Now the social stability of a monarchy depends, as Balzac saw,
on the intellectual and moral qualities of its aristocracy. In *La
Duchesse de Langeais,* Balzac reproaches the Faubourg Saint-
Germain for snobbishly refusing to bring into its ranks the aristocrats of nature, for not seeking out some "genius" "in the cold
garret where he might have been dying." Without intelligence
—"a broad skull"—the nobility cannot survive; it has imprisoned
itself in aristocratic forms which are no longer enough. "Instead
of throwing aside the insignia which offended the masses and
secretly keeping its power, it allowed the bourgeoisie to seize
power, while the nobility has fatally clung to the insignia, and
has consistently forgotten the laws prescribed to it by its numeri-
cal weakness." [61] *Le Lys dans la vallée* dramatizes these criticisms.
The novel takes place during the first years of the Restoration,
and in a few rapid but powerful strokes, Balzac paints a gloomy
picture of the moral climate brought to France by the return of
the Bourbons. We don't follow Félix's career at the court in much
detail, but he indicates the tone of court life by a couple of
sketches of Louis XVIII. When Félix remembers fatuously congratulating himself for controlling the lives of two such superior
women as Henriette and Lady Dudley, he attributes his "evil
thoughts" to the contagious cynicism, the "deflowering wit" of
the king (986). He is, of course, being morally evasive, but we
do see in the novel the court's indifference to Henriette's fate, and
this indifference clearly means much more than a lack of interest
in a provincial lady's private affairs. Only at Clochegourde are
the interests of this society being passionately defended. But
Henriette's extraordinary attempt to make her love for Félix
strengthen rather than destroy her sense of social duty provides
merely an occasion for epigrams at the Tuileries. The real business of social life is the politics of self-advancement, that "fierce
eagerness" to jump on the Restoration bandwagon which had

61. V, 147–50.

disgusted Félix at the reception in Tours, early in the novel, for the Duc d'Angoulême (784). When the Duc de Lenoncourt announces to the king that his daughter is dying, Félix leaves alone for Clochegourde; Lenoncourt, "more a courtier than a father," stays with the king and will probably "play Monsieur's daily game of whist" after the ceremony of the king's retirement for the night. And Louis XVIII brutally suggests how politically frivolous Félix's love is:

> At La Croix de Berny, I met His Majesty who was coming back from Verrières. The king accepted a bouquet of flowers which he let fall to his feet, and he gave me a look full of those royal ironies whose depth is overwhelming, and which seemed to say to me: "If you want to be something in politics, come back! Don't amuse yourself parleying with the dead!" The duke waved to me with melancholy. The two stately coaches each drawn by eight horses, the colonels in gilded uniforms, the escort and the swirls of dust passed by rapidly to the cries of Long live the king! It seemed to me that the court had trampled on madame de Mortsauf's body with the insensitivity that nature shows for our catastrophes. (993-94)

The comparison is instructive: the court, as it were, gives cere-monial forms to "nature," which is not the same thing as saying that it civilizes nature. *Le Lys* dramatizes different versions of how social life may adjust to the instinctive voraciousness of in-dividuals. The threat to society comes from the natural egoism of desire, and yet in *Le Lys*—which is anything but a novel of renunciation—Balzac also emphasizes those natural impulses which guarantee social cohesion. Like the philosopher Saint-Martin, whose doctrine Félix summarizes for Natalie, Balzac is trying to imagine a way of feeling which could "free duty from its legal degradation . . ." (812). Only the family links social institutions to nature, makes of Henriette's theory of moral duties the development of a biological impulse. Ultimately, Hen-riette's sense of social responsibility depends on a feeling with-out which her social conscience would be a fragile abstraction:

her need to protect her children. There is no sentimentality about motherhood in *Le Lys,* but Madame de Mortsauf's love for Madeleine and Jacques is in effect presented as the *only* guarantee of social morality. In Henriette's feelings for her children, self-concern coincides with love for others. "Me! . . . which *me* are you speaking of?" she sharply asks Félix, who, in a curiously cruel compliment, has just praised her for not being willing—as he is—to give up eternity for a single day of happiness. "I feel many 'me's' in myself! These two children, she added pointing to Madeleine and Jacques, "are *me*" (938). What stings her in Lady Dudley's passion for Félix is Arabelle's inconceivable readiness to sacrifice her children. We see, in Henriette's admiration and horror of her rival's criminal greatness, how many inherited ideas Balzac's deceptively simple heroine has already brushed aside. "What! there are women who sacrifice their children to a man? Fortune, society, I can understand that, eternity, yes, perhaps! But one's children! to deprive oneself of one's children!" (960) Far from the social arena of Paris, Henriette reinvents social order as a natural necessity; her inability to break up her family, to abandon her children to the hysterically self-absorbed count, is her sublime version of self-protection.

Images of social disintegration in *Le Lys* are consistently images of family disintegration. At its worst, the caricature of family life becomes an idolatry of empty form. Félix rightly sees the connection between Lady Dudley's arrogant defiance of social conventions and a fanatical attachment to conventions. Her portrait is, to be sure, wildly improbable, and since she becomes, predictably, "the type" of the Englishwoman, Balzac treats us to a comically demonic vision of England. Nonetheless, Balzac's England is a metaphor for precisely that mechanical adherence to law which he himself seems at times to be advocating. There is no contradiction between Arabelle's spectacular adultery and her worship of the laws she breaks. The perfection of social rituals, meant to regulate morality so completely that "the practice of virtue seems to be the necessary functioning of machinery which operates on schedule" (944), leaves a conveniently wide margin for *un*regulated self-assertion. Félix speaks of that irritation with excessively developed forms, with "a constant perfection in things, a methodical regularity in habits," which leads women like Arabelle to "the adoration of the romantic and the difficult" (945). And her cultivation of the scandalous, of the extraordinary, is nothing more than a perverse way of proving herself worthy of the distinctions she is far from willing to give up for the sake of love: ". . . admit," she confesses to Félix, ". . . that given our insipid modern manners, the aristocracy can no longer distinguish itself except by something extraordinary in the realm of feeling. How can I teach the bourgeoisie that the blood in my veins is not like theirs, if not by dying differently from the way they die?" (949) The aristocrat's superiority consists in being able to demonstrate publicly the irrelevance of any social commitments to the most exquisite social performance. Thus, ". . . by a horrible mockery, [Lady Dudley] continued to observe the proprieties while making a display of herself with me in the Bois" (991).

Both Félix and society are, for Arabelle, occasions for self-glorification. She subverts love and social life by such an exaggerated devotion to both that she makes them look trivial compared to her superior inventions for serving them. ". . . No proof of love," Félix says of Arabelle, "surprised her; she had such a great desire for agitation, for noise, for the sensational, that probably nothing lived up to her ideal in that sort of beauty, which explains her frenetic efforts at love; in her extravagant imagination, she was concerned with herself and not with me" (991). The difference between Henriette and Lady Dudley is not, as Félix would like to think, one of "divine love" and "carnal love" (948). That trite opposition hardly does justice to the struggle with sexuality which has both nourished and threatened the love between Henriette and Félix. The dubious tribute of "divine love," as Jacques Borel has perceptively suggested, is probably the guilty Félix's euphemism for his own indifference.[62] Much more pertinently, Lady Dudley provides the "solution" which, once Henriette envisages it, causes her death: the mockery of *all* attachments by an apparent worship of one attachment. The unsatisfied appetites from which Henriette dies—she has refused food for over forty days and her life has been reduced to a constant hunger—menaces not only her family, but, most profoundly, her love itself. Lady Dudley illustrates the Balzacian lesson of discontinuity between appetite and *any* order, social or sentimental.

Henriette, as we shall see in a moment, is perhaps the most original of Balzac's creations in that, with greater care and a more humane intelligence than any other character in *La Comédie humaine,* she seeks to imagine and create nonrepressive forms, forms that would both discipline and satisfy desires. Arabelle, in contrast to Madame de Mortsauf, worships social forms as a dispensation from self-containment, and social hierarchy merely sanctions the superiority she feels to social obligations. Henriette is far from being moralistically shocked by her rival's flouting of conventions. She recognizes in Lady Dudley's flamboyant passion its most frightening element: an indifference to Félix consistent with an indifference to anything *but* that passion. ". . . She seems to me to place herself a little too boldly above conventions," Henriette says of Arabelle to Félix; "the woman who does not recognize any laws is very close to listening only to her caprices. People who are so restless and so anxious to shine have not received the gift of constancy" (975). The parody of social obedience thus inspires Balzac's most interesting argument for obedience to law: the harmony between such obedience and generosity of feeling, the continuity among *all* attempts to sublimate appetite into a desire for community.

No one is less naïve about the realities of social life than Henriette. All her advice, in the astonishing letter she writes as a

62. *Le Lys dans la vallée et les sources profondes de la création balzacienne* (Paris, 1961), p. 201.

guide to Félix's career in Paris, hinges on what she almost explicitly defines as a contract of hostility or alienation between the individual and society. Her "theory of duties" is a tactical conclusion, and she makes it clear that she is speaking "neither of religious beliefs, nor of feelings" when she advises Félix "to obey the general law in all things, without questioning it, whether it serves your interests or works against them." "The theory of individual happiness skillfully pursued at everyone else's expense" is an *imprudent* way of assuring just that happiness; an obedience to customs and laws provides the best strategy for social domination. Henriette sees the secret resources for personal success in precisely those virtues which society sanctifies as a brake to personal ambitions: ". . . rectitude, honor, loyalty, are the surest and quickest instruments of your fortune" (887–88). Her concise maxims compose a code of behavior for the most carefully calculated ambition. In fact, Henriette's picture of social life is really not too different from the one Vautrin draws for Rastignac. Like him, she sees the *salon* as not much more than a plush jungle. And while the ideal of Clochegourde is not quite the "patriarchal life" with two hundred Negro slaves which Vautrin dreams of leading on an American plantation, Henriette, like the great criminal, imagines a society both closer to nature and more congenial to feelings of solidarity. Certainly Clochegourde, unlike Vautrin's more theoretical paradise of inversion, can survive only if it takes Paris into account. Henriette's letter is a manual for survival, not an invitation to revolt. The social realism of *Le Lys* could be thought of in terms of an allegorical complexity: Félix's career in Paris is a way of testing the possibility of Clochegourde against more violent appetites. Henriette thus invites Félix to leave an immense margin for the destruction of what they have been carefully building; but he will finally return to the valley as one of the "tigers" from the jungle.

Appetite in *Le Lys* is primarily sexual. A single kiss threatens the fragile order of Henriette's marriage. "Do you still remember your kisses today?" Henriette writes to Félix in the letter he reads after her death; "they have dominated my life, they have furrowed my soul; the ardor of your blood awakened the ardor of mine; your youth penetrated my youth, your desires entered my heart." In her attempt to tame that "imperious pleasure" (1018-19), Madame de Mortsauf comes as close as any Balzacian character to finding nontautological forms for the magical power of desire, that is, forms capable of satisfying desire while transforming it. Sexuality makes of Henriette's and Félix's lives a drama of ingenuity. They have to invent the fictions which, far from denying their physical need, will provide it with satisfactions so extravagant and unexpected that desire can be deceived about its own nature.

Balzacian fantasies of androgyny serve this experiment. *Séraphîta*, which Balzac finished at the same time as *Le Lys* (in the fall of 1835), gives a mystical version of an optimistic doctrine capable, so to speak, of changing the emotional coefficient of sexual indistinctness. The "passage" from masculine to feminine can, as we have seen, be a dissipation of energy, a castration following the explosion of will. But this fearful fantasy, expressed in other terms, could be conceived of as an immense hope, that of restoring a lost unity between the self and the world by breaking down the barriers between the sexes. The mystery of dual sexuality in a single person solves the greater mystery of division, of separateness. The marriage of angels in Swedenborg, described by Monsieur Becker in *Séraphîta*, realizes this sexual merger: "In this union, which produces no children, man has contributed UNDERSTANDING, woman has contributed WILL: they become a single being. A SINGLE flesh here on earth; then they go to heaven after taking on the celestial form. On earth, in the state of nature, the mutual inclination of the two sexes toward physical pleasures is an EFFECT which entails fatigue and disgust; but in its celestial form, the couple, having become *the same* Spirit, finds in itself a constant source of pleasures." [63]

63. X, 511.

In *Le Lys,* desire is tamed partly by a more realistic version of merged sexual identities. Félix's timidity and his fragile, deceptively boyish appearance when Henriette first sees him at Clochegourde seem to allow her to forget the effect of his kisses and to interpret her feelings as protective and maternal. She probably thinks he is only fourteen, and when she learns his age she is almost grateful to him for having lived so long, as if his robust health could guarantee the survival of her own sickly children. Henriette dulls some of Félix's aggressiveness by treating him with the same authority she uses with Jacques and Madeleine; and she succeeds because Félix himself, never having had his mother's affection, hesitates between his new wish to assert himself sexually and his old need for maternal love. Henriette is ingenious at these family fictions. She subdues Félix by treating him like her child, and at the same time she safely confesses her own weakness by asking him to advise and protect her as her aunt had done: "Love me as my aunt loved me . . ." is the refrain meant to transform Félix's aggressiveness into avuncular guidance (917). Félix will be "less than a lover, but more than a brother": the latter is to contain but not destroy the former (854). Such family games, by prolonging Félix's childhood, keep him sexually amorphous; Henriette kisses Félix's hand "letting a tear of joy fall on it" when she learns that Louis XVIII laughingly calls his virginal aide "mademoiselle de Vandenesse" (912). But this defense can be only temporary, and when Félix returns to Clochegourde after two years in Paris, Henriette is terrified to see "the young man there where she had always seen a child." After making him repeat that he still loves her "like a sister" and "like a mother," she half-playfully reminds him that "if your strategy is to be a man with the king, you must know, sir, that here it is to remain a child. As a child, you will be loved!"—for the child "can't want anything I can't grant" (913–15). But already at Félix's previous visit, after only eight months away from Clochegourde, Henriette had recognized the defeat of these tac-

tics. "You have grown . . . ," she says simply to Félix, thus recognizing his physical presence as a threat to the family rather
than as a reinforcement of her family loyalties (907).

There is also an attempt to modulate the magnetism of will in
Le Lys. Generally a bombardment of the world, thought becomes
an appeasing influence at Clochegourde. The shift from WILL
and POWER to KNOWLEDGE takes the form of an emotional clair-
voyance. Henriette has the gift of Specialty, defined in Séraphîta
as "a kind of inner vision which penetrates everything," [64] but
she can exercise this "surprising faculty" only to predict the future of those she loves: her children and Félix (906). Instead of
the pyramidal hoarding of energy which makes of Gobseck's or
Bette's will a formidable armory, Henriette's self-denials give her
a protective (rather than destructive) power over the world.
The harsh melodrama of Splendeures et misères des courtisanes
and of Le Père Goriot is replaced by a certain sentimentalism;
conserved energy finds its way back into the world not as a pro-
jectile, but as waves of benevolence.

In their attempts to find stabilizing forms for their desires, the
lovers in Le Lys borrow imagined orders from the past. Félix
speaks of "my passion, which began the Middle Ages again and
brought back chivalry" (941). He compares Henriette to "the
Beatrice of the Florentine poet, the spotless Laura of the Venetian
poet" (883), and he prefaces the story of his childhood by telling
Henriette that at the reception in Tours she became for him "the
Lady in whose hands shines the crown destined to the victors of
the tournament" (829). These literary allusions are Félix's attempt to draw his own feelings into line with more distant and
helpfully conventionalized images of feelings (principally, those
of courtly love). Anxiously suspenseful about the form their
passion will take, he and Henriette use literary models as a kind
of prompter for their own emotions. And while more modern
literature trains us to think how difficult it is to shed the fictions

64. X, 523.

of the past (and how violent our parodies must become in order
to accomplish that),[65] Balzac illustrates the almost heroic nature
of *conformity* to the past. *Le Lys* is a tragedy of a failure of coincidence, that is, of the unbridgeable gap between this work of
fiction and other fictional models. It may seem peculiar to speak
of what is, after all, Balzac's originality as a failure, but his very
fidelity to his own imagination seals Henriette's doom. Nothing
would serve her love better and Balzac's work more poorly than
the success of Félix's appeals to medieval heroes and heroines.
Courtly love, as Félix seems to understand it, is precisely that
compromise between desire and order which his love needs in
order to survive. It is the sentimental luxury of a society where
the business of marriage excludes love, a noble if devious effort
to reconcile personal happiness with the preservation of social
order. And, exalted as courtly love may be, the lady stays married, and the lover's desires are (at least ideally) sublimated into
a life of service. So, far from feeling a need to free themselves
from memories and references irrelevant to their particular love,
Félix and Henriette welcome these memories in the hope that
they will adequately define their love. But an impersonal past
can be lighter than we perhaps like to think when we speak of
the so-called burden of history, and Balzac's lovers finally recognize the terrible originality of their desires.

The most inventive—and most precarious—line of defense in
Le Lys is suggested by the novel's title. Nature is the principal
artifice in the struggle against appetite. Félix's reveries about the
correspondences between his feelings and nature probably begin
the day he sees the Mortsauf château in the Indre valley for the
first time, at the end of his long walk from Tours to Frapesle.
Even before knowing her, Félix identifies Henriette as "the lily
of this valley" when he notices the "white point" of her percale
dress in the distance. And he immediately enrolls the landscape
in the service of his feelings. Unable to contain his desires, he

65. See Richard Poirier, "The Politics of Self-Parody," *Partisan Review*,
XXXV (Summer 1968).

makes them part of the scene: "Infinite love, with nothing to feed on other than a scarcely glimpsed object which filled my soul, seemed to me expressed by that long ribbon of water which runs in the sunlight between two green banks, as well as by those lines of poplars which embellish this vale of love with their swaying lace-work, by the oak forests which stand out between the vineyards on slopes which the river rounds off in constantly different ways, and by those blurred horizons which recede in contrasting patterns" (788–89). Alain has said that the view of the valley in *Le Lys* "elevates the soul less than it benumbs it. It constantly sets before us an excess of matter, and a happiness entirely contained in a fertile pulp." "Everything there is an invitation to the most earthly, most material happiness." In their struggle against the imperious demands of their own nature, Henriette and Félix find themselves in a country where ". . . everything cries out to us that nature is sufficient and even fulfills all our needs." [66] Alain rightly reminds us how hostile the landscape is to any asceticism, but the sensual variety and richness of nature are also *cultivated* by the lovers as the most important strategy of their extraordinarily liberal and indulgent self-discipline. Throughout the novel, metaphors from nature describe feelings, and feelings are read into all the details of the natural scene. These correspondences are a way of detouring passion into a richly satisfying view of the world; spirituality in *Le Lys* is never a denial of the senses, but rather consists in the lovers' invention and enjoyment of spectacles which constitute a new field for the play of the senses.

Perhaps the most famous passage in the novel describes the bouquets Félix composes for Henriette, those "symphonies of flowers" which express, discipline, and yet also provoke the lovers' desires. A floral language is substituted for the forbidden declaration of passion; these "fugitive allegories" provide "neutral pleasures" which, Félix writes, "were a great help to us in beguiling desires irritated by long periods of contemplating the

66. *En lisant Balzac* (Paris, 1935), p. 33.

loved one, as well as by those looks which take immense pleasure in shining into the very depths of the forms they penetrate. For me (I cannot say if the same was true for her), it was like the cracks through which the water held back in an indestructible dam gushes forth, and which often prevent a misfortune by making some concession to necessity" (859). Desire, the organizing principle of Félix's fantastically ingenious bouquets and of the landscape, becomes appeased by being transformed into a principle of spatial composition. Nature exorcizes sexual impulses by mediating them. The valley, the river, the flowers transform passion from a fantasy of explosive energy into a relatively stable symbolic fiction. The needs of desire are circumvented by the care with which they have to be composed, and this symbolization in nature perhaps exemplifies the process by which we modulate our aggressiveness toward the world by patiently testing the world as a field for self-dramatization. We plot its relation to the self and in this way refine more naïve illusions of the world as a mere, already given, extension of the self's substance.

That refinement takes place in Le Lys dans la vallée, although no single passage documents it adequately. Judged in isolation, the description of one of Félix's bouquets, for example, has undeniably ridiculous moments. The successful use of nature as a controlling metaphor for passion in Le Lys depends less on the quality of individual passages than on the casual persistence with which the strategy is applied throughout the novel. There is hardly a page on which images from nature—primarily of flowers, water, and animals—are not made to carry the burden of psychological description. On the first page, Félix, as he begins to tell Natalie about his childhood, imagines a "moving elegy" which would portray the "torments suffered in silence by souls whose still tender roots find only hard pebbles in the domestic soil, whose first foliage is torn to pieces by malevolent hands, whose flowers are stricken by frost just as they open" (771). Henriette imagines love as "an immense lake whose depths can never be sounded, where storms may be violent, but infrequent and contained within inviolable limits" (976), and Félix uses another water image to describe how his work-filled, chaste life in Paris helps to trace "the furrows of duty" in his heart and renew his love for Henriette: "Feelings always run rapidly in those deep-bedded streams which hold back the waters, purify them, incessantly refresh the heart, and fertilize life with the abundant treasures of a hidden faith which is like a divine source where the unique thought of a unique love multiplies" (941). Henriette's "obscure and full life" is like "those thickly wooded, flowery and unknown places" which Félix admires while picking the flowers for his bouquets (941). But after Félix's betrayal, Henriette's words "gave out some peculiar odor of flowers irrevocably cut" (952), and he finds her physically "mortified like the fruit on which bruises begin to appear and which an internal worm makes prematurely turn yellow" (956). These carefully developed, insistently repeated analogies tend to make the artifice seem natural, and an immense range of psychological nuance is expressed in metaphors which generally keep their literal distinctness. Richly detailed but never merely ornamental, the images from nature prevasively but unobtrusively carry the psychological substance of the story.

Certainly there are moments when, for example, the meteorology of feeling becomes excessive. Henriette's soul runs the risk of being *too* clearly visualized as a prairie when Félix describes how jealousy devastates it: "The hurricane of infidelity, similar to the Loire when it swells and permanently covers a part of the land with sand, had passed over her soul making a desert of opulent green meadows" (952). But we learn, because of the dramatic urgency in Félix's images, because of all that is at stake in this transference of feeling into landscape, not to *stop* uncomfortably (as we might in Flaubert) at such examples of metaphorical strain. The surest sign of success in this plot to civilize feeling by naturalizing it is perhaps a kind of graceful banality in Balzac's nature images in *Le Lys*. I find this appealing simplicity in the description of the valley's final tribute to Henriette just before her death: "The murmurs of evening—the melodious breeze in the foliage, the birds' last warbling, the insects' refrains and humming, the voices of the water, the plaintive cry of the tree-frog—the entire countryside was saying good-bye to the most beautiful lily of the valley, to her simple and rustic life" (1009). Or in Félix's explanation of the Indre's "consoling charm": "The agitation of a love full of desires held in check harmonizes with the water's agitation, the flowers which man's hand has not perverted express his most secret dreams, the pleasurable swaying of a boat vaguely imitates the thoughts floating through the soul" (926). And, as a last example, the contrast between the valley when Félix first saw it (". . . wasn't it freshly green, wasn't it all ablaze at that moment just as my desires and thoughts were freshly green and all ablaze?") and its autumnal gloom when, initiated into the drama of Henriette's life, he leaves Clochegourde to make his way in Paris: "Now the fields were bare, the poplar leaves were falling, and those which were left had the color of rust; the vine-branches were burned, the treetops presented the solemn hues of that *tanned* color which kings used to adopt for their costume and which hid the imperial purple of power under the brown shades of sorrow. Always in harmony with my thoughts, the valley, where the yellow rays of a weak sun were dying out, was offering me another vivid image of my soul" (884-85). Instead of escaping into nature in order to hear more clearly the complaints of their own injured spirits (the romantic way of minimizing nature), Félix and Henriette create a more complex sympathy between themselves and the world. They depend on the taming powers of nature, but they themselves must of course cultivate those powers. They must make nature contain, articulate, and plot the course of feelings whose violent energies would otherwise terrorize the lovers.

I have been speaking somewhat deviously of "success," deliberately confusing *Le Lys*'s quality as a novel with Félix and Henriette's attempts to contain their desires. The obscure irony of

the book is that the lovers' principal strategies are elaborated
with the greatest care when there is no longer any chance that
these efforts will save their love. Now, it could be argued, the
stakes are merely literary. But the distinction is, I think, superficial: the lovers' search for containing forms could be thought of
as a psychological metaphor for problems of literary creation.
They want to discipline their desires by giving them the composition of familial feelings, of prestigious historical models, and of
scenes from nature; and the discipline would result from the suggestiveness of these other structures, from their inspirational
value. The container would, hopefully, determine the nature of
the contained. Félix and Henriette seem to expect nature not
merely to detour their desires but also, so to speak, to infiltrate
the very substance of desire. Their metaphors are meant to be
psychologically contagious, and their experiment raises the literary question of the extent to which any composition can abolish
or at least make irrelevant its psychological antecedents or causes.

Is Félix, then, rather absurdly hoping for a greater artfulness in
retrospect, one which would effectively substitute "neutral pleasures" for those desires which have killed Madame de Mortsauf?
Or are we to understand the elaborate metaphorical composition of
Le Lys merely as a nostalgic literary bouquet to the memory of
his first love? If so, in writing that improbably long letter, Félix
acts both sentimentally and vainly; he—and as a result the drama
at Clochegourde—would be diminished in our eyes if we were
to see him simply as a complacent verbal embroiderer. He is partly
that, but, more profoundly, only the letter can demonstrate the
inevitability of Henriette's death. In a sense, their experiment
was obscured by the contingency of their love and their hope; it
is *now* that their strategies are most rigorously tested in the ideal,
"pure" conditions of a literature without hope. The nature and
function of metaphor in this literary composition are the keys to
Henriette's death. For there is little difference between the lovers'
and the writer's inventions; both are experiments in the possibility of psychological renovation through the development of new

forms. And Félix's letter to Natalie is perhaps Balzac's most
pessimistic statement about a phenomenon which we can now
look at more closely: the mysterious circularities of containment.

What are the reasons for failure in *Le Lys?* In a sense, nothing
is more natural, since Henriette's hopes are naïve. Having somehow never known sexual excitement until the day Félix kisses her
at the reception in Tours, she is overwhelmed by these new desires and yet seems to think that their satisfaction can be indefinitely postponed. With Lady Dudley, as Borel puts it, Félix
"finally escapes from that childhood which seems to be prolonged by a love which tries to be only maternal." [67] And Alain
defines Henriette's jealousy as a sudden perception of sensual
pleasures, pleasures which she understands—too late—that she
could save.[68] There are, of course, numerous signs of rebellious
desires in the novel long before Lady Dudley appears. We see
them most clearly in Félix, who wavers between docile obedience
and helpless rages against the pact of sexual continence which
he and Henriette have made. The case is more complicated with
Henriette, who, presented from Félix's point of view, seems generally to be taking the role of a sexual censor. Now when Félix
writes his letter, he knows about the struggles which Henriette
had apparently kept hidden from him. When he says: "If Henriette loved, she knew nothing of the pleasures of love nor of its
storms" (928), he has already heard her cry out for those pleasures on her deathbed. He can remember her wondering if life
is a "bitter joke," if God and virtue exist, if Lady Dudley is
"right" (963). And as he speaks of the saintly Madame de Mortsauf, Félix's mind contains the image of that "nameless something of Bossuet, which was struggling against nothingness, and
which hunger and disappointed desires were pushing into the
selfish combat of life against death" (1003). He has heard her,

67. *Le Lys dans la vallée et les sources profondes de la création balza-*
cienne, p. 198.
68. *En lisant Balzac,* p. 36.

dying, challenge Arabelle's hold over him: "You won't escape from me anymore! I want to be loved, I'll be as wild as Lady Dudley, I'll learn English so that I can say *My Dee* right" (1005). He has, finally, read the letter in which she tells him that she had sometimes hoped for some violence from him, that ". . . if in those moments when I became doubly cold, you had taken me in your arms, I would have died from happiness" (1019).

   These revelations come toward the end of the novel; they begin with Félix's return to Touraine with Lady Dudley, when Henriette's jealousy and suffering reveal to Félix, apparently for the first time, the violent and demanding nature of her love for him. Until then we see Madame de Mortsauf from the point of view of Félix's half-admiring, half-irritated idealization of her character, and some of the early incidents have to be revised in the light of what we learn later on. The advantages of this reticence on Félix's part are obvious. Instead of making a large part of his story irrelevant by crudely telling us that Henriette was more passionate than much of what he remembers suggests, he rightly shows how important his mistaken view of her was to their love: they helped to make him more timid, to discipline the desires which threatened their union more than he knew. And this tension between the blindness Félix faithfully re-creates and the occasionally suggested violence of Henriette's feelings gives to *Le Lys* a narrative reticence rare in Balzac's fiction. His most interesting characters—as I have shown with Vautrin and Bette—have a complexity which the narrator never succeeds in completely "covering," but we nevertheless usually feel in Balzac the *intention* of making narrative comment perfectly adequate to the meanings which his stories dramatize. In fact, Balzacian action can often seem like an unnecessary bonus: it may simply illustrate (without enriching or contesting) the comprehensive expositions which precede it. In *Le Lys*, on the other hand, there is an unusual distance between narrative awareness and dramatic example, and Balzac, as we shall see when we look at

Félix more closely, may be unwilling to close the gap entirely even at the end of the novel. With Henriette, Balzac relies more heavily on action than on exposition for accurate characterization, which means that words and gestures in Le Lys have both an exceptional density of meaning and an exceptional margin of obscurity. Henriette's desires escape Félix for a long time; they are contained in mysterious remarks or movements which briefly light up areas not being analyzed. Perhaps only retrospectively do we understand all the despair in Henriette's "I have not counted the days . . ." (879) when Félix reasonably announces that after almost three months at Frapesle he has to think of returning to his family, or the sexual fears in her noting that Félix, after his first long absence, has "grown up" (907), or the self-accusation in Henriette's extraordinary response to Félix's promise not to demand more from her than she is willing to give: "Your generosities kill me . . ." (939). While the lovers attempt to re-create their love by identifying it with a system of rich metaphorical inventiveness, Le Lys simultaneously demonstrates the approximative nature of language. Far from transforming feelings by their powerful suggestiveness, Henriette's words often drily and inadequately point to those feelings as inexpressible and unchangeable. The pessimism of the litote qualifies the exuberance of metaphor.

Much more obscure than Henriette's desires, however, are the reasons why Félix fails to notice them. The impact of "Your generosities kill me" is due largely to the impression Félix has been creating of himself as less able to control his sexual demands than Henriette. One or two other remarks suggest that while Félix may now know more about Henriette than he did in the past, he still knows very little about himself. "As for you, Félix . . . ," Henriette tells him even after he has betrayed her with Lady Dudley, ". . . you are the friend who could not do any harm. . . . How many times I found you superior to me! you were high-minded and noble, while I was petty and guilty! There, it is said, I can only be a faint light you look up to, a cold and sparkling but unalterable light" (973). That "only" startles us: it suggests Henriette's distaste for the roles which she and Félix have invented, her sense of their experiment as perhaps an insult to that more richly human intuition which made her immediately see a "shared emotion" in the erotic stimulation provoked by Félix's kisses at the ball in Angoulême (1018). And how are we to take this whitewashing of Félix—as sentimental generosity, as a lover's blindness, as the self-accusation of an overly scrupulous, naïvely pious woman? Another interpretation is of course possible: this moral praise accurately characterizes Félix. How passionate and demanding has he really been?

I suppose the following remarks on Félix should be somewhat tentative, in part because *Le Lys* can be coherently understood without them. If Félix betrays his love for Henriette, it may simply be because, as he tells her in rather more complicated language, a man cannot live without sex indefinitely and keep his health. The psychological coherence of *Le Lys dans la vallée* does, however, strike me as less crudely "realistic" than that. If tentativeness is called for, it is because Félix is one of Balzac's most obscure self-projections, perhaps slightly too ambiguous to be completely successful as a character within conventions which tolerate great complexity but not psychological incoherence or disintegration. We do not really know what Balzac thinks of Félix, and, since Balzac is not Gide, there is no reason to feel that he is deliberately dropping clues throughout the novel designed to justify Natalie's indictment of Félix. The epistolary form conveniently makes possible a limitless complicity with character as well as a limitless duplicity about character.

In her nasty answer to Félix's confession, Natalie accuses him of having "killed the most beautiful and the most virtuous of women on your entrance into society." He punished Henriette for not being Lady Dudley, Lady Dudley for not being Henriette; "what is going to happen to *me*, since I am neither one nor the other?" Natalie ends by advising Félix never to tell his story again: "Every woman would notice the hardness of your heart, and you would always be unhappy" (1031–32). *Une Fille d'Eve*, where Félix reappears, is not too much help in determining Balzac's attitude toward him in *Le Lys*. True, it seems to be a certain "dryness of heart" in Félix which makes his wife anxious to enjoy the excitement of an adventure with the flamboyant Raoul Nathan. We see Félix as a coldly gentle husband whose irreproachable devotion to Marie includes everything but passion. But we also see Natalie de Manerville again, and not in a very favorable light: she and Lady Dudley (among others) do their best to promote the cuckoldry of Félix. Marie's betrayal is their revenge, and Natalie's letter in *Le Lys* may be the first step in that revenge: a "friendly" warning about his character as a way of striking back at him for having loved other women. She is unfair because she is furious. It seems right to speak, as Natalie does, of Félix's lack of "tact" in writing to her about Henriette's and Arabelle's perfections, but does Balzac really want us to see him as a murderer?

Perhaps not; but even if we leave a wide margin for Natalie's jealousy, her accusations do correspond to something subtly cruel in Félix. He is peculiarly insensitive to the signs of passion in Henriette. When the count falls ill, for example, Félix bizarrely interprets Henriette's depression and anxiety as a sign of her "purity"; he sees himself as only an "accident" in Henriette's life, and angrily reproaches himself for not having attached her to him "by the chains of indisputable rights which possession creates." "Surely," he concludes, "she loved as Laura de Noves loved Petrarch, and not as Francesca da Rimini loved Paolo: what a frightful discovery for someone who dreamed of uniting these two kinds of love!" (928–29) Félix is a subtle reasoner, as Henriette sarcastically points out when he justifies his affair with Lady Dudley by a theory on the dangers of chastity (961–62), and he uses his reasoning less to calculate his chances of success with Henriette than to prove to himself that she is less tempted to give in to him than we know she is. Who is the chaste, untroubled partner in the scene where, desperate at the idea of Félix's departure after the count's recovery, Henriette leads Félix into her bedroom, kneels before him, and gives him a lock of the hair she has lost since knowing him: "I leaned slowly toward her forehead, she did not bend down to avoid my lips, I kissed her chastely, without any guilty intoxication, without any thrill of sensual pleasure, but with a solemn tenderness and compassion. Did she want to sacrifice everything? Was she only going, as I had done, to the edge of the precipice? If love had led her to surrender herself, she would not have had that deep calm, that religious look, and she would not have said to me in her pure voice:—You're not angry with me anymore?" (940–41)

Félix is a master in the art of containment. It is perhaps his tranquil asceticism, his "generosities" which make Henriette suffer more effectively than any aggressive sexual pursuit. Confronted with the astonishing ease and rapidity with which he passes from a dangerous but flattering passion to a sort of pale spirituality, Henriette understandably accuses only herself at this spectacle of desires so skilfully tamed. Félix learns his lesson too well; his demonstrations of self-control are parodies of the much more liberal compromise Henriette seems to have imagined between desire and discipline. "Why shouldn't I have her?" Félix asks himself after his first return to Clochegourde, and, "tormented by mad ideas which unbearable desires inspired," he spends an hour that night crying "with rage" in front of Henriette's door, but his abrupt transition to total calm is almost comical: "When I began to feel cold, I went upstairs again, got back into bed and slept calmly till morning" (908–9).

Félix is the most menacing presence of Le Lys. He brings into this rare Balzacian effort to imagine desire as both expansive and nondestructive the more primitive fantasy of an emotional hoarding harmful both to the self and the world. The version of containment which I mentioned earlier—that partial castration

for the sake of omnipotence—reappears in the curious pleasure
Félix experiences in refusing to satisfy his desires.[69] "I don't
know," Félix writes referring to his hour of rage outside Henriette's bedroom, "how to explain (is it something predestined,
some mystery of character?) the pleasure I find in going to the
edge of precipices, in probing into the abyss of evil, in questioning its depths, feeling its coldness and coming away deeply
moved" (908–9). "The abyss of evil" means nothing here; it is
a fancy way of obscuring the real subject of the sentence, which
is the pleasure not of flirting with evil but rather of frustrating
desire. Félix sentimentalizes this masochistic satisfaction in another passage where he tries to explain why he and Henriette
keep postponing their first long talk together: "Perhaps she
liked as much as I did those shudders similar to the emotions of
fear, shudders which ravage the sensibility, during those moments when one holds back a life ready to overflow, when,
yielding to the modest reticence which disturbs young girls
before they show themselves to the husband they love, one hesitates to reveal one's heart" (826–27). How adequately does a
bride's sexual timidity describe the exhausting rhythm of self-
excitement and self-mutilation suggested in the first part of the
sentence? Finally, speaking of the need he felt not to "offend"
Henriette with his desires, of the care with which he kept

69. This sensual asceticism is the main point of resemblance between
Le Lys and the novel to which it has been most frequently compared:
Sainte-Beuve's *Volupté*. But the differences between the two works are
more numerous and more important than the similarities. Henriette is
one of Balzac's most beautifully realized creations; Madame de Couaën,
about whose feelings we know almost nothing, hardly exists. Most important, in *Volupté* there is no attempt even to imagine a liberal solution to
the problem of fearful desires. Amaury is interesting *only* because of his
inability to connect sexual satisfaction with emotional involvement. The
psychological interest of Sainte-Beuve's novel lies in his rather murky
portrait of Amaury's anguished promiscuity and, more deeply, of his
fears of impotence. The pathos of *Volupté*—which makes it profoundly
nonBalzacian—is that the only "therapy" Sainte-Beuve can imagine for
his hero's troubled sexuality is the total renunciation of sex in the priest-
hood.

hidden from her a passion whose corrosive heat he compares to that of a red-hot iron, Félix admits to Natalie the secret pleasures of unfulfilled desires: "Furthermore—shall I confess it to you, you who have such a deeply feminine nature?—this situation offered moments of bewitching languors, of divine sweetness, as well as the satisfactions which follow sacrifices tacitly agreed to" (850). But there is no reason to think that Henriette is less of a woman than Natalie, and not once does Henriette mention those "bewitching languors," or the "divine sweetness" of an incomplete love. Félix alone appears to enjoy deliberately aborted stimulations, a kind of emotional *coitus interruptus,* and it is perhaps this artfully controlled playing with their love which gives him the coolness and the poise which Henriette pathetically interprets as moral superiority.

Such self-containments subvert Félix and Henriette's efforts to appease their desires by recomposing them as luxuriant images of nature. And Balzac suggests the inevitability of his hero's undermining the experiment he apparently agrees to try with Madame de Mortsauf. The first part of *Le Lys* is called "The Two Childhoods," and, after hearing Félix's memories of his unhappy life at home and in school, Henriette makes the natural but dangerous mistake of confusing his childhood with hers. Both were unloved by their parents but, interestingly enough, Henriette, unlike Félix, had in her aunt, the Duchesse de Verneuil, a model of maternal affection, of a generous, uncalculating love. Félix, on the other hand, much more abandoned, reacts with "a horrible mistrust of myself" (775); in front of the mockery or coldness he finds each time he tries to be expansive, he withdraws proudly into himself and learns to hold back his feelings and develop "a strength which grew from being put to use and predisposed my soul to all sorts of moral resistance" (772). By the time he leaves school, he has "a temperament of iron" and, he adds, because of his prolonged puberty, "no young man was better prepared than I was to feel, to love" (781). The conclusion is somewhat unexpected. It would seem more accurate to

say that Félix's childhood has prepared him for precisely the kind
of self-torture and torture of others which I think he brings to
his love for Henriette. The affective pattern from which Félix
seems unable to free himself is that of a generous expansiveness
followed by a startlingly sudden drying up of feeling; his most
impulsive advances become abrupt retreats.

Félix's self-control is as ambiguous as Gobseck's satiety. The
hoarding of energy, as we have seen, magically keeps the self
intact at the same time that it gives a surer, more devastating
aim on the world. *Le Lys* demystifies this solution and actually
gives it a kind of psychological plausibility. In *Gobseck* and *La
Peau de chagrin*, Balzac merely affirms the mysterious strength
of conserved energy. In *Le Lys*, he translates his theory into more
psychologically concrete terms. Félix demonstates the power of
indifference as an instrument of revenge. The philosophical
elaborations of spent and conserved energy are absent in *Le Lys*,
and we see Félix at least partly engaged in what strikes me as
a permanent revenge against an unloving woman. It is as if he
had to find his mother's indifference in all the women he loved,
and punished them for their anticipated coldness with a deep
reserve in himself. Furthermore, by so consistently placing Henriette in the rarefied regions of disembodied love, Félix reduces
her spirituality from a creation to an instinct. Perhaps nothing
threatens their love more than Félix's falsely generous assumption that only *his* desires have to be disciplined. A strangely
excessive good faith thus undermines a joint creation. In a sense,
it is Félix's passivity which brings violence into *Le Lys*; his
idealizations isolate Henriette and camouflage those "moral resistances" which he had developed long ago as a tactic of revenge
and domination.

Finally, each of the women who love Félix is taunted by the
spectacle or the memory of a love greater than hers. And in this
amorous competition, Félix measures the love he inspires by the
suffering he causes; as he leaves Clochegourde to rejoin Lady
Dudley, he is surprised by "a feeling of pride at knowing I was

the arbiter of two such exceptional destinies, at being the idol, for such different reasons, of two such superior women, and from having inspired passions so great that, in both cases, death would come if I failed them" (986). Indeed, perhaps only death can convince him of love—a condition which Henriette promptly satisfies. But death is separation, and, curiously enough, Félix's behavior seems also designed to plunge him back into the unhappy solitude of his childhood. Henriette dies; Lady Dudley and Natalie leave him; and Marie neglects him for Raoul. He provokes the very hostility he fears and again becomes the unloved boy whom these extravagantly loving women were meant to rescue.

With all this, Félix is somehow not unappealing. He has so much conscious good will, such generous intentions and such dignified reasonableness, and, perhaps above all, such a mysteriously lonely fate in *La Comédie humaine* that he easily elicits our sympathy. There is nonetheless a strong dose of brutality in his character. His blocked effusiveness is, first of all, brutal to the self: Félix's "conservation" of desire dissipates energy in a way perhaps analogous to the self-draining effects of the "knowledge" Balzac imagined as less dissipating than "will" or "power." Félix's "dryness of heart" parallels and prefigures that drying up of his creative powers which Balzac complained of toward the end of his life. And what I have called Félix's indifference to sexual satisfaction is the condition of a more profound Balzacian satisfaction: the reticence and unreliability of his passion help him to dominate and even destroy other wills. Arabelle and especially Henriette "spend" themselves in their passion. Félix's cool play of one against the other is the subtle strategy of his appetite for power, the "civilized" version of instincts which he himself recognizes when he wonders if he belongs to "the race of tigers."

Le Lys contains its *dénouement* from the start. "The Two Childhoods" points to the defeat of an experiment made in the

hope of by-passing psychological determination. "Yes indeed,"
Henriette profoundly says to Félix when she forces him to take
her to see Lady Dudley, "my life is consistent in its greatest as
well as in its smallest circumstances" (971). The "theme" of
her life has resisted all her efforts to compose it differently: her
mother, her husband, her children, and finally Félix have all col-
laborated in the monotonous design of suffering. The deep
pessimism which Henriette reveals during her first long talk
with Félix is a skeptical view, before the fact, of their love; it
expresses her sense of an irrelevance in the variety of human
choices. In order to change the course of their lives and to modulate the violence of their desires, Félix and Henriette admirably
but futilely exploit that variety in their effort to seduce into new
patterns a future they already contain within themselves.

There is also complicity between the brutality of desire and
the language of modulated desire. Nature is an order which
contains the threats to containment. The very richness of the
natural world provides occasions for disrupting harmony without
disrupting metaphorical consistency. The valley of the Indre,
intended as an alternative to the jungles of *La Comédie humaine*, ends by attracting the noxious vegetation and the wild
life of *Le Père Goriot* and *La Cousine Bette*. Lions and tigers
menace the swallow, the nightingale, the swan. The count's face
"vaguely resembled that of a white wolf with blood in his snout"
(803); when he is angry, his eyes sparkle like "those of tigers"
(823); and as he advances to strike Henriette, his yellow eyes
"made him look like a starving beast coming out of a forest"
(874). Lady Dudley hides her jealousy of Henriette "with the
energy of the hunter who doesn't notice a wound as he rushes
toward the fiery moments of the kill." The care with which she
keeps Félix a prisoner makes him think of "the lioness who has
grabbed in her mouth and brought back to her den some prey to
nibble at" (949). Will Félix himself be the devouring tiger, the
aggressive lover who pursues his victim with "the hunter's painful patience" (822), or will he surround Henriette, the lily,

"with a triple hedge of thorns, in order to protect her from storms, from all contact, from all injury" (849)?

There is a zoological, a botanical, and even a meteorological suspense in Le Lys. The swan's song may occasionally appease the more ferocious animals, and the lily's whiteness diffuses ideas of moral purity, but the floral and animal worlds which Félix creates in order to protect Henriette are also particularly vulnerable to attack. Henriette bends "like a lily heavy with rain" under the weight of Félix's betrayal (952), and the image of this delicate flower seems to awaken impulses of strangulation, symbolized and perhaps encouraged by references to more sinister natural growths. The difficulties of Henriette's family life have their "roots" and their "boughs" which, "similar to lianas, stifled, inhibited the family's movements and its breathing, enveloped the running of the household in slender but multiple threads, and delayed the growth of their fortune by complicating the most necessary acts . . ." (852). Félix remembers his joy at being able to come to Clochegourde without exciting the count's suspicions; ". . . the previous events of my life," he adds, "led me to spread myself out like a climbing plant in the beautiful soul where the entrancing world of shared feelings was opening up for me" (850). The image of course suggests more than emotional harmony; the hint of Félix's desires as parasitic and smothering is incongruous with the more pious version of his motives at the end of the sentence. Nature also provides the frankly brutal images which describe the count's frustration at no longer being able to torment Henriette, who has become indifferent to everything but her jealousy of Lady Dudley: "No longer finding any soft earth in which to drive his arrows, this man had become as anxious as the child who does not see the poor insect he is tormenting move anymore" (954). Henriette, infinitely richer than any of Balzac's other "virtuous" characters, nevertheless shares the fate of all those who authentically sacrifice their aggressiveness in La Comédie humaine, and the metaphors used to describe her emphasize the suicidal nature of such renunciations. The world is a reservoir of images diversified enough to accommodate *any* feelings. Metaphorical confrontations between the swallow and the tiger give a "natural" logic to the *dénouement* which the metaphorical detours of *Le Lys* were meant to elude.

Nature provides a complex and ambiguous inspiration in *Le Lys dans la vallée*. The lovers' hope is that the valley will tame desire by redefining it as a peaceful landscape, that Félix's bouquets will satisfy the senses without exciting sensual appetites. The future of their passion will presumably be determined by the forms in which they carefully and artfully choose to recognize their passion. But the "circuit" of desire traps them. Henriette accepts Félix's bouquets in the hope of appeasing her desires, but she finds in them a seductive new version of her desires. The floral transposition of passion has become so successful that the mere sight and odor of flowers are enough to provoke Henriette's rebellious cries just before her death. "Thus the flowers had caused her delirium," Félix concludes after writing that the doctor had removed from the sickroom the bouquets "which were acting too strongly on the nerves" of Madame de Mortsauf; "she was not responsible for it" (1008). But the flowers violently agitate Henriette's senses precisely because of that complicity between their desires and the landscape which she and Félix have established. Félix's presence is no longer even necessary; the unmistakable imprint of desire on the landscape has made of the valley an inescapable, continuous temptation.

The subject of *Le Lys* is, then, the self-contesting logic of containment. Félix and Henriette's inventions or appropriations —the fictions of family, of history, or of nature—have, in principle, a disciplinary function. Desires "settle" into these containing forms; they become composed, in the sense of more tranquil, by being submitted to an art of patient composition. And the containers of desire are meant to effect an alchemy of desire. They give to the Balzacian fantasies of energy a reassuring intelligibility which, it is hoped, will inspire the nature of desire itself. But where does that intelligibility really come from? Félix and Henriette undermine the disciplinary nature of those containers by the very care with which they "pour" their desires into them. The fictions they adopt about their passion merely give an elaborate formal consecration to passion. An imperfectly, often incoherently articulated fantasy of the dangers of appetite is thus promoted to a systematic interpretation of *all* experience. The language of desire appropriates nature, makes of the world a spectacle of passion. By a logic implicit in the word containment itself, the content of that which is meant to control destructive impulses coincides with those very impulses. Because the self fills the container with the desires it seeks to contain (to modulate and even to transform), language and the world merely provide seductively diversified forms for a remarkably tenacious, repetitive theme. They both stimulate and give shape to the Balzacian fantasies of dangerous energy. Finally, there is not only the "spatial" conformity between mental structures and the patterns of language and of nature, but also a temporal continuity between beginnings and ends. In a sense, very little happens in *Le Lys*; time is merely another illusory resource for re-creating the self. Both Félix and Henriette attract fates already contained in their childhoods. Everything that follows, including their love, has the superfluity characteristic of a Balzacian novel, where the *dénouement* often strikes us as an almost unnecessary proof of the predictive, containing powers of the exposition.

Of course, to see only these conformities in Félix's and Henriette's lives would be to miss their richly inventive—if finally unsuccessful—attempts to escape from those conformities. In the same way, the prophetic profiles of buildings and persons in a Balzacian exposition can never include the diversity of character and situation which accompanies the working out of a plot often fixed and exposed before the action even begins. Nevertheless, in both cases Balzac illustrates his profound skepticism

about the particular occasions of time and of language. One of
Louis Lambert's thoughts is that " 'the events which testify to
Humanity's action, and which are the product of its intelligence,
have causes in which they are preconceived, as our actions are
accomplished in our thoughts before being reproduced in the
external world; forewarnings or prophecies are the *perception*
of these causes . . .' .' "[70] As Georges Poulet has said, Balzac
invites us to move back from present, concrete realities to a "more
and more abstract anteriority," to the causes which contain a
character's destiny before it is lived.[71] In its most extreme version, this sense of tyrannical causality leads Balzac to a serious
defense, in *Le Cousin Pons*, of the art of palm-reading. Our body
expresses our fate, our hands express our body: "thus we have
palmistry." If someone can read your past, he can just as easily
predict the future which existing causes will produce.[72] Prophecy
is possible because contingency is irrelevant; the world merely
reproduces events already enacted in the mind.

In a sense, this extraordinary devaluation of whatever actual-
izes mental life (time, language, novelistic action) expresses
Balzac's immense confidence in the power of thought: the world,
as I said earlier, docilely becomes what is willed or desired.
And this primitive identification between desires and events
explains the paradoxically abstract nature of Balzac's fiction. His
work may include more *things* than that of any other novelist,
but their systematic relevance to easily recognizable patterns of
significance makes all those objects peculiarly weightless. They
provide a wider field for the realization of preconceived designs,
but they seldom threaten the unity of those designs. Thus, Balzac's often tiresome descriptions and digressions are both unnecessary and never irrelevant. He is always ready to stop his story
for a piece on the organization of the underworld, on the tyranny

70. X, *Louis Lambert*, 400.
71. *La Distance intérieure*, in *Etudes sur le temps humain*, II (Paris,
1952), 181 and 159.
72. VI, 625–26.

of journalism, or the decadence of the French nobility, but his immense range of reference hardly affects the astonishing consistency of his narrative. The diversified occasions of a Balzacian novel add little that is problematic or unexpected to its development; it is as if he indulged in the most extraordinary diffusiveness only to illustrate his invulnerable coherence. Balzac himself may very well have been dazzled by his powers of absorption. The more his work grew, the more clearly he saw its coherence, and his belief in the materiality of will was undoubtedly confirmed by the less magical but perhaps no less impressive spectacle of a compositional victory over a potentially chaotic variety.

I have said that this power, while it exhilarated Balzac, seems also to have terrified him; he is always trying to imagine ways of protecting himself and the world from his explosively possessive energies. Balzac often thought of this danger in terms of physical violence and brutal social antagonisms. *Le Lys dans la vallée* restates his fears in a way both psychologically and artistically more sophisticated: Félix and Henriette suffer from the tautological nature of their self-inventions. They seek to escape from the power which allows us to fit every occasion into a familiar structure, which gives to our lives a unity and a conformity so adequately expressed in each of our acts and utterances that life itself becomes irrelevant to its meaning. The pathos of *Le Lys* is that Félix should reenact and even intensify his effort to escape from that willed fatality when the circuit of self-imprisoning forms has already been completed. But perhaps because of its very futility, Félix's letter can examine, with more leisure and in greater detail, both his resources for self-re-creation and the reasons for his failure. Now he is "freer" than ever; he can transform *all* the events of the drama at Clochegourde into the suggestive metaphors originally designed to change the course of those events. And as each incident, each character, each digression is drawn into the metaphorical network which Félix's language composes, the verbal consistency of *Le Lys* retrospectively helps us to explain the inevitability of Henriette's fate.

The expressive resources of nature, instead of inspiring more
flexible, modulated desires, merely make intelligible, as an objective fact about the world, the violence of desire from which
Henriette dies.

Le Lys dans la vallée, almost entirely constructed as an exercise in metaphorical ingenuity, is Balzac's most important statement on the limitations of realistic fiction. The metaphorical
richness of the novel corresponds to the dramatic variety of La
Comédie humaine itself. Balzac's attempt to cover all the forms
of social life could be thought of as a way of testing the self-
expanding possibilities of imaginative activity. The observer of
French society would treat material so diversified that the self
would finally coincide with a variety irreducible to any single
psychological scheme. The godlike power which Balzac dreamed
of would perhaps have consisted in that totally unrecognizable
presence of the author which the realistic novelist aims at in his
ideal of art as the mirror of reality. But Balzac's attachment to
the notion of unity—among phenomena and between the self
and the world—commits him to a different kind of power.
". . . Everything hangs together in the real world," he writes
in Le Cousin Pons. "Every movement in it corresponds to a cause,
every cause is connected to the whole; and, consequently, the
whole is represented in the slightest movement." [73] But this
theory of the particular as a container of the universal means
very little except as an expression of Balzac's confidence in his
own unifying powers, in his ability to make even minor fictional
occasions of La Comédie humaine adequate representations of
his whole enterprise. It is in this sense that, as Poulet has profoundly said of Balzac, the act of writing becomes curiously
superfluous. Action is a "useless repetition" of the Idea.[74] Everything is contained in its cause, including the work itself; and
Balzac's most arrogant—and most self-limiting—claim is undoubtedly that an effect is nothing but a cause made actual.

73. VI, 627.
74. La Distance intérieure, p. 191.

That is, by denying the imbalance between intention and realization which attests the uncontrollable richness of the contexts in which intentions must be played out, he defies experience to mystify him, to disorganize him, to coerce him into a less rigid posture of will. His power is to make time irrelevant, a power which, as we have seen in *Le Lys*, merely imprisons the self in the circle of its own repetitive representations. The "conformities" of Félix's and Henriette's lives illustrate the melancholy invulnerability of spatial form.

Our conclusion was, in an appropriately Balzacian fashion, contained in our beginning. *Le Lys dans la vallée* has been our "digression" into Balzac's most impressive effort to reconcile psychological and social stability with an exuberant indulgence of the self's desires and energies. But Balzac's principal literary strategies (analogous to his advocacy of social hierarchy) for maintaining order, or, more exactly, for transforming a single, explosive act of will into the distinct units of a novelistic space, are an extraordinarily systematized narrative presentation and a mania for classification. These strategies resemble the mechanical defense against passion which Henriette finds in the monotonous discipline of her needlework (871), and which Félix welcomes in his physical work at Clochegourde during the grape-picking season. "I enjoyed the ineffable pleasure of external work, which carries life along by regulating the course of passion, for passion, without this mechanical movement, might easily set fire to everything" (862). By proclaiming the divisibility of will into a panoramic image of social "species," Balzac was able to explain and approve of the variety of *La Comédie humaine* and thus escape the logic of silence implicit in the notion of containment. And while that notion may strike us as preceding from a naïve fantasy about the self's power over the world, it does raise the question of the extent to which literature —indeed any expression—re-forms or merely repeats images of the self. By illustrating, in a world as diversified as that of *La Comédie humaine*, the tautological nature of imagined orders,

Balzac suggests the gap between the richness of our experience and our resources for interpreting experience. His uniqueness undoubtedly lies in the curious mixture of an undaunted, Gargantuan enthusiasm about all life's occasions and an inability to exploit them as promoters of psychological change. Perhaps only a man less concerned with power—more indifferent, in one sense, to some of life's opportunities—could present convincing images of such exploitation. In the history of the French novel, such self-revising nonchalance belongs only to Stendhal.

II

STENDHALIAN PRISONS AND *SALONS*
[*La Chartreuse de Parme*]

Stendhal's favorite image for politics in a novel is that of "a pistol shot in the middle of a concert." [1] In his enthusiastic account of *La Chartreuse de Parme*, Balzac not only fails to complain about the disruptive noise; he seems hardly to be aware that it interrupts more harmonious sounds. *La Chartreuse*, Balzac writes, is *"The Modern Prince*, the novel that Machiavelli

1. See, for example, *Romans et nouvelles*, ed. Henri Martineau, 2 vols. (Paris, 1952), I, 105 (*Armance*), 576 (*Le Rouge et le noir*), and II, 405 (*La Chartreuse de Parme*). For *La Chartreuse* quote, see *The Charterhouse of Parma*, tr. Lowell Bair, introduction by Harry Levin (New York, 1960), p. 349. Subsequent page references to *La Chartreuse* will be given in the text; the first reference in each case will be to the English translation, the second to volume two of the Pléiade edition of Stendhal's *Romans et nouvelles*. Quotations from Stendhal's other novels will also be from this French edition.

Except for Bair's English versions of *La Chartreuse*, I have translated all the passages in French referred to in this chapter. Bracketed passages in a translation, here and elsewhere where I have used available English translations of the novels I discuss, are my substitutions for parts of a translation which I have felt needed some modification.

would write, if he were living banished from Italy in the nine-teenth century." Gina, Mosca, and Ferrante Palla are the Bal-zacian heroes of *La Chartreuse*; Fabrice is little more than the colorless *jeune premier* who lacks a "grande pensée," a "feeling which would make him superior to the people of genius who surrounded him." Consequently, on the important question of that elite audience whom Stendhal is addressing in *La Char-treuse*, Balzac can confidently write: ". . . the greatest obstacle to the fame which M. Beyle deserves comes from the fact that *La Chartreuse de Parme* can find readers capable of appreciating it only among diplomats, ministers of state, observers, the most eminent society people, the most distinguished artists; in short, readers from among the twelve or fifteen hundred people who are at the head of Europe." [2] It would indeed be difficult to imagine Fabrice and Clélia "at the head of Europe," but we may hesitate to dismiss them as easily as Balzac does in his generous misreading of *Le Chartreuse de Parme*. Are Balzac's figures of power the men to whom Stendhal is speaking most intimately, The Happy Few to whom *La Chartreuse* is dedi-cated?

Stendhal's pictures of society are both incisive and crude, or, more exactly, they have the incisiveness of an intelligent but total rejection of almost all forms of social participation. Society in Stendhal is primarily politics, the behavior by which social life is shaped into hierarchies of power. And politics, especially in *La Chartreuse de Parme*, can be easily summed up: it is the frantic, unscrupulous attempt to gain the power necessary to guarantee a constant satisfaction of vanity. The importance of vanity in the story can hardly be overestimated; major political events, shifts of power, take place because someone's image of himself has been either flattered or attacked. The favor Mosca enjoys during the reign of Ernest IV is due largely to his skill in keeping the prince from feeling ashamed of looking in terror

2. "Etudes sur M. Beyle," in *Œuvres complètes*, ed. Marcel Bouteron and Henri Lognon (Paris, 1912–40), XL, 374 and 402.

under all his beds for Jacobins. Fabrice is thrown into prison because the prince cannot forgive Gina for her insolent airs of independence the night she threatened to leave Parma and forced Ernest IV to write a letter promising not to sign the order for Fabrice's arrest. And Mosca's credit with Ernest V is dangerously precarious because the young prince has heard that Mosca referred to him once as " 'that child' " (354; 411).

The picture of Parma could be thought of less as an attempt to detail the complex machinery of government than as a dramatic expression of Stendhal's—and Fabrice's—opinion of government. We can already see one of the ways in which the portrait of society is a function of Fabrice's temperament: Stendhal seems more interested in justifying his hero's scorn—and isolation—than in the plausibility of his portrait. Indeed, the real importance of the courtiers of Parma in the novel is as a kind of negative of the truly aristocratic personality. While aristocracy in Stendhal is essentially the ability to imagine, recognize, and cultivate the "delicate plant" of happiness (134; 167), politics is the area in which Stendhal illustrates an inaptitude for happiness. Stendhal's obsession with vanity is an obsession with the vice most incompatible psychologically with the virtue of happiness. The vain person has to be *told* he is happy. A title of nobility for Rassi and a Louis XIV pose for Ernest IV are the signs by which others are expected to recognize satisfactions which are in fact deduced from other people's envy. And the nastiness of vanity is in its intolerance of the absence of vanity. What the courtiers hate in Gina and Fabrice is their scandalous indifference to flattery, their talent for being independently happy. ". . . The court as well as the public," Stendhal significantly says about the joyful reaction to Fabrice's imprisonment, "took spiteful delight in Fabrizio's misfortune: he had been too fortunate before" (260; 307).

Political behavior in *La Chartreuse* is almost completely devoid of ideological considerations. There is no difference of policy between the ultra and liberal parties of Parma; the words are convenient labels around which more personal antagonisms are organized. After the assassination of Ernest IV, Mosca, until then the leader of the conservative faction, discovers to his amusement that he is now at the head of the liberal party. There are, it appears, real liberals in the city, but Stendhal generally treats them as unsympathetically as he does the nominal ones at the prince's court. Their opinion is, first of all, controlled by the news an absolute monarch chooses to feed them; when they hear that eight of the soldiers who supposedly helped Fabrice escape from prison have been shot by the police, they blame the executions on Fabrice's "imprudence" (341; 396). They would, in any case, be doomed to inactivity by their lack of imagination for defiance or rebellion. Even the genuine liberals are shocked by the duchess's illumination of her castle at Sacca in celebration of Fabrice's escape, finding, Stendhal writes, "that she had callously endangered the poor suspects being held in various prisons, and uselessly exasperated the sovereign" (342; 397).

The political pessimism reflected in Stendhal's representation of the ultra and liberal factions at Parma was undoubtedly encouraged by the state of European politics in Stendhal's time. Recent events in Modena and Parma itself (where Austrian troops had intervened to put down a rebellion) corroborate Mosca's prediction of what would have happened had he not defended the monarchy during the short-lived revolt following Ernest IV's death: " '. . . there would have been three days of fire and slaughter (for it will take a hundred years to make a republic anything but an absurdity here), then two weeks of looting, until two or three regiments sent by some foreign power finally came in to restore order' " (357; 413). Perhaps even more important, any enthusiasm Stendhal may occasionally feel for republican government is dampened by a temperamental repugnance at the idea of living in a republic. His tastes are as finicky and aristocratic as his hero's, and a certain sympathy on Stendhal's part for representative government seems somewhat theoretical compared with his instinctive disgust at the idea of how bored he would be in a country like America. If ". . . any man who approaches a court jeopardizes his happiness . . . , on the other hand, in America, which is a republic, one must accept the endless boredom of currying favor with shopkeepers, and become as stupid as they are; and in America there is no opera" (374; 431).

There is nothing of the revolutionary in Stendhal.[3] If he has a certain admiration for the patriot-poet Ferrante Palla, he also insists on his eccentricities, his freakishness. *Le Rouge et le noir* is, in this respect, revealing. Not only are Stendhal and Julien uninterested in changing society; the novel's "purpose," one feels, is to kill the ambitious energy which constitutes the hero's only social involvement. One of Stendhal's comments on Julien is, almost word for word, what Hoederer's attack on the idealistic Communist Hugo will be in Sartre's play, *Les Mains sales*. At the Valenods' dinner party, Julien comes close to giving up his exhausting calculations in disgust when he thinks of all the moral compromises he will have to make to succeed in this society, and Stendhal writes: "I confess that the weakness Julien shows in this monologue gives me a poor opinion of him. He would be worthy of being the colleague of those conspirators in yellow gloves, who claim to change the whole way of life in a great country, and do not want to have the smallest scratch for which to blame themselves." [4] The fine irony in this unexpected comparison is that Julien not only is uninterested in changing "the whole way of life in a great country"; neither does he really care (although he doesn't realize this yet) for the recognitions he appears to be seeking. He is fit to be neither a revolutionary nor a parvenu because his social ambition includes very little interest in society; instead, he wants to be powerful enough to be able to do without society. Julien sees Napoleon not as the man who changed society, but rather as a historical metaphor for his own

3. This point is also made by Jean Starobinski, in "Stendhal pseudonyme," *L'Œil vivant* (Paris, 1961), pp. 235–36.
4. I, 348–49.

dream of a secure solitude in which people will no longer be able to hurt him. And Stendhal's irony toward Julien's ambition is a way of protecting that dream while Julien goes about trying to satisfy it in the wrong way. What we might call anachronistically Stendhal's Sartrean comment is a perfectly accurate statement of Julien's incapacity for social action, but Stendhal can, in his image, comfortably confuse revolutionary motives with a strictly personal thirst for power because *he*—at least as the narrator of the novel—has already rejected the social action that both of these imply. In spite of his tough comment, he is, in a sense, more fastidious than Julien, and his casual mockery of both Julien and delicate "conspirators" does not suggest someone who has chosen "dirty hands"—compromises—but rather someone who has pulled out of the fight. Julien will pull out too, and his attempt to kill Madame de Rênal at the end of the novel is the way he destroys his self-destroying successes. His murderous impulse has saved him, and prison provides both him and Stendhal with the only environment in which a hidden longing to be indifferent to society can be ideally satisfied.

It is perhaps the element of political passivity in Stendhal which has led some of his readers to overemphasize the farcical intention of the political portrait in *La Chartreuse*. Society in the novel is both laughable and powerful, and it is important to remember that at every moment in the story we see evidence of its power. The comic figures at the court of Parma are capable of producing tragedy; if their style is ridiculous, their power is ominous. Stendhal makes it clear from the start of the novel that the laughably vain world in which his heroes live is potentially a dangerous, even murderous world. As a result, there is nothing really unexpected or surprising about the end of *La Chartreuse*; to suggest that it destroys the tone of the novel is not to see all the possibilities that tone allows for. The ending is, however, somewhat cramped; all the events from the night Clélia begins to receive Fabrice again to Gina's death, a period of about four years, take up only six pages in the Pléiade edition. Stendhal's publisher, disturbed by the length of the book, was anxious to avoid any additions to the text. Stendhal complied, but with reluctance. He found his style too elliptical, his characters' feelings inadequately delineated, and he apparently intended to redo and expand the hurried last pages of *La Chartreuse*. It could, however, be argued that a certain structural imbalance in the work as it stands, as well as the spareness and dryness of commentary in the last few pages, give to the story an added poignancy which we would be sorry to lose for the sake of a more even, harmonious composition. The essential balance of the novel is a precarious one between life in society and happiness; it is upset not by any expository deficiency, but rather because Stendhal and his heroes have run out of escape valves. There is, it would seem, no longer any way to protect the vision of The Happy Few, and the very brusqueness of the novel's conclusion movingly expresses the defeat of the novel's *raison d'être*. Parma, not the Farnese tower, imprisons Fabrice and Clélia, and it finally destroys both their lives and the novel, which has, after all, been an investigation into what can be achieved in spite of Parma. Unlike Balzac, and although he set about, with remarkable docility, revising *La Chartreuse* along the lines suggested by Balzac, Stendhal had no convictions about or interest in fullness of exposition. If his conclusion is thin, it is because it *is* a conclusion, that is, an episode which could only be described for itself, an episode without promise.

The role of politics in *La Chartreuse* is therefore crucial, but, it seems, only as an instrument of destruction. Political life takes up an extraordinary amount of space in Stendhal's fiction without ever providing a satisfactory way of life for his heroes. And what is true of Stendhal is true of the other major French realists. The same inability to imagine a compromise between the self and society, to conceive of a relationship between the two that would not be disappointing, corrupting, and destructive characterizes Balzac, Flaubert, and Proust. In this respect, the French novel is close to the American novel; in both, and in sharp contrast to much of British fiction, social experience, instead of providing the terms and conditions for self-awareness and self-fulfillment, educates the hero into a definitive alienation from society. What is especially distinctive about French novels such as *La Chartreuse* and *L'Education sentimentale* is the detail with which a rejected alternative is presented, detail which we are expected to recognize as faithful to the realities of social life. American novelists tend to by-pass politics more explicitly, either by ignoring it or allegorizing it, by what often seems like a deliberate carelessness about the probability of social portraits. There is nonetheless in much of French and American fiction the same uncompromising, melodramatic distribution of values: happiness is unimaginable in any other terms than those of a private dream. And society and politics are taken seriously only because of their power to spoil and destroy that dream.

Furthermore, while the space given to politics in *La Chartreuse* corresponds to the destructive influence of politics in the lives of Stendhal's heroes, it expresses the *attention* only Stendhal gives to politics. Maurice Bardèche, a fervent admirer of Stendhal the political analyst, speaks of "the poetry of moral indifference" in the Stendhalian hero, but his approval of Fabrice's aristocratic scorn of a mean and corrupt society prevents him from seeing the peculiarity of a work in which the hero virtually ignores a subject to which the reader is constantly being forced to pay attention.[5] The "pistol shot" of politics is by no means an occasional interruption in a "concert" of happiness; rather, the brutal noise only rarely stops to permit a brief interlude of happiness. There is something mysterious about Stendhal's preoccupation with politics, something which an appeal to his realistic conscience (an appeal frequently made by Stendhal himself) only partially explains. Both the meticulous attention and the impatience which Stendhal brings to his pictures of social life are most interestingly intelligible, I think, in terms of that aspect of his work to which social life seems most hostile: the hero's "chasse au bonheur." The

5. *Stendhal romancier* (Paris, 1947), pp. 371 and 364.

full significance of Parma in *La Chartreuse* can be appreciated only if we look closely at the different stages of Fabrice's essentially antipolitical and antisocial pursuit of happiness. As we shall see, each is implied by the other; politics and happiness are the opposite, complementary poles in a single fantasy of threatened harmony between the self and the world.

The French occupation of Milan—from May 15, 1796, to April, 1799, and then, after thirteen months of boredom under the Austrians again, from 1800 to 1813—is the first version of happiness in *La Chartreuse de Parme*. Napoleon's army brings to Milan everything Stendhal loves: passion, courage, gaiety, music, and youth (the French soldiers "were all under twenty-five years of age, and their commanding general, who was twenty-seven, was known as the oldest man in his army" [3;27]). Napoleon's soldiers are the most un-French of Frenchmen; besides, as Stendhal is careful to point out, they reawaken a valor the Lombards had shown in the Middle Ages before their Austrian conquerors made them soft and effeminate. But the return of Austrian troops to Milan in 1813 puts an end to "all those brilliant festivities which marked the too short reign of the charming Prince Eugene" (10; 35). The defeat of Napoleon's army destroys a brief harmony in *La Chartreuse* between happiness and life in society. Gina's stay at Grianta after her husband's death is the first image in the novel of another sort of happiness, that of a small, isolated, threatened group.

The countess's first impressions at Grianta are of nature; Stendhal describes Lake Como and the surrounding hills from the point of view of Gina's enthusiastic admiration. Her "astonished eyes" take in a favorite Stendhalian landscape: uncultivated land, "hills of uneven height covered with clumps of trees planted by chance," the far-off sounds of bells ("softened as they float over the water") from villages hidden, except for their steeples, among the trees, and, beyond the hills, the "stern austerity" of the snow-covered peaks of the Alps. A boat is bought and decorated, and a

life of games and small adventures, of braving storms on the
lake during the day and studying the "science" of astrology at
night, begins for a chosen few. The enemy is Fabrice's father and
brother and their "spies," the world of sour, solemn men who had
fled to the country when Napoleon's young soldiers gaily invaded
Milan (20–21; 45–47). Fabrice, his mother, his aunt, his sisters:
the happy society in Stendhal is an alliance of women and youth.
The hostile outsider is the man, the father. Only the studious,
unaggressive, impotent "grandfather"—the Abbé Blanès here,
the Abbé Chélan in *Le Rouge et le noir*, and Henri Beyle's
grandfather Gagnon in *La Vie de Henry Brulard*—is allowed
entry into Stendhal's paradisical world of mothers and children.

What is the importance of these familial alliances and hostili-
ties in Stendhal's fiction? He remembered the Oedipal fantasies
of his childhood with astonishing clarity. A famous passage in the
autobiographical *Vie de Henry Brulard* reveals an almost suspicious willingness to confess these fantasies: "I wanted to cover
my mother with kisses and I would have preferred that there be
no clothes. She loved me passionately and often kissed me, I re-
turned her kisses so ardently that she was often forced to run
away. I hated my father whenever he came and interrupted our
kisses. I always wanted to give them to her on her breasts." [6] We
find in Stendhal's novels feelings considerably more complex
than this disarmingly frank passage might lead us to expect. Hostility toward the father is, first of all, balanced by the Stendhalian
hero's need for the loving attention of an older man. Fabrice's
father (or rather the man he takes for his father: he is really the
son of the charming French lieutenant Robert), like Julien
Sorel's, is brutal and stupid, but Fabrice bursts into tears when
he learns of the Marquis del Dongo's death. " 'Am I a hypocrite?' " he wonders, " 'I used to think I did not love him at all' "
(304; 356). Stendhal does in fact provide his young heroes with
the affection of fatherly figures, but there is always something

6. *Vie de Henry Brulard*, in *Œuvres intimes*, ed. Henri Martineau (Paris,
1955), p. 60.

lacking in these devoted older men: intelligence in Octave's father in *Armance,* moral flexibility in the Abbé Pirard, strength in the extremely old Abbés Chélan and Blanès, temperamental sympathy in Lucien Leuwen's father, and, until very late in *La Chartreuse,* a knowledge of Fabrice's love for Clélia in Mosca. It is as if Stendhal's abhorrence of an intrusive, unsympathetic father made it impossible for him even to imagine an ideal father for his heroes; these devoted older men are all images of loving inadequacy.

But is Stendhal unable to give his heroes (and himself) the kind of father he felt he never had, or is he unwilling to do so? There are hints in his novels that Stendhal refuses a father's love perhaps more insistently than that love may have been refused to him. I am thinking especially of *Lucien Leuwen,* where, for the first time in Stendhal's work, we have an exquisitely intelligent, tactful, and loving father. Monsieur Leuwen is, to be sure, temperamentally different from Lucien, and his brusquely and ironically expressed affection contrasts with his wife's effusive protectiveness toward Lucien, but this very reticence of feeling, in both father and son, helps to make of their relationship a uniquely moving one in Stendhal's world. It is, then, somewhat surprising that this indulgent and tender father (comically irritated by his own tenderness) should, toward the end of the novel, be emotionally repudiated by his son. We learn, in a curious passage, that Lucien suddenly suffers from a "burning remorse for not feeling any friendship or tenderness for his father." And what we have come to admire in Monsieur Leuwen as a rare blend of wit and feeling, of worldliness and vulnerability, is just as suddenly denied by Stendhal with a ruthless and meticulous insistence:

> The *chasm* between these two people was too deep. Everything which, rightly or wrongly, seemed sublime, generous, tender to Lucien, all the things he thought it was noble to die for, or beautiful to live with, were considered by his father as deceptions and as worthy only of being joked about. They were perhaps in

agreement on only one feeling: an intimate friendship strengthened by having been put to the test for thirty years. Actually,
M. Leuwen was exquisitely courteous; his politeness almost
touched the *sublime* and even reproduced the real thing when
it was a question of his son's weaknesses; but this son was shrewd
enough to guess that what was sublime in his father was the
product of intelligence, of a subtle mind, of the art of being
polite, delicate, irreproachable.[7]

The loving father is perhaps more difficult for Stendhal to tolerate than to imagine; it may be precisely his inadequacies which
make him acceptable.

Applied to Stendhal's life, these remarks are necessarily conjectural; his fiction does, however, at least suggest an aversion
to the loving father as strong as the need for him. Even the most
appealing older men in Stendhal's novels are somehow crippled,
put at a disadvantage; the Stendhalian hero enjoys every privilege
which Stendhal himself lacked except that of an ideal father.
Biographically, this gap in the compensatory pattern of Stendhal's
fiction suggests that Henri Beyle both compulsively relives his
own painful alienation from his father in his heroes' lives, and
also punishes that father by making him either brutal and stupid
or pathetically unable to reach and touch a son he loves. But a
closer look at Stendhal's work suggests a hypothesis more useful
for the analysis of the novels themselves. If his heroes are consistently deprived of a loving father, it is precisely an ideally protective, intelligent, and sympathetic father who presents the
Stendhalian hero to Stendhal's audience. It is as if Stendhal were
too jealous of this role to give it to anyone but himself. His refusal to dramatize a role which he is perfectly capable of imagining for his narrator leads us to what is perhaps the most secret
aspect of his Oedipal feelings: the desire to be his own father.[8]

7. I, 1316.
8. See Norman O. Brown's brilliant discussion of the *causa sui* project
in *Life Against Death* (New York, 1959), pp. 118ff.

This unrealizable desire to be the author of one's own existence can, in Stendhal's fiction, be satisfied only by a novelistic *dédoublement*, by the paternal relation of an omniscient narrator to his dramatized (and idealized) self. Thus, Stendhal creates Fabrice's and Julien's "real" fathers in order to replace them; the only father he allows his heroes is Stendhal himself, and the pleasures of that relationship are, necessarily, all for Stendhal. The perfect father is both absent and omnipresent in Stendhal's fiction. He is nothing more and nothing less than the narrator's voice. It could even be argued that if an unsympathetic father had not existed in Stendhal's life, he would have had to be invented in Stendhal's fiction, in order to make of the son's (the hero's) existence, throughout the novels, a continuous *creation* of the "original" son's (the novelist's) imagination.

We can go one step further. There are, I have suggested, three kinds of fathers in Stendhal's fiction: the sympathetic but inadequate older men (the Abbés Blanès and Chélan, Monsieur Leuwen, even Mosca), the ideal narrator-father, and, finally, the cruel and stupid enemy. In a sense, the most important of these is the last, for he is generalized into the Stendhalian portrait of society itself, which is as destructive and vain and narrow-minded as old Sorel or the Marquis del Dongo. The hostile father is therefore as necessary a presence in Stendhal's fiction as he is an abhorred presence: he is the only opening for the hero into the world of politics and history. Without him, the Stendhalian hero would be immobilized in the isolated (and imprisoned) world of mothers and children. He is, as it were, structurally necessary in order to create social involvements, conflicts, dramatic action. The illusion of the Stendhalian hero is that he can enter society without being destroyed by the father, although the bruises he suffers at the hands of society also conveniently justify his return to scenes of childhood from which the father is excluded. It is as if society existed in order to vindicate the hero's repudiation of society, a repudiation which seems actually to precede social experiences and—as we shall presently see—perhaps even to determine its nature.

Fabrice's abortive attempt to enter history by leaving Grianta and joining Napoleon's army in France illustrates very well the ambiguous nature of his political involvements. His reasons for admiring Napoleon are an amusing and significant mixture of public and private motives: " 'He tried to give us a fatherland, and he loved my uncle,' " he explains to Gina (24; 49), thus unconsciously suggesting that the cause he will be defending at Waterloo is as much that of a happy family as it is that of modern Europe. Fabrice's "chasse au bonheur" is, although he does not realize this until his stay in prison, always a search for an intimacy similar to but more intense and more complete than the intimacy at Grianta with Gina, his mother, and his sisters. His military adventure—or anti-adventure—in France and Belgium is a result of a generous illusion not only about the nature of warfare but also about the nature of his own aspirations. The celebrated Waterloo episode in *La Chartreuse* is, as it has often been said, a satire of the conventions of heroic war literature; the origins of Fabrice's naïveté are the battle scenes in Tasso and Ariosto. For the panoramic views of *Jerusalem Delivered* Stendhal substitutes the close-up: the blood-soaked trousers of a dead soldier, "the curious spectacle of all the little branches flying in either direction as though cut off by a scythe" as bullets shoot through them (35; 61), the hoofs of a wounded horse digging into its own entrails, and the deafening sound of cannons. And instead of the welcome he expected as a volunteer ready to die for Napoleon's noble cause, Fabrice also discovers the political realities of war. A few patriotic words to a French officer get him thrown into prison; he learns with shock of the betrayals of Napoleon's officers; and the "battle" he comically looks for is, for the most part, an uninspiring view of the French army in frightened, disorganized retreat.

The fiasco at Waterloo in *La Chartreuse* is the public event which makes historically probable and even necessary Fabrice's theological "studies" and Mosca's project of having him named as successor to the Archbishop of Parma. In a Europe paralyzed by the fear of another Revolution and another Bonaparte, the only careers available to a man of Fabrice's birth are, as Mosca finally convinces the disappointed Gina, elegantly riding an English horse on the streets of Milan or choosing the Church as an instrument of personal prestige and power. But while Stendhal thus gives to his hero's life a seal of historical authenticity, the image of Fabrice in battle suggests more personal reasons for the shape his destiny will take. Fabrice's naïveté is detailed in interesting ways. He does not simply discover the differences between literary battlefields and real battlefields; his reactions reveal expectations irrelevant to *any* version of military life. Fabrice is, first of all, much less of a quixotic warrior inflamed with moral passion than a young aristocrat of the most delicate esthetic sensibility. He is "outraged" by the noise of the battle (36; 63); "he was struck above all by the dirty feet" of the first dead soldier he sees (32; 59); and he cannot help but judge the boring repetitions in Corporal Aubry's and the vivandière's talk by the standards of conversation learned in the Comtesse Pietranera's Milanese *salon*.

Even more significantly, Fabrice's impulse to find a congenial little group is at least as strong as his desire to help Napoleon save Europe. He spontaneously transforms historical catastrophe into just another scene for personal relations. He wonders if he can "demand satisfaction" from the general who swears at his horse (36; 62), and he defiantly repeats his reference to the retreating French as "sheep" long after the soldier who had told him to shut up has forgotten that "he had insulted their nation" (48–49; 95–96). Such indignations are the other side of his joy when people are friendly to him, when his childlike dreams of soldierly camaraderie are briefly realized. His fury at the men who steal his horse is a bitter sense of having been betrayed "by that

sergeant he had loved so much, and by those hussars he had regarded as brothers! That was what broke his heart" (42; 69).
And perhaps the deepest irony of Fabrice's military venture—an
irony less important for its military or political implications than
for what it reveals about Fabrice's nature—is that nothing that
happens at Waterloo touches him more deeply than the friendship he strikes up with a vivandière. She and Aniken, the Flemish
girl whose family shelters Fabrice and treats his wounded arm,
and to whom he later writes a letter in which "there was certainly some love" (64; 93), are the most memorable encounters
of this heroic expedition. The major role of the motherly vivandière in these chapters is naturally something of a joke, given
the heroic rhetoric with which Fabrice set out for battle; but it
points unmistakably to a need, still unrecognized by Fabrice, for
which a "field" has not yet been found. The humor of the Waterloo section is largely in the incongruity between the occasion being described and the kind of attention Fabrice brings to this
occasion. Only the Farnese tower will provide the setting in
which Fabrice's simplicity can be convincingly redefined as his
profundity and his heroism. The journey to Waterloo therefore
emphasizes Fabrice's attachment to the values of Grianta. Finally,
if this adventure is, in one sense, presented in order to be dismissed, its presentation enriches the novel's substance. Fabrice's
mistake helps to save Stendhal from the dangerous thinness of a
work about games at Grianta.

The shift from the battlefield to the court puts us—and Fabrice
—in a setting where, as we have seen, ugliness, betrayal, and
hypocrisy are the daily fare, the style and substance of social in-
tercourse. Fabrice's return to Grianta to consult the Abbé Blanès
is a self-protective move, an escape from the moral contamination
of political life: " 'All the complicated interests of that petty little
court have made me petty too . . .' " (140–41; 175). Not exactly
petty or mean, but unsure of himself, out of character: troubled
by his discovery of how Gina feels about him and unable to find
a way of being truthful with her without hurting and insulting

her, Fabrice has allowed his "whim" for the actress Marietta
(". . . at his age," Stendhal exclaims, "his cares had already reduced him to having whims!") to become a "pique d'amour-
propre," a challenge to his vanity (129; 162). The trip to Grianta
is a cure, a cure which consists of a return to nature and to childhood.

The whole episode takes up only two chapters in *La Chartreuse*, and yet its weight in the novel is immeasurably greater
than the space it occupies. The conditions for happiness are difficult to come by; their infrequency may obscure the extraordinary
simplicity of the state of happiness itself. Almost nothing happens during Fabrice's journey, and yet we are somehow made to
feel that during much of the novel and much of his life Fabrice
is exiled from such moments. Stendhal's success is all the more
astonishing since the apparent theme of the passage is the most
worn out of romantic clichés: the escape from a corrupt, unhappy
society to the innocent joys of nature and childhood impressions.
Stendhal's success is, I think, due precisely to a certain indifference to these themes. Unlike Chateaubriand, for example, in
his treatment of René's melancholy wanderings throughout
Europe, Stendhal never generalizes Fabrice's situation in order
to obscure and indulge in an uneasy but overwhelming sympathy
with his hero's psychological peculiarities. Chateaubriand's inflated rhetoric glamorizes the abstract themes which save him
from directly confronting the full extent of his complicity with
René. But while his eloquence thus directs our attention to large
views of history, the very continuities which Chateaubriand takes
for granted between his hero and history reveal an irrepressible
sympathy with the much more particular phenomenon of René's
narcissistic love of solitude. Stendhal, as we shall see, can be
equally self-protective, but his defensive mechanisms do not include asking us to think of his book in terms of themes which
might have given a kind of historical justification to his hero's
psychology. It is a sign of Stendhal's willingness to make Fabrice
entirely responsible for his own nature (rather than a victim of

the nineteenth century) that, as we read the Grianta section, it
may never occur to us that it is a "romantic" passage.

Stendhal's presentation of the scene which moves Fabrice to
tears is a good example of his descriptive reticence:

> The road ran through a little forest whose trees projected the
> black outlines of their foliage against a sky that was filled with
> stars but veiled by a light mist. The water and the sky were pro-
> foundly peaceful; Fabrizio's soul could not resist that sublime
> beauty: he stopped and sat down on a rock that jutted out into
> the lake, forming a little promontory. The universal silence was
> broken only, at regular intervals, by the gentle ripples of the lake
> as they came in to expire on the shore.
>
> •   •   •
>
> A morning breeze was beginning to temper the overwhelming
> heat that had reigned during the day. The faint white glow of
> dawn was already outlining the peaks of the Alps that rise to
> the north and east of Lake Como. Their massive shapes, snow-
> capped even in June, [stand] out against the azure of a sky
> which is always clear at those immense altitudes. A spur of the
> Alps reaching southward into happy Italy separates the shores of
> Lake Como from those of Lake Garda. Fabrizio cast his eyes over
> all the spurs of those sublime mountains. As the dawn grew
> brighter, it revealed the valleys that separated them, illuminating
> the fine mist rising from the bottoms of the gorges. (132–33;
> 165–66)

The characteristic sobriety of this description is largely a question
of an attitude toward language. "The anti-lyricism of Stendhal,"
as Jean Starobinski has said, "is a refusal to grant the slightest
value to the intensity of speech; language is always at a certain
distance from what it claims to express." [9] In an age when writers
rely on inflated rhetoric both to express and make up for their
spiritual *désœuvrement*, for what they themselves complain of as
an emptiness of experience, Stendhal is unique in his use of

9. "Stendhal pseudonyme," p. 232.

understatement merely to outline a fullness of being, to hint at the intensity of a briefly felt harmony between the self and the world. There is, at most, a muted eloquence in Stendhal's style at such moments. The abruptness, the choppiness of the analytical passages disappear; an orderly description proceeds with an even, leisurely rhythm. And the effect on the reader is analogous to the emotional effect of these rare moments on Fabrice. In the same way that they interrupt for him the agitated rhythms of political life, they introduce a new tempo for us, and our enjoyment is increased by the contrast with the stylistic tensions and shocks which surround these occasional islands of verbal *détente*.

The aspect of nature as a metaphysical irritant, as a reminder of man's exasperated ignorance about the universe (in Sénancour, most notably), is totally absent in Stendhal. The passage I have quoted describes a moment of perfect happiness; the shapes and rhythms of nature momentarily provide sensations which the Stendhalian hero recognizes as his particular form of happiness. Romantic eloquence is often an attempt to use language as a means both of expanding consciousness and making the universe significant; mystery and profundity are projected into the world in an effort to create an adequate scene for the mind's excitement. The impulse revealed by Stendhal's text is just the opposite: the economy and undisturbed quality of his decription suggest an already achieved equality between the mind and the world, a successful reduction of external stimuli to a formula for individual fulfillment. The nature of the Stendhalian formula has been admirably defined by Jean-Pierre Richard. The combination of clear designs and a semi-transparent mist, the emergence, at dawn, of demarcations in the landscape along which the eye moves with pleasure, the regular rhythm of the lake's waves against the shore, and, at Grianta, the remembered sound of the *mortaretti* "heard from a distance across the lake, and softened by the rippling of the water" (142–43; 177): the world becomes a spectacle for happiness in Stendhal when, as Richard writes, its elements concretely satisfy a need for both clarity and continuity, for sharply distinct sensations and impressions of fusion and unity.[10]

Alone in the tower, visited only by the ailing Abbé Blanès who gives him protection and advice, hidden from hostile eyes, Fabrice realizes another aspect of the Stendhalian dream: he discovers *details* as a source of ecstasy. With "an astonishment bordering on delirium," Fabrice sees the Abbé Blanès's lantern in a long and narrow window of the clocktower; his sudden memories of the simplest things "flooded Fabrizio's soul with emotions and filled it with happiness": "This map of the heavens [the abbé's planisphere] was stretched over a large earthenware vase which had once held one of the orange trees of the castle. In the opening of the bottom of the vase burned the tiniest of lamps. Its smoke escaped through a little tin pipe whose shadow marked north on the map" (136; 170). Similarly, he is moved by the view of some sparrows searching for bread crumbs on the balcony outside his father's dining room and of "a great number of orange trees in large earthenware vases" (140; 174). During the procession in honor of Saint Giovita, the sound of the *mortaretti*, "a running fire of sharp explosions, thoroughly irregular and ridiculous," and "which had so often delighted him in his childhood," chases away his fear of the gendarmes; and, finally, the sound of each stroke of the oars from the peasants' boats returning home after the procession "enraptured him . . ." (142–43; 177). *La Chartreuse* is a novel of happy and unhappy details. The opposition between two kinds of life is documented, to a large extent, as an opposition of an enthusiastically joyful attention to details and a discouraged, tired, but necessary surveillance over details. The labyrinthine intrigues at the court of Parma constitute the hell of details; their paradise is the "running fire of sharp explosions" of the *mortaretti* and, in the Farnese tower, Fabrice's making a hole in the shutter in order to continue seeing Clélia, which is nothing less than an experience of ecstatic carpentry.

10. "Connaissance et tendresse chez Stendhal," *Littérature et sensation,* preface by Georges Poulet (Paris, 1954), pp. 32 and 76–78.

The detail is, as it has often been said, a source and guarantee of truth for Stendhal. The only truth is detailed, *circonstancié*; as Richard has remarked, detail, by localizing and putting its "stamp" on a sensation, transforms it into intellectual perception.[11] And to tell a story well, to give your listener an exact and enjoyable sense of what happened, requires not a talent for summary but rather an effort to remember every gesture, every nuance, every word. "Overwhelm me with details . . . ," Stendhal wrote to his sister Pauline,[12] and Monsieur Leuwen is no less insistent that Lucien remember every detail of his trip with Coffe to Campagnier and Caen.[13] In the passage describing Fabrice's stay in the clocktower at Grianta, we see the affective function of detail which in part explains the intellectual and conversational value which Stendhal attributes to it: only the remembered detail can awaken past sensations, can bring back a happy immediacy of contact between the self and the world. Such contact has been made all the more difficult by "the complicated life of a court" (143; 177), where the unloving father has, so to speak, been expanded into a society of political enemies. And at Grianta, in Austrian territory, the presence of gendarmes—with the menace of the Spielberg prison they evoke—casts a shadow over Fabrice's joy. But his dangerous and seemingly useless return to Grianta is justified by the exalting revitalization of memory which it brings. "All the memories of childhood thronged back to besiege his mind . . . ," and as a result, ". . . that day spent imprisoned in a belfry was perhaps one of the happiest of his life" (140; 174–75).

The resurrection of the past at Grianta is, incidentally, only superficially Proustian. The value of affective memory in Stendhal is not, as it is in Proust, in the evidence it affords of a permanent self. The importance of involuntary memory in *A*

11. "Connaissance et tendresse chez Stendhal," p. 29.
12. *Correspondance*, 10 vols. (Paris, 1933–34), II, p. 109.
13. "More details, more details, he said to his son, originality and truth are only in details . . ." (I, *Lucien Leuwen*, 1275).

la Recherche du temps perdu, as we shall see, depends on a kind of ontological anguish in Marcel, on a persistent and explicit sense of the self's instability from which Stendhal's heroes do not suffer. Furthermore, memory does not have in Stendhal the self-protective and self-re-creative function which it has in Proust. Nothing in Stendhal's writing suggests the Proustian use of literature both to impose a continuous style on what had seemed like a fragmented history of discontinuous selves, and also to create a future in the process of an apparently faithful recording of the past. And the gaiety with which Fabrice relives past impressions is vastly different from the trance-like intensity into which an involuntary memory plunges Marcel, for whom the taste of the *madeleine*, for example, performs the service of dematerializing present reality. It suspends him momentarily in a purely mental space between the past and the present. Fabrice is much more directly aggressive toward an uncongenial present. Rather than subvert it by drowning it in history, he exploits history in order to be able to give himself entirely to the present.

It is essentially the extraordinary strength implicit in Fabrice's ability to change his relation to the world *now* which makes us take more seriously than anything else in the novel a state of mind which Stendhal daringly invites us to consider as deliriously childlike. In a sense, it is of course childlike: Fabrice recaptures a confidence about the world which we lose as soon as we perceive the world as potentially dangerous, as an environment distinct from the self and even uncongenial to the self. And a certain gravity in the gayest scenes of *La Chartreuse de Parme* can, I think, be explained by the fact that the intensity of happiness is directly proportionate to its impossibility. The experience surrounding these exceptional moments is such a weighty reminder of the duality and antagonisms between the self and the world that Stendhal instinctively portrays happiness as a *ravissement*, a transport, almost a hallucination. That is, he portrays it as an illusion; the incongruity between the stroke of an oar and Fabrice's ecstasy is also a subtly established distance between Fabrice and the reader, the distance of our melancholy awareness of the fragile support which the world offers Fabrice's expansive self.

The final version of the fantasy of happiness in *La Chartreuse de Parme* is, of course, Fabrice's love for Clélia Conti. The military and political lives are detours in the "chasse au bonheur"; friendship, solitude in nature, a return to childhood scenes are only partial realizations of the fantasy; only an exclusive, all-absorbing intimacy with one other person satisfies the rigorous demands of this Stendhalian dream. Fabrice's imprisonment saves him; in the "folly" of his love for the cell from which he can see Clélia every day, he finally becomes Stendhal's ideal hero, a man who, instead of vaguely wondering if he is doomed never to experience what he naïvely has called "the noble and intellectual aspect of love" (204; 244), now knows what Mosca, in his painfully but generously lucid jealousy, had recognized as the "message" of Fabrice's presence: ". . . love and the happiness it brings are the only serious things in the world" (123; 156).

Love in *La Chartreuse* is the "goal" of a fantasy of happy union with the world. Henri Beyle the seducer *manqué* finds an extraordinarily flattering image of his awkwardness in the Stendhalian lover's fear and trembling. The novels erase the frustrations of Stendhal's experience: the helplessly timid lover becomes the successful lover. More important, love is Fabrice's only involvement, and it is an absolute involvement. Once he realizes he loves Clélia, nothing, the rest of his life, including his fantastic celebrity at Parma at the end of the novel, will be able to turn his attention away from that love. Even his disastrous decision to abduct their son Sandrino is a "caprice de tendresse" which directly concerns Clélia: " 'Since an unparalleled fate has deprived me of the happiness, enjoyed by so many other loving hearts, of living with the woman I love, I want at least to have someone with me, who will remind me of you, and replace you to some extent' " (427–28; 489–90).

The pleasures of love are proportionate to the terror it inspires. There is no rhetorical exaggeration either when Stendhal calls one of Fabrice's first intuitions of Clélia's love for him "the happiest moment" of his life, "beyond all comparison" (273; 322), or when Fabrice, seeing Clélia at the theatre after months of not having even a glimpse of her, "thought he would choke with joy; he had such extraordinary sensations that he said to himself, 'Perhaps I'm going to die!'" (413; 474) He does, after all, die from his grief at Clélia's death, and there is, rightly, not a trace of irony in Stendhal's voice when he describes Fabrice's "terror" in prison as he discovers his feelings for Clélia: "He felt all too clearly that the happiness of his whole life [was going to force him to reckon with the governor's daughter], and that it was within her power to make him the unhappiest of men" (274; 323). Fabrice in love, it has been said, is already Fabrice in the Charterhouse; passion removes him from the world as irreversibly as a monastic vow. Love is the Stendhalian version of a religious vocation.

Indeed, Clélia's beauty is an invitation to leave the world as much as it is a promise of happy love. "'She would be a charming prison companion,'" Fabrice prophetically says to himself when he sees her for the first time on the road from Como to Milan (69; 99). Stendhal describes Clélia as "pensive" (99; 130, and 226; 269); when Fabrice meets her again the day of his imprisonment, "he was especially struck by the melancholy expression of her face" (225; 268). The very shape of her forehead suggests both withdrawal and expectation; it might, Stendhal remarks, have told "an attentive observer that her noble air, her demeanor so far above ordinary graces, sprang from a profound indifference to everything ordinary. It was the absence, not the impossibility of interest in anything" (229; 273). But if Stendhal rightly defends Clélia's capacity for human involvements, there is an interesting comparison between Clélia and Gina which helps to explain why Stendhal's preference is much less marked, more hesitant than Fabrice's: "It was noticed that evening [of

Fabrice's imprisonment] that Clélia's face was more animated than usual. Now animation, the appearance of taking part in what was happening around her, was the main thing that was lacking in this beautiful girl. When her beauty was compared to that of the duchess, it was especially the impression she gave of not being moved by anything, of being above everything, that tipped the balance in her rival's favor. In England or France, countries of vanity, the opposite opinion would probably have prevailed" (227; 271). This observation beautifully illustrates Stendhal's brusquely casual way of taking it for granted that life is superior to his own imagination of what might be most exalting in life. The appeal of Italy here is not only as an alternative to France, but also, in a sense, to Fabrice and Clélia. The metaphors of Italy and of France can be more complex than they might at first seem. In the passage just quoted, Stendhal is expressing a preference for Gina over Clélia for precisely those reasons which immediately draw Fabrice to Clélia and make him prefer her to Gina. Clélia's detachment, her impassivity and inaccessibility—which would be considered by Proust as a universally necessary condition for inspiring interest and desire—would make her seem more appealing than Gina only in countries where love is a satisfaction of vanity, the pleasure of making an impression on someone difficult to impress. The moral health and beauty of the ideal Italian sensibility is that it responds to openness more than to secretiveness; it seeks to possess whatever will bring it into a more energetic and immediate contact with all experience.

La Sanseverina, unlike Clélia, is fantastically attentive to everything. Indeed, her great mistake is to be excited by the prospect of life at Parma; she thinks of its dangers as entertaining. But even the vain princes of Parma love her, as if by possessing her they could "catch" her style of life, learn to create happiness by being exuberantly inventive over every occasion. Clélia can, of course, give herself as spontaneously and generously as Gina, and she would naturally be as out of place as the duchess in Stendhal's

England and France. But while we feel that an exclusive passion for Fabrice would, in a sense, diminish Gina, it is what brings Clélia to life. The duchess's temperament is eminently social; she misses the pleasures of conversation during her stay at Grianta early in the novel, for, as Stendhal remarks, ". . . she was too intelligent not to feel occasionally the boredom that comes from not being able to exchange ideas with anyone" (22; 47). The appeal of Gina in *La Chartreuse* is something like the appeal of a brilliant *salon;* what Fabrice immediately responds to in Clélia is an invitation, which he had read on her face long before he became her father's prisoner, to solitude, even to enforced confinement. Nothing could be more different from what draws Mosca and Gina together, from the essentially social nature of *their* intimacy. Mosca is never happier than when he betrays his prince in order to help Fabrice escape from prison (that is, in order to show his devotion to Gina), but we don't feel that his love for Gina requires being alienated from society, that its natural element is secrecy or privacy. We think of Gina and Mosca receiving guests even in a prison cell; we just as early think of Fabrice and Clélia transforming a *salon* into a secluded cell. In a sense, the antagonistic society of Parma threatens but also serves their love.

Love removes the Stendhalian hero from society; it also seems to remove him from sexuality. Neither in *Le Rouge et le noir* nor in *La Chartreuse* is the happiness of love associated with sexual passion. There is in Stendhal's fiction a reticence or *pudeur* about sexual matters which is perhaps more deeply characteristic of him than the cynical, outspoken pose of some of the letters and the marginalia. This reticence is linked to what seems to have been a strong fantasy (but, apparently, not the reality) of impotence in Stendhal. The course of this fantasy in Stendhal's fiction is one of a steady sublimation. Its most unsatisfactory version is in *Armance,* where Octave is in fact sexually impotent. This disability, coupled with Stendhal's reticence about it, makes for confusion and mystification. Octave's insecurity and his taste for solitude may be incomprehensible if we have not been given the key to his eccentric behavior. And because impotence in *Armance* is a motive which is never dramatized as a motive, the end may strike us as a gratuitous stroke of chance: Stendhal is reduced to having Octave kill himself not because he can neither love nor inspire love, but because he mistakenly thinks Armance wrote a letter confessing to a friend that she has never loved him. In *La Chartreuse*, the fantasy of impotence is promoted to something richer, a comical and poignant uncertainty in Fabrice: is he doomed merely to physical pleasure, never to know "la partie noble et intellectuelle de l'amour"? These doubts express both Fabrice's naïveté (he hardly suspects how this "intellectual" experience will absorb his whole being) and his instinctive sense that all his other adventures are mere preludes to his love. This appealing lack of self-confidence is lost in what we have of *Lamiel*, where the pattern of doubt recurs, but from a position of excessive strength. There is curiosity without need in Stendhal's strangely desensitized heroine. Lamiel's cold speculations about whether or not she is insensitive to love, and her very real indifference to sex, reduce her to the most rarefied (and psychologically protected) version of the Stendhalian theme of erotic inadequacy or absence.

Victor Brombert has spoken perceptively of the Stendhalian narrator's reticence about sexuality, of his "*escamotage*, or juggling away, of sex." [14] Passionate love is of the greatest importance in the novels (and Stendhal's heroes can of course be sexually demanding), but Stendhal is remarkably silent about the pleasures of passion. It is as if his concrete dramatic images of love (as distinct from the theorizing of *De l'Amour*) left Stendhal— and his hero—speechless. Fabrice's amorous transports have none of the sensual particularity of Félix's tributes to Henriette in *Le Lys dans la vallée*, and Stendhal makes a detour around his lovers' happiness by simply telling us how long it lasted. The

14. *Stendhal et la voie oblique/L'auteur devant son monde romanesque* (New Haven and Paris, 1954), p. 163.

reason for this characteristic reticence is that happiness is discovered to be *by nature* indescribable, and by this I do not mean that Stendhal is short-cutting a problem of expression by banally insisting that joy is ineffable, but rather that the movement toward happiness is, psychologically, a regression to a love essentially nonsexual and even nonverbal. *Le Rouge et le noir* and *La Chartreuse* may follow recognizable, realistic patterns of seduction, passion, and the consequences of passion, but the importance Julien and Fabrice attach to physical union is much less convincing than the peculiar power of what could be called scenes of blissful childhood.

This is not said as a criticism of Stendhal for something "incomplete" in his images of love, but rather in order to suggest the radical use to which he is putting his novelistic form. I do not feel, incidentally, that we get close to Stendhal's most original talent by assimilating his work to what Gilbert Durand has called a movement toward the *moment romanesque,* that is, toward a moment when "intimate jubilations win out over the values of the epic exploit." Durand sees Stendhalian *pudeur* as the secrecy necessary for all intimacy; reason and analysis would be a threat to *la voyance mystique*.[15] Durand's book on *La Chartreuse* is lovely, but the mythic realities which interest him obscure *La Chartreuse*'s particularity. Part of Stendhal's extraordinary achievement lies in the fact that in novels dominated by one of the most worldly, sophisticated, "adult" voices in all fiction, we are led to believe that happiness lies in the paradise of asexual play which Julien and Fabrice enjoy cavorting in Madame de Rênal's garden and making up word games in the Farnese tower. The garden and the tower, it could be said, are sexual enough, but the point is precisely that they are sexual *symbols* and not *scenes of* sexuality. That is, in a manner reminiscent of children's play, possibly sexual choices (on Stendhal's part) provide only the setting for behavior which, instead of merely accompanying sexu-

15. *Le Décor mythique de la Chartreuse de Parme/Contribution à l'esthétique du romanesque* (Paris, 1961), pp. 135, 109, and 176.

STENDHALIAN PRISONS AND SALONS

ality, replaces it. Stendhal's narrative *pudeur* (and the undoubtedly related fear of impotence) seem to express a refusal
of sexuality, an implicit conviction that sex is alien to the particular kind of intimacy which constitutes happiness.

The chances which this fantasy leads Stendhal to take with
the very life of his novels will seem enormous if we consider the
novelistic thinness of the love between Fabrice and Clélia. The
fullest account of the activities of happiness is given during
Fabrice's stay in prison. They mainly consist of ingenious games,
inventive solutions to the problem of communication between
Fabrice's cell and Clélia's aviary. Fabrice's "chasse au bonheur"
is—in spite of all the obstacles to his love for Clélia—completed
in the Farnese tower, and to the extent that this pursuit determines the shape and progress of *La Chartreuse* itself, his imprisonment is also the "goal" of the novel. The fact that this goal
is reached, and that it is reached relatively early in *La Chartreuse*,
allows for a greater exploration of its novelistic possibilities than
in any of Stendhal's other works. Except for some brief moments
early in *Le Rouge et le noir*, Julien stops resisting his love for
Madame de Rênal only after he has tried to kill her. Stendhal,
partly by his mockery of the Napoleonic love strategies which
Julien uses in his effort to seduce Madame de Rênal, has suggested from the start that his hero can be happy only by abandoning himself to his love for this mother-mistress with whom he
could finally be what he has never been: the loved child. But
Julien's blindness to his own nature postpones the testing of
that love; his pathetic attempts to remain faithful to his wrong
choices have, in the meanwhile, provided the novel with its dramatic substance. There is, so to speak, a minimum of novelistic
pressure put on Madame de Rênal's visits to Julien's cell, which
are essentially only an epilogue to Julien's life. They are powerful,
at this late and tragic point in the story, simply as an absence of
tension, a ceasing of struggle and resistance.

Fabrice's very different temperament, and his "luck" in finding Clélia, raise a crucial question for Stendhal's fiction: what are

the inventive potentialities in a fantasy of ecstatic play? Fabrice's
pleasure in his prison games, even though the games are meant
to make Clélia communicate with him and finally agree to a meeting with him, makes it clear that happy love in Stendhal would
have no other project than its own leisurely playfulness. Any conflicts which passion might generate are prevented by the absence of sexual passion in Stendhal's dramatization of love. The
exclusion of society, guaranteed both by its hostility and by the
invitation to retreat which is an important part of Clélia's appeal,
eliminates involvements and interests beyond the lovers' involvement with each other. In other words, the love between Fabrice
and Clélia contains almost no possibilities for dramatic conflict,
variety, or progress; indeed, its very ideality would seem to depend on a spiritual immobility. It perhaps also realizes, more
generally, a wish for a peaceful, somewhat monotonous harmony
with the world, which is to say that it overcomes the divisions,
the differentiations which create pain but which are also the inspirations of language and of novelistic invention.

Stendhal uses the painful divisions and antagonisms of life to
save both his work and himself from the infantile fantasy which
is his hero's dangerous paradise. The charm of the part of the
novel describing Fabrice's stay in prison, a charm which helps
us to accept it, surprisingly enough, as the most serious part of
the novel, is due largely to what Stendhal has been doing
throughout the story to more conventional images of seriousness.
Imprisonment comes to Fabrice as a relief, and we find ourselves
willing to believe that the most important problem in the hero's
life is how to saw away part of the shutter and make an alphabet
with which to send messages to Clélia. But the atmosphere of
play is, of course, somewhat deceptive; it is transformed into one
of urgent vigilance by the fact that Fabrice's life is in danger
as long as he stays in prison. Fabrice is indifferent to this danger,
but the lovers' prison games would have much less interest for
us if their inventiveness were not a question of life and death.
The society excluded by Fabrice's cell continues to provide

threats which inspire the activities of prison life. And happiness "exploits" society in this way throughout the novel. The substance, the matter of fiction is provided by the enemy of its highest pleasures: Parma. The space of the novel is filled with political detail which suffocates The Happy Few but at the same time creates the tension, the drama, the life that keep the story moving. It interrupts a happiness about which, finally, there is very little to *say*. The profound importance of politics in *La Chartreuse* should now be clear. Stendhal's tireless attention to a society which destroys the paradise of play also creates the verbal environment in which happiness—essentially nonverbal and unnovelistic—can be evoked as that which is missing.

Missing, and yet, by a curious final twist, referred to by this society just as surely as this type of social image is implicit in the Stendhalian image of happiness. The hostile father and the hostile society are necessary both to bring the hero into the world and to vindicate his retreat from the world. Politics and happiness as I have defined them are the two magnetic poles of Stendhal's fiction. They provide what might be called the structural differentiation of a single fantasy of threatened and threatening unity between the self and the world. The court at Parma is the "natural" partner of the idyll in the Farnese tower, the ideally divisive complement to an ideally harmonious union. The type of society we find in *La Chartreuse* is implied by images of happiness which are consistently images of flight and seclusion. The paradise of the Stendhalian hero is a kind of death-in-life, and the deepest needs of Fabrice and Julien are actually best served by the society they live in. What other alternative than a retreat to the peace and safe isolation of childhood is left to them by this cruel, agitated world of men? Society saves the Stendhalian vision of happiness from the self-containment and purposelessness of mere being, but its very hostility also reinforces the hero's choices, justifies his joyful self-imprisonments.

Is there, then, no escape from the politics of destruction and the imprisoned immobility of love other than an unillusioned awareness of their mutual destructiveness? Stendhal's attention to Parma in *La Chartreuse* makes it possible for him to tell a story, but it also intensifies the appeal of a love which threatens story telling. The role of politics in the novel is therefore an ambiguous solution to the dangers of the Stendhalian vision of happiness. It keeps Stendhal from losing himself—and his work —in that vision, but it also confirms what Fabrice's indifference to society implies: if Stendhal, unlike Fabrice, saves himself, there is nothing to save himself *for*.

Other solutions, possibly livable compromises—for both the characters and the narrator—do, however, emerge during the course of the novel. The possibility of such solutions for Stendhal's characters seems to depend, first of all, on their ability to find historical models capable of reclaiming and transforming the present. The only alternative to the self-defeating fantasy of a secret and besieged love would be the revival in the present of a social context in which a harmony between the hero and the world could be achieved through historically meaningful gestures. But such a revival depends on a continuity between past and present about which Stendhal is consistently pessimistic. His characters' attempts to relive the heroisms of the past, for example, are always occasions for comedy, for parodies of heroism. Julien's Napoleonic stance is absurdly out of place with the trembling and tender Madame de Rênal; Mathilde's cult for the extravagant energies of her sixteenth-century ancestors leads only, especially in a world terrified by energy and imagination, to the eccentric and the macabre. The court of Parma is a low comedy version of Italian Renaissance courts and of Versailles; Ernest IV poses under the portrait of Louis XIV so that his courtiers may mistake the pretense for the reality and confuse the farcical monarchy with the glorious one. History, while it obsesses Stendhal's characters, is unavailable to them except as nostalgia and parodic gestures, and the polarization I have described between social life and happiness is undoubtedly reinforced by Stendhal's refusal to allow historical nostalgia to blind him to the unavailability of past styles to the present. His work, instead of romanticizing the past in order to make a private fantasy seem like a social fact for more privileged generations, contains the implicit recognition that the "chasse au bonheur" is not inspired by any historical truth other than that of a personal dream-world.

Now in *La Chartreuse* Stendhal creates a couple less ideal than Fabrice and Clélia and closer to Stendhal himself. It is as if, while writing a book in which the "chasse au bonheur" leads to secrecy and even imprisonment, he were also exploring the possibility of a happiness capable of creating its own social environment. The society imagined for Gina and Mosca would, it seems, exclude the kind of political involvements forced on them at Parma; it would be indifferent to politics without being victimized by politics. The *salon* would replace the court without either escaping its jurisdiction or arousing its hostility. It is impossible to emphasize too strongly the importance of the *salon* for Stendhal's imagination as perhaps the only way of socializing happiness, of adjusting the intensities of passion to the pace and scope of a larger community. A frequent scene in his fiction is that of the *homme d'esprit* in a drawing room unworthy of him, surrounded by boring, vain people. In *La Chartreuse*, the prospect of a satisfactory *salon*, in which the *homme d'esprit* would be the rule and not the exception, is made historically plausible by "the too short reign of the charming Prince Eugene" in Milan. The only reference to the past which escapes parody is to a past provided by the novel itself. The years when "the charming Countess Pietranera" was "one of the most distinguished women at the court of Prince Eugene, Viceroy of Italy," are only briefly referred to at the beginning of *La Chartreuse* (10; 34–35), but the memory of those years gives added strength to the condemnation of Parma. It also nourishes Gina's illusions about what life at Parma will be like, and in fact her early successes at Parma reinforce her idea of court life as a

"fascinating game" (111; 143). The "fatal stupidity" of coming
to live in the court of a tyrant to whom each of his victims seems
like a "defiance to his power" is made painfully clear by Fabrice's
imprisonment, when the duchess thinks bitterly of what she had
expected to find at Parma: ". . . I was thinking of the attrac-
tions of a pleasant court, something inferior, it's true, but something in the style of the happy days of Prince Eugene" (237;
282), "whose kindness," Stendhal says elsewhere, "has left such
a lasting memory" (395; 455).

Contemporary Italian life makes impossible that harmony between the *salon* and the court which made of Eugene's reign the
Golden Age both of Milan and of the novel, but when Mosca
describes the kind of life still available to him and Gina in
Naples, he evokes an image of at least peaceful coexistence between the state and The Happy Few: " 'Neither of us has any
real need of luxury. If I have a horse and a seat in a box at the
San Carlo in Naples, I will be more than satisfied. It will never
be the degree of luxury in which we live that will give us a position in society: it will be the pleasure which the intelligent people of the city may find in coming to your house for a cup of
tea' " (356; 413). The special lustre of luxury will be missing,
but the most essential aspect in the Stendhalian notion of aristocracy is undoubtedly to be found in the count's interesting
connection between distinction or rank and the ability to attract
a spiritual elite—"les gens d'esprit du pays"—for the pleasures of
conversation. And the *salon* as a compromise between the court
and the Farnese tower is almost realized toward the end of the
novel: "We have," Gina writes to Fabrice from Naples, "a concert every Thursday and an evening party [conversation] every
Sunday; our drawing rooms are always packed" (411; 471).
Gina's passionate interest in Fabrice perhaps dictates this invitation, but the importance of the letter is much greater than her
motives in writing it. The duchess's *salon* is the *only* escape from
the two prisons of Parma and of a love condemned first of all
by its very nature. Only the wittily humane talk of a cultivated

elite converts the Stendhalian image of happiness into a livable social reality.

But, in a work which contains the blissful love in the Farnese tower, La Sanseverina's *salon* is not a strong enough alternative. Gina herself "combined all the appearances of happiness, but she lived only a short time after Fabrizio, whom she still adored, and who spent only a year in his Charterhouse." Mosca, once again in the prince's favor, is merely "enormously rich," left to view with something less than enlivening irony the contentment of Ernest V's subjects, "who compared his rule to that of the Grand Duke of Tuscany" (431; 493). The *salon* as society for The Happy Few is, then, explored but finally rejected in *La Chartreuse*. And the failure of this alternative is perhaps the strongest evidence of the structural inflexibility of this superficially sprawling, leisurely novel. The polarization of Stendhal's imagination into the antagonistic aspects of the fantasy I have been describing seems to have severely limited the range of play which might have come from the writing of *La Chartreuse*. At least as far as his characters are concerned, Stendhal does not find in novelistic invention a temporary, at least literary liberation from the rigid assumption of a world totally inhospitable to a totally unworldly dream of happiness. The "integrity" of this fantasy is maintained throughout the novel; as a result, there is no escape from it in terms of those dramatic relationships imagined as a rigorously faithful expansion of the fantasy.

An escape is, however, provided by the voice which records the inability to escape. The difference between Stendhal and his hero is recognizable as a difference in style between the two, and the style which the Stendhalian narrator creates for himself is the alternative proposed in *La Chartreuse* both to Parma and to Fabrice. As I have said, Stendhal, unlike Fabrice, pursues the dream of happiness while attentively elaborating the social realities which thwart it. This very attention requires a personality different from Fabrice's, one which escapes the psychological rigidity of the novel's theme in the very process of detailing its elements. Given the nature of society in the novel, the temperamental differences between Stendhal and Fabrice can be thought of as a self-protective strategy on the part of the novelist. In the same way that we recognize the rightness—as well as the sadness—of Mosca surviving alone in a world he alone has understood and been willing to live in, we can also see in Stendhal's attention to politics a certain wisdom which makes survival possible. Writing about society is an education about the dangers of society, or, more accurately, a way for Stendhal to learn that his image of social life is incompatible with his image of happiness. His involvement with history dramatically confirms the unhistorical nature of the kind of fantasy pursued through Fabrice's "chasse au bonheur." The realistic convention of portraying real sequences of real social and political events thus saves Stendhal from any illusions about his fantasy prospering in a context of historical time. And so he protects himself from the destructiveness of society by making himself—like Mosca again—just slightly unworthy of his own dream of an ideal humanity. By his attention to society, Stendhal puts himself at a certain distance from Fabrice and suggests, by this self-preserving gesture, his inability to imagine any way of saving his hero. He separates himself from Fabrice by a sophistication, by a knowledge about and an attention to the world which are much less appealing than his hero's naïveté, but which enable him to keep sight of the dangers of naïveté.

The Stendhalian narrator's personality is not, at first glance, very appealing. Mosca's cool irony is at least balanced by his love for Gina, and the generosity in his jealous admiration of Fabrice more than ensures our sympathy. The most irritating presence, the most grating voice in the novel is Stendhal's. The price Stendhal pays for not being Fabrice is the narrative surface of tiresome irony in La Chartreuse de Parme. There is, first of all, the continual shadow-boxing with a hostile audience. The absurd self-defense in the Avertissement to La Chartreuse, for example, is nothing more than an attack on his audience. Who can doubt the narrator's preference for "Italian hearts" over "French hearts" after reading this "apology" to the reader:

> I am publishing this novel without changing anything in the manuscript of 1830. This may have two drawbacks:
>
> The first one concerns the reader: the characters, being Italians, will perhaps interest him less, since hearts in Italy are quite different from French hearts. The Italians are sincere, straightforward people who, unabashed, say what they think. They have only spasmodic outbursts of vanity; it then becomes a passion and takes the name of *puntiglio*. And to them, poverty is not a subject of ridicule.

As if this were not clear enough, Stendhal hypocritically assures us that he casts "the strongest moral censure" on much of his characters' behavior, although he "admits" having done nothing to make their behavior more acceptable to the reader. "What would be the use of giving them the lofty morality and social graces which distinguish the character of the French, who love money above all else and almost never sin from hatred or love?" (xiii–xiv; 23–24)

The *Avertissement* is a warning recurrent in Stendhal's fiction: to resist his lovable heroes is to run the risk of becoming the villains of his stories, of being treated like cold, vain, money-loving French readers. The reader is to share Stendhal's enthusiasms before questioning them. We see in such passages the superficial resemblance between Stendhal and Fielding, whom Stendhal admired. The latter's insincere apology offers us the same cozy and facile satisfaction of belonging to the "right side" that we enjoy in Fielding's deliberately unconvincing defenses of Blifil and criticism of Tom. Stendhal, like Fielding, seems to be creating the unsympathetic reader in order to do away with him. A certain kind of audience is made impossible—frightened away —by the manner in which it is addressed. *La Chartreuse* is dedicated to The Happy Few—those capable of loving Stendhal's hero, who also know that "'. . . love and the happiness it gives are the only serious things in the world' "—but they are a secret audience, one Stendhal almost never addresses directly. What happens in the story calls for such readers, assumes that they do exist, but Stendhal *speaks* to the others, ironically flatters them, attacks them, defies them not to recognize the superiority of his heroes.

Fabrice is by far the most appealing of Stendhal's heroes, but we are seldom allowed to enjoy his naïveté and spontaneity without being reminded that other readers might *not* enjoy them. The nervously and aggressively mocking narrator hardly ever relents in his effort to make us view our own sophistications (about life and about fiction) with the same indifference or condescension with which, it is feared, we might be inclined to regard Fabrice's simplicity. The latter's most lovable gestures are prefaced (especially in the first half of *La Chartreuse*) by these tedious intrusions on the part of his worried creator. The more moving an episode is, the more precautionary Stendhal becomes. For example, the sublimity of what is to follow can be guessed from Stendhal's way of introducing Fabrice's return to Grianta to consult the Abbé Blanès and to recapture "the freshness of his feelings at the age of sixteen": ". . . the object of his expedition, and the feelings that agitated [our hero] during the fifty hours it lasted, are so absurd that, in the interests of our story, it would no doubt have been better to pass over them in silence" (131; 165). The beauty of Lake Como, the surrounding woods, and a starry night move Fabrice to happy tears, for which, predictably, Stendhal "apologizes": "Fabrizio had an Italian heart, and I ask that he be excused for it; this defect, which will make him less likable, consisted chiefly in the fact that he had only spasmodic outbursts of vanity, and that the mere sight of sublime beauty moved him deeply and took away the sharp, bitter sting of his sorrows" (132; 166).

The behavior of other characters can set off the same mechanism. When Mosca proposes to Gina that she marry the old

Duke Sanseverina so that she may live in Parma as his, Mosca's, mistress, Stendhal hastens to absolve himself of any guilt for having set down the details of such an objectionable bargain: "Is it his fault [that of the historian] if the characters, seduced by passions which, unfortunately for him, he does not share, descend to actions that are profoundly immoral? It is true," Stendhal adds—and once again the French reader is meant to feel ashamed of not being Italian—"that such things are no longer done in a country where the only passion that has survived all others is the love of money, a means of satisfying vanity" (93; 124). As Robert M. Adams has said of this passage: "The passionate truth of the story is affirmed by inventing someone to sneer at it, and then sneering at that person." [16] It is difficult not to find such passages in *La Chartreuse* heavy-handed and obvious; they have in fact alienated many of the readers whose sympathies they obliquely seek to ensure. Nothing, after all, seems less spontaneous and innocent, more calculated, than the irony by which Stendhal would break down our resistance to spontaneity and innocence. Finally, the Stendhalian defenses and disguises are astonishingly transparent; as Georges Blin has put it, the ease with which we see through these strategies is directly proportionate to the energy Stendhal spends in developing them.[17]

Stendhal, unlike Fabrice, is extraordinarily sensitive to what others might think of his hero. And his manner of dealing with an imagined hostility (which he himself brings into his story by his constant effort to prevent it from spoiling his story) expresses a personality full of those vulnerabilities which, it seems, Stendhal could at least temporarily overcome only in the creation of a hero like Fabrice. Victor Brombert, Jean Starobinski, and Georges Blin have given admirable portraits of the Stendhalian pathology. Stendhal, as Brombert sharply argues, is militant and aggressive out of timidity; the attack on the reader

16. *Stendhal: Notes on a Novelist* (New York, 1959), p. 65.
17. *Stendhal et les problèmes de la personnalité* (Paris, 1958), I, 299.

presented as an attack on the hero is Stendhal's strategy for moving us without compromising himself, for making us share emotions he does not dare show directly. Beyle's penchant for pseudonyms and mystifications (at the beginning of *La Chartreuse* he manages, for example, to lie about when and where he wrote the novel as well as about its sources) expresses, as does his irony, a terror of being seen directly, of becoming the unprotected object of someone else's attention. And so, as Starobinski has shown, Stendhal conducts the search for *le naturel* with a baffling assortment of masks; a system of disguises is designed both to confuse others and to overcome an original feeling of alienation from the self.

Now even the most intelligently sympathetic analyses of Stendhal's compulsive need to couple every self-exposure with a self-denial do little to change the effect of that need on his novels. Stendhal's ironic apologies for what is most lovable in Fabrice remains, I think, the least interesting aspect of his attempt to transcend the mutually exclusive worlds of Fabrice and society. If, however, his irony does not really spoil the novel for us, it is not, it seems to me, because we choose to think of it in the context of Stendhal's life, but rather because the context of *La Chartreuse* itself gives to it a significance somewhat different from the one suggested by other evidence in Stendhal's life. His irony does not, at any rate, strike us *only* as a continuous shirking of responsibility for his own enthusiasms, as a sign of his pathological timidity and terror of exposure. Both Fabrice's fate and the nature of society in *La Chartreuse* give to the narrator's irony a certain depth or urgency, as if that constant reference to hostile points of view were necessary as part of the narrator's poignant struggle against both the appeal and the dangers of his own story, as part of an attempt to achieve psychological *balance*. The hostile reader is brought into the story as an urgently needed presence. Stendhal's irony thus helps to adjust his vision of happiness to his vision of society: it makes of their opposition an occasion for some form of social communication.

Furthermore, the inclusiveness of the narrative point of view in *La Chartreuse* does not always depend on this summoning into the story of a hostile presence. There is in the novel a certain resistance to "Italy" and to Fabrice more subtle than the coarse, "French" insensitivity which Stendhal is continually attacking. The first chapter of the novel, "Milan in 1796," makes it clear that the militancy of the *Avertissement* will not be Stendhal's only mode of address. The carefree, joyous atmosphere which Napoleon's soldiers bring to the Italians is marvelously evoked, but here and there Stendhal's enthusiasm is just slightly reticent:

> An entire people realized, on May 15, 1796, that everything they had respected till then was supremely ridiculous and sometimes odious. The departure of the last Austrian regiment marked the downfall of the old ideas. Risking one's life became fashionable; people saw that, in order to be happy after centuries of insipid feelings, they had to love their country with genuine love, and seek heroic actions. They had been plunged into profound darkness by the long, vigilant despotism of Charles V and Philip II; they overturned these tyrants' statues and suddenly found themselves flooded with light. (1–2; 25–26)

The modulations of the narrator's voice here are incomparably richer than in the passages I quoted earlier from the *Avertissement*. A kind of airy nonchalance in Stendhal's style suggests the exhilaration of release, the joy of unreflective bravura. But there are details, juxtapositions, which make us smile. Stendhal subtly insists on the suddenness of this change in the Milanese's lives: he gives us exact dates for a whole population's complete reversal of values. The Italians see their past as ridiculous on May 15, 1796, and all the old ideas "fall" as the last Austrian regiment leaves. There is also something absurd in the way the Italians gaily and resolutely jump on the bandwagon of hero-

ism; overnight it becomes "fashionable" to risk one's life, "they
had" to be sincerely patriotic and "seek" heroic actions. Finally,
the causal sequence is most frankly comical in the last sentence
of the passage: the act of knocking down Charles-Quint's and
Philippe II's statues is enough to flood the Italian mind with
a new spiritual light.

Now in these early pages Stendhal is creating an atmosphere
for which we (like Gina) will be nostalgic once we are hopelessly involved in the petty intrigues of the court at Parma. He
is, as I have suggested, providing a past for the rest of his novel,
something which will make the dream of happiness an historical
memory rather than just wishful thinking. But this privileged
time is being described by someone who cannot help but find
something slightly ridiculous in the very temperament which he
has set out to exalt. At the very least, it surprises him. It is as if
the creation of this temperament were accompanied by an amused
astonishment in the man creating it. As Stendhal's yearning for
an admirably free and happy life "leaves" him to become, in the
novel, the state of affairs in Milan in 1796, it takes on a slightly
foreign look. And the narrator seems spontaneously to put a certain distance between himself and the values which he usually
tries to make us accept unreservedly. His voice is, then, from
the beginning of La Chartreuse, trying out an alternative to both
the "French" and the "Italian" sensibilities. This slight resistance
to the latter at the very start of the story suggests, furthermore,
limitations and impossibilities in the Italian way of life which
the novel will, indeed, document. The "necessity" of the plot,
of his characters' fate, is at least implied in Stendhal's protecting
himself from them before their fate has been worked out.

We occasionally see, in Stendhal's treatment of Fabrice, a
similar reluctance to give to his favorite characters an unqualified
approval. Stendhal's irony with Fabrice is generally of the sort I
have pointed out in the passage describing Fabrice's return to
Grianta: he wants to increase our delight with his hero's beautiful gestures by pretending to be ashamed of them. But there
are passages in which Stendhal is soberly unironic in his judg-

ment of Fabrice. On his way to visit the Abbé Blanès, "his true father," Fabrice wonders if astrology can be considered a respectable science, "a *proven* science, in the same category as geometry, for example." He tries calmly and objectively to remember all the incidents in his life when prophetic signs proved false, but, Stendhal notes, ". . . his attention lingered happily over the cases in which the omen had been clearly followed by the [fortunate or unfortunate accident which it seemed to him to predict]." With such a method Fabrice's reasoning doesn't get very far and, instead of attacking an analytic "French" mind for being insensitive to the charm of Fabrice's wobbly logic, Stendhal, firmly if not unsympathetically, diagnoses and condemns his hero's assumption that reality can be ignored and reasoned about at the same time:

> He was still too young; in his moments of leisure, he delighted in savoring the sensations produced by the romantic circumstances with which his imagination was always ready to supply him. He was far from employing his time in patiently observing the real characteristics of things in order to discover their causes. Reality still seemed dull and sordid to him. I can understand that one might not like to look at it, but in that case one ought not to reason about it. And one certainly ought not to raise objections with the various components of one's ignorance. (134–36; 168–70)

Stendhal's position is complex. He is not exactly reproaching Fabrice for not paying attention to "the real characteristics of things." Indeed, Stendhal might almost envy Fabrice's "half-belief" in prophetic signs, for what Stendhal sees, and what his hero does not see, is that this belief is "a religion, a profound impression received at the beginning of his life. To think about that belief was to feel; it was happiness" (134; 168). In a sense, Fabrice can be blamed only for diluting his joy; he is wasting his time in trying to give scientific dignity to what makes him happy. In his criticism of Fabrice, Stendhal is therefore, in part, defending the religion of feeling. But there isn't any scorn in

this passage for the operations of reason. If Fabrice's superstitions are justified because they bring him joy, Stendhal's language, by its careful discriminations and its concise definition
of what true reasoning consists of ("regarder avec patience les
particularités réelles des choses pour ensuite deviner leurs
causes") adequately expresses his own respect for a human faculty which his hero—at least at this point in his life—both
scorns and misuses. Reason may be the end of happiness, but
Stendhal, in his hymn to happiness, cannot help but come to
the defense of reason.

Fabrice, Stendhal writes, "would have felt invincible repugnance for anyone who denied the validity of omens, especially
if the denial had been made with irony" (135; 168). Stendhal
is, on the whole, more gentle, but he never hesitates to make discriminations unavailable to his intellectually naïve hero. Fabrice,
praying in San Petronio in Bologna, asks forgiveness for having
killed Giletti, but, ". . . it is remarkable that it never occurred
to him to number among his sins his plans to become an archbishop solely because Count Mosca was Prime Minister and
regarded that position and the majestic life that went with it as
suitable for the duchess's nephew" (174; 211). Having learned
from the Milanese Jesuits not to think "*about unaccustomed
things,*"

> . . . although he did not lack intelligence and, above all, the
> ability to reason logically, it never once occurred to him that
> the use of Count Mosca's influence in his favor might be a form
> of simony. Such is the triumph of a Jesuit education: it incul-
> cates the habit of ignoring things which are as plain as day.
> A Frenchman, brought up amid the self-interest and irony of
> Paris, might, without dishonesty, have accused Fabrizio of
> hypocrisy at the very moment when our hero was opening his
> heart to God with utter sincerity and deep emotion. (174–75;
> 212)

The last sentence is a good example of a typically Stendhalian
poising of attitudes. The Frenchman is treated remarkably well

(his accusation would be disinterested), although we are reminded again of the ungenerous society he lives in; and it is
really Stendhal who is accusing Fabrice of hypocrisy, although
the superlatives at the end of the passage bring our attention
back, after the sophisticated cultural and moral digression, to
the admirable honesty and depth of Fabrice's feelings. The
Jesuits are bearing the brunt of Stendhal's attack here, but in
certain respects Fabrice is their product. The result of his education, at any rate, is by no means out of harmony with his
natural disposition. Fabrice simply does not always have as much
esprit as his Parisian counterpart might naturally have, and this
eminently French word is a positive word in Stendhal's vocabulary. Fabrice's moral myopia in the church, his confused reasoning about the scientific validity of astrology, and the Milanese's
sudden passion for heroism on May 15, 1796, all illustrate, in
different ways, a failure of the critical spirit, an intellectual passivity which only an inference of causes from "les particularités
réelles des choses" could cure. Stendhal, by the distance he maintains in such passages, dominates the experience to which his
characters, however joyfully, only submit.

There is, of course, nothing surprising in a defense of analytical intelligence from the admirer of Condillac, Helvétius, and
Destutt de Tracy. Such defenses in the novel are, however, less
interesting as symptomatic of Stendhal's intellectual tastes than
as an expression of a personality flexible enough to judge the
values which the novel exalts. The urbanity and sophistication
with which we are addressed throughout the novel prevent both
Stendhal and us from becoming dangerously involved in an
inflexibly polarized fantasy. They save us from the melodramatic
primitiveness of that fantasy by an irony about what constitutes
it. Now this saving presence in *La Chartreuse* depends, perhaps
more than on anything else, on the pace at which the story
proceeds. Stendhal himself and numerous commentators have
recognized his talent for improvisation. He had a horror of outlines, for the interesting reason that they require being remem-

bered, which was enough to disgust him with the work yet to
be done. "I do the outline," he wrote, "after writing the story
as my heart dictates it; otherwise the appeal to memory kills the
imagination (at any rate, that's the way it is in my case)." [18]
Given this absence of a predetermined unity, the speed at which
La Chartreuse was written—it took about seven weeks, from
November 4 to December 25, 1838—undoubtedly helped to
guarantee continuity among different episodes. In a more important way, it also made for a freer relation between Stendhal at
the moment of writing and the psychological structures which,
as we have seen, the novel expresses. The appeal to memory, as
Stendhal seems obscurely to have realized, would have meant
not only a dependence on a preconceived plan, but also a greater
subservience to those structures and themes which such a plan
might have made excessively transparent.

The novelist's outline—analogous in this respect to the Balzacian exposition—could be thought of as a way for his past to
control his novel's future. The obligation it imposes is one of
fidelity to a kind of order and intelligibility already articulated.
Stendhal's hurried improvisations helped, as Brombert has emphasized, to reverse what might at first seem the more natural
relation between autobiography and fiction. As the marginalia
(especially of *Lucien Leuwen*) indicate, Stendhal's memory, instead of serving as a conscious inspiration for what was about
to be written, was awakened by what he had already written.
This *a posteriori* self-recognition in Stendhal as a reader of his
own fiction[19] thus suggests considerable receptiveness, at the
moment of composition, to influences not recognizably autobiographical. The novel's future is more open, at least an appearance
of compositional freedom is created by Stendhal's having to discover simultaneously his fictional material and the manner of
confronting it. The Stendhalian method of writing is a way of

18. *Mélanges intimes et Marginalia*, 2 vols. (Paris, 1936), II, p. 262.
19. See Brombert's discussion of "spontaneous reactions" in *Stendhal et
la voie oblique*, pp. 101–27.

allowing the suggestiveness of the narrator's talk, as he proceeds with the story, to compete with the suggestiveness of psychological depth.

Stendhal's writing has the immediacy and unpredictability of those passionate deliberations which characterize his heroes at moments of crisis. (Jean Prévost has spoken of simultaneous "movements" of "invention" in the author, of "passion" in Stendhal's heroes, and of "sympathy" in the reader.[20]) The scenes describing Mosca's jealousy, Gina's pain and rage the night she learns of Fabrice's imprisonment, and Fabrice's confusion about how to deal with Gina's feelings for him could be taken as models of the kind of composition I have in mind. With their abrupt shifts of mood, pace, and direction, they compose a future for the Stendhalian characters out of a dialectical struggle between passionate outburst and an attempt to look calmly at the "particularités réelles des choses." It is during these monologues, with their psychological detail and the reversals of direction which even make parts of the monologue seem superfluous in retrospect, that the time of Stendhal's novelistic composition most closely parallels the time of his characters' lives. And this coincidence of creation throws further light on what has often been praised as the freedom of the Stendhalian hero. He is free, essentially, from those narrative summaries of psychological states which, in Balzac, Flaubert, and Proust, by their very aid to intelligibility, partially enclose and prefigure a character's future. The effect of such summaries is to make visible what could be called the space between the novelist's imagination and his fable; they make of his story a more transparent metaphor for the ways in which he tends to give order and structure to the world. They emphasize and perhaps increase the extent to which novelistic characters are limited to a future defined by their creator's past. The many attacks, since Flaubert, on analytical summaries of psychological states in fiction are at least partly understandable

20. *La Création chez Stendhal/Essai sur le métier d'écrire et la psychologie de l'écrivain* (Paris, 1951), pp. 347–48.

in terms of the novelist's attempt to free his characters from his own past, that is, to free *himself* from that past as he writes.

The autonomy of characters of fiction is, of course, an illusion. What we call their freedom perhaps depends on the range and stability of those mental configurations which inspire the novelist at the moment of writing. Stendhal's compositional method obviously does not free his characters from all psychological determination; it does, however, make the range of determining factors as broad as possible by allowing Stendhal himself partially to evade the pressures of his most persistent psychological themes. "For each incident," he writes in his notes for *Lamiel*, "ask yourself if it should be told philosophically, or in the narrative mode, according to Aristotle's doctrine." And his preference for *"the narrative account of an event"* over *"the intellectual résumé of an action"* is more than a choice in favor of dramatic liveliness.[21] It suggests, more significantly, Stendhal's desire to shift his narrative inspiration from an idea conceived at a certain distance from narrative detail to the richer suggestiveness of the various details themselves. Each moment of his writing would, ideally, become more important for the future of his writing than the thematic structures which resist the local inspirations of particular contexts.

Literature, as I am suggesting throughout this study, is perhaps always a compromise between these two sources of inspiration. A writer's individuality can be discussed as the particular shape which this compromise takes in his work, as his special version of a struggle between self-immobilizing themes and the pull away from such themes toward a greater variety of response to the world and to language. For Stendhal's characters, the progress of *La Chartreuse*—in spite of the novel's dramatic variety—exposes and reinforces a rigid imaginative structure from which nothing in the novel saves them, notwithstanding the freedom which Stendhal appears anxious to allow them. I agree

21. Quoted by Martineau in his preface to *Lamiel*, in *Romans et nouvelles*, II, 862.

with Adams that, "without enemies," Stendhal's heroes tend to "wither away," but I do not think that this is because ". . . they are almost without natures . . . ," or because Stendhal's fiction has "no core or center." [22] Blin takes a similar line when he speaks of the "psychological autonomy" of heroes without heredity, without a past.[23] But Stendhal's characters do not, I feel, have the openness which might come from their living entirely on life's surfaces. Only the narrator profits from the indeterminacy at which his method aims; he alone escapes his characters' fate by his very elaboration of its inevitability. Stendhal's writing both consecrates and subverts the rigid psychological diagrams which shape his characters' lives. These lives are easily recognizable as victimized by what is undoubtedly their creator's psychological history, but the narrator's improvised responses to his story also improvise a self superior to its own history. His voice, poised between the Stendhalian images of happiness and of society, creates a "third presence" in *La Chartreuse* which reinvents fantasy as worthy of entertaining the most maturely subtle intelligence. Such, hopefully, is the intelligence of the reader Stendhal would invent while appearing to neglect him, of The Happy Few who make up the strictly literary *salon* of Stendhal and his audience.

22. *Stendhal: Notes on a Novelist*, pp. 59–60.
23. *Stendhal et les problèmes du roman* (Paris, 1954), p. 107.

III

FLAUBERT AND THE THREATS
OF IMAGINATION
[*Madame Bovary*]

Before marriage she thought herself in love; but since the happiness that should have followed failed to come, she must, she thought, have been mistaken. And Emma tried to find out what one meant exactly in life by the words *bliss, passion, ecstasy,* that had seemed to her so beautiful in books.[1]

*   *   *

"But isn't it amusing," he sometimes said to himself, "that I'm immune to that exclusive, passionate obsession known as love? . . . Could it be that what's known as love is only another lie? I feel love, of course, just as I feel hunger at six o'clock!

1. Gustave Flaubert, *Madame Bovary,* edited with a substantially new translation by Paul de Man, based on the version by Eleanor Marx Aveling (New York, 1965), p. 24. *Madame Bovary,* in *Œuvres,* ed. A. Thibaudet and R. Dumesnil, 2 vols. (1951–52), I, 356. Subsequent page references to *Madame Bovary* will be given in the text; the first reference in each case will be to the English translation, the second to volume one in the Pléiade edition of *Madame Bovary* in *Œuvres.* References to Flaubert's other fiction will also be to this French edition. All other translations here (except for the one cited in note 2) are my own.

Could it be that liars have taken that rather vulgar propensity and turned it into the love of Othello, of Tancred? Or should I believe that I'm made differently from other men? Is my soul lacking in one passion? Why should it be? That would be a strange fate!" [2]

Novelists, as these passages from *Madame Bovary* and *La Chartreuse de Parme* suggest, are apt to take what may seem like a cruel pleasure in exposing their heroes' naïve confidence in novelistic versions of life. It is as if the writer of fiction were intent on advertising the void of fiction, even on making us distrustful of his own efforts to entertain and deceive us. In his curious deprecation of his medium, the realist, as Harry Levin has said, seeks to approximate truth by relentlessly exposing the artifices of literature.[3] Seduced by the glamorous associations (mainly literary) of such abstractions as "love" and "bliss," Fabrice and Emma idly and absurdly wait for experience to adjust itself to their words. As a result, it would appear that they are doomed to a constant and comic puzzlement: is the whirring of bullets at Waterloo what men call a "battle"? where is "the noble and intellectual part of love" in the vain pursuit of La Fausta? does submitting to Rodolphe's sexual expertise constitute "ecstasy"? Were these the kinds of experiences behind such words when other men and women used them? How, in short, can we ever be certain that what we are living corresponds exactly to what we have anticipated as life's most exciting promises?

But Stendhal's distrust of the vocabulary of passion proceeds from an even greater confidence in the reality of passion. Fabrice loses his naïveté about the promise of passion not as a result of repeated disappointments, but because of his happy love for Clélia. Love *is* waiting for Fabrice, and words are simply inade-

2. *The Charterhouse of Parma*, tr. Lowell Bair, introduction by Harry Levin (New York, 1960), p. 186. *La Chartreuse de Parme*, in *Romans et nouvelles*, ed. Henri Martineau, 2 vols. (Paris, 1952), I, 224–25.
3. *The Gates of Horn/A Study of Five French Realists* (New York, 1963), p. 51.

quate to express the intensity and richness of feelings which
Stendhal is nevertheless reduced to celebrating verbally. *La
Chartreuse,* as I have said, provides an environment both necessary and irrelevant to love. Parma is a negative way of extolling
life in the Farnese tower, and the very language of the novel
could be thought of as a mere expediency for hinting at an essentially inexpressible ecstasy. Stendhal, so to speak, always rushes
beyond his writing; something more important than language
keeps him from excessively worrying about the shape or artistic
"rightness" of particular passages. A certain impatience with
style expresses his exuberant sense of personal style as untrans-
latable. At best, his writing can simply suggest the improvised
rhythms of passion which no exaggerated respect for the writing
process itself could ever express.

In Flaubert the easy flow, the transparency of language disappear. Nothing could be more alien to Flaubert. Whereas Fabrice is
only mildly and temporarily comical when he muses about the
meanings of words, Emma Bovary kills herself because of her
failure to find a situation worthy of her vocabulary. The only
important question in her life is to know what "bliss," "passion,"
and "ecstasy" mean, and it is inconceivable to Flaubert's heroine
that any experience imperfectly formulated could bring happiness, could even be worth living. Emma tests each episode in
her life in the light of the language she has learned from books,
and while Flaubert is ruthlessly satirical in his judgment of her
absurd expectations, we recognize in her folly a distorted reflection of the excruciating process by which Flaubert himself tested
the rhythmical and dramatic appropriateness of each of his
phrases.

In Flaubert the easy flow, the transparency of language disappear. Perhaps a certain nonchalance about language is crucial
to the realism of Stendhal and of Balzac. That is, even if, as in
La Chartreuse, words are incapable of translating the highest
feelings, neither Stendhal nor Balzac thinks of language as
sufficiently opaque and autonomous to prevent our perception
of the real. To argue that art mirrors reality is not necessarily to

assert a similarity of nature between the two; if the novelist claims that words "reflect" life, it may be because he feels they have no life strong enough to resist the passionate projects—the pursuit of power or of happiness—which words are made to serve. With Flaubert, the reflecting nature of language becomes both imperative and immensely problematical. In spite of her silly sentimentality, Emma Bovary raises a question fatal to the realistic illusion: does language have its "source" in life, is life really "behind" language? The urgency with which she lives this question displaces the subject of fiction: no longer focused in a relatively uncomplicated way on the world, Flaubert's work examines its own instrumentalities. The word as object tends to replace the world of objects, and it is this crucial shift of attention which defines Flaubert's spectacularly subversive role in the history of realistic fiction.

My study of Flaubert will be necessarily more abstract, less psychologically concrete, than my discussions of Balzac and of Stendhal. For Flaubert's fiction is less about specific personalities than about the problematic relation between the fictions of language and *any* personality. The recurrent design of his work appears peculiarly affectless: even with a character as rich as Emma Bovary, Flaubert is less interested in her psychological particularity than in her capacity to produce fictions and suffer from their unreality. Immensely different characters can lend themselves to this design: Bouvard and Pécuchet resemble Emma because their passion for knowledge involves the same illusions as Emma's dreams of passion. In fact, as the evolution of Flaubert's work shows, psychology can be considered as an obstacle to the treatment of his theme: the straw men are the best characters because they have no character, because nothing personal interferes with their being used as vehicles through whom the abstract and empty nature of mental life can be illustrated.

Furthermore, the kind of criticism which Flaubert's work invites would have nothing to say about the author of that work. Impersonality is a profound subject of his work rather than a technique applied to other, more traditional subjects of fiction. If we respond to what is most original in Flaubert, we are, I think, bound to see the inappropriateness of attempting to infer a biographical self from his work, or even of trying to construct a thematic self wholly within his work. For such critical procedures are irrelevant to what Flaubert's novels are most interestingly about: the arbitrary, insignificant, inexpressive nature of language. Language never fits the world or the self; a novel never fits its subject or its author's personality; and, finally, criticism can never fit the object it chooses to discuss. The content of particular statements is, we might say, a secondary, even accidental characteristic of language. Fundamentally, language refers to nothing beyond its own impersonal (and discouraging) virtuosity. And while such a position, if we fully subscribed to it, would naturally condemn in advance any discussion of Flaubert at all, our criticism can at least trace the logic of a certain argument about literature which has been a major source of both inspiration and paralysis for all modern art.

In the history of the novel, Flaubert is perhaps second only to Dostoevski as an observer of pathological symptoms. But, characteristically, he discourages psychological interpretations of the very cases which seem to lend themselves best to complex psychological analyses. We can see this in the most curious and extreme example in Flaubert of an apparently psychoanalytic fiction *avant la lettre*. "La Légende de Saint Julien l'Hospitalier" traces the biography of a sadist whose saintly self-immolation is the punishment he inflicts upon himself for his murderous fantasies. Raised by parents who think of him as "marked by God" and who "give him infinite respect and attention," Julien displays both a mildness which makes his mother think he will become an archbishop, and a breathless interest in warriors' tales of "the prodigious wounds" inflicted in the battles of their youth which leads his father to see in him a future conqueror. But one day in church this spoiled and deceptively submissive boy sees a white mouse whose reappearance on subsequent Sundays fascinates, troubles, and "importunes" him. "Taken with hatred" for the animal, he "resolved to get rid of it," and, having killed the mouse with a stick, he begins his career of fantastic slaughter.[4]

Julien becomes a hunter in order to satisfy his thirst for blood, and with a supernatural power which seems to objectify the insatiable nature of his urge to destroy, he kills with exhilaration an incredible number of animals until one day a great stag, before dying from an arrow Julien has shot into his head, curses him and predicts that he will murder his father and mother. Horrified, Julien gives up hunting, leaves home, becomes a famous warrior, and marries an emperor's daughter who, when he tells her of his fears, ridicules his superstitions and encourages him to take up hunting again. When he does, the animals he shoots at mysteriously survive his attacks, surround and follow him ominously (with their "cunning looks . . . they seemed to be meditating a plan of revenge . . ."). Terrified and exasperated, Julien pounces on some red partridges who inexplicably disappear under the cape he hopes to smother them with. "His thirst for slaughter came back; since there was a lack of animals, he would have liked to massacre men." The occasion at once presents itself. His parents, after years of searching for their son, have arrived at his castle and are put up for the night by Julien's wife in the younger couple's bedroom. There Julien, mistaking them for his wife and a lover, savagely kills them. He then leaves his wife and his land, asking her only "to pray for his soul, since from now on he no longer existed." He begs, wears "a hair-shirt with iron points,"[5] seeks death in all sorts of perilous adventures, finally decides to live in order to serve others, and dies one night in the embrace of a horrible leper (kissing his bluish, foul-smelling mouth, and pressed, naked, against his cold and scabby body in order to give the leper some of his own warmth). The leper, suddenly transfigured, reveals himself as

4. II, 625–27.
5. II, 640–44.

Christ and, as a reward for Julien's absolute charity, carries him
triumphantly up to heaven.

Flaubert presents his tale as an exercise in hagiography: "And
that," he writes at the end, "is the story of saint Julien the
Hospitaler, almost as it is told on the stained-glass window of
a church in my region." [6] The narrator's matter-of-factness
throughout the story indeed suggests an attempt merely to tran-
scribe the different scenes of Saint Julien's life as they might be
represented in the stained-glass panels of a church window.
And, except for an occasionally false note, when the narrator's
indulgent, sophisticated restraint is a bit too obvious (as when,
speaking of Julien's pious mother, he writes: "By dint of praying to God, a son came to her"),[7] the unemphatically literal
rendering of the legend, the lack of analytical comment, do help
to make Julien's extraordinary fate seem almost natural. But a
similarly matter-of-fact account of Julien's upbringing and of the
progress of his sadistic impulses provides the commentary which
Flaubert refrains from giving explicitly. A more transparently
reductive analysis might have undone the legend by simply
translating it back into the more probable history (or secret
fantasies) which it transforms but also exposes. The advantage
of Flaubert's method would seem to be that instead of a speculative commentary appended to or inserted in a supernatural tale,
we have an internal analysis provided by the tale itself and which
indirectly suggests the metaphorical status of the events being
recorded.

But having chosen to imitate rather than explicate the pictorial version of the legend, Flaubert gives us much more than
a psychological reading of the miracles. The supernatural is no
more imaginary than the natural; or rather, both psychology and
hagiography come to have the same inventive distinction because
the literal rendering of both makes them equally historical and
equally fictive. There is no "reality" which the legend both

6. II, 648.
7. II, 624.

makes sacred and obscures. While Julien the saint appears to be a pious sublimation of Julien the self-punishing murderer, both sadism and sainthood could be thought of as creative fantasies equally capable of producing events. That is, they are both versions of the same fable, and both add something substantial to history: on the one hand, the murder of Julien's parents, on the other, the veneration of Julien the saint. In a sense, remarkable as Flaubert's "case-study" is, he goes beyond his own psychological sophistication into an implicit equalization and critique of *all* fictions. There is no need to question the events of Julien's life since no representation of reality has priority over any other representation. Psychology is as interpretive as hagiography, which is to say that while they may both be metaphorical, neither one is more "original" than the other, and both illustrate the same tendency to multiply fictions about human experience. Thus the natural and the supernatural can be treated almost as different esthetic tastes in an unremittingly literal narrative.

The way in which Flaubert de-emphasizes any psychological depths which might be behind Julien's saintly behavior puts us on the track of his suspicious view of easy correspondences between expression of any sort (whether it be a descriptive phrase or a murderous act) and preexistent realities. We will, however, have to go much further, and I want first of all to consider how, more generally, an interest in extreme psychological states can be the beginning of a devaluation of psychology in literature. The writer can subvert certain kinds of significance in mental life by indicating a superfluous richness in the life of the mind, a richness inexplicable except perhaps in terms of the imagination's receptiveness to the proliferating nature of language itself. In expanded or hyperbolic states of consciousness, when the stimulated mind is "producing" in excess of what can be accounted for by its environment or even by its past, we see what might be called the anxiously free imagination. And the treatment of this phenomenon in literature depends on the varying emphases which writers give to the disturbing symptoms of anxiety on the one hand, and, on the other, to the possibilities of self-renewal in the apparent freedom.

The attention which writers may devote to these extreme mental states implies, most radically, an indifference to the traditionally *explanatory* function of literary fictions. Romantic anguish may be incurable, but it is generally not unintelligible. There is a "sufficient cause" for the suffering of Werther, René, Oberman, Ruy Blas, and Chatterton, and the rhetorical effort of romantic writers (especially in France) is aimed less at the description of a specific state of mind than at a "justification" of extreme states by a strenuous appeal to historical, psychological, or metaphysical causes. Romantic despair is, as a result, dignified and can even be optimistic. Behind those majestic poses lies the sense of a universe somehow adequate to a noble (if suicidal) consciousness of it. The hero may be aware only of futility, but even the futile and the meaningless become tragic, that is, richly stimulating facts about the world for Oberman and René. If Hugo and Vigny often seem didactic, it is because they think of the poet's anguish not as an inexplicable fact of consciousness, but as a historical circumstance which an enlightened society could change by heeding its prophets. And even in the most radical irrationalists of French literature—think of the ambitions of Nerval, Rimbaud, and Breton—the world of dreams can, in a sense, be salvaged; it is as if there were no mental experience which is by nature absolutely impermeable to any kind of intelligible discourse. Only in writers we have begun to listen to rather recently—most notably, Georges Bataille and Maurice Blanchot —do we find in French an insistent allusiveness to something more extreme than irrationality, to a mode of being which, unlike the irrational, is inaccessible to reason and which literature may take as the invisible subject it attempts *not* to express.

The neutral, impersonal language which Blanchot dreams of would not be psychologically descriptive; ideally, it would be entirely devoid of any particular personality. But perhaps the origins of such startling ambitions lie in self-dramatizations so

hyperbolic that they tend to abstract personality from its environment and make imagination appear autonomous and impersonal.
Literature's apparent function of making life intelligible begins
to be subverted as soon as it takes for a subject an agitation
neither adequately projected on the world nor adequately accounted for by the world. There is already something of this in
the *Lui* of Diderot's *Le Neveu de Rameau*, which is perhaps
why that work strikes us as more modern than the swarm of romantic books it seems both to announce and to mock. The *Lui's*
manic restlessness, for all his brilliance, is comical and disturb-
ingly trivial, but that is his originality. The character is interesting
not for the reasons why he behaves as he does (his laziness, deliberate hypocrisy, self-disgust, failure as a composer), but for the
essentially absurd inventiveness which his idleness makes possible. For the reasons are inadequate to the range of invention,
as indeed the setting (the terrace of the Café de la Régence)
seems inappropriate to the performance. The contrast between
this extraordinarily turned-on or expanded consciousness and the
poverty of the occasion as well as of the character's life make him
both ridiculous and irreducibly mysterious. The comedy is crucial,
and Diderot is suggesting the absorbing insignificance of a mind
idly exploring its own limits. Some of Musset's heroes strike a
similar note. Although they tend to reflect on absurdity in "serious" metaphysical terms, in their freest moments their speech
may be simply garbled. In *Les Caprices de Marianne*, for example, vaguely philosophical talk about reality as a "mirror" on
which things merely glide is far less interesting than the inarticulate, undignified, and "empty" irritability which Octave displays
after his scenes with Marianne (when he complains of the bells
grating on his nerves, or when only a silly "Drig! drig!" or a "Tra,
tra, poum! poum!" can express the disarray of a totally disinterested, unattached mind which Marianne has temporarily set afloat
again, dislodged from the comparative security of debauchery).[8]

8. Alfred de Musset, *Théâtre complet*, ed. Maurice Allen (Paris, 1952),
pp. 155, 170, and 794–95.

There are, of course, immense differences among all these treatments of unspecified and extreme mental states. The exuberant activity of Diderot's *neveu*, for example, is a far cry from the poet's leaden melancholy in those pieces of *Les Fleurs du mal* where Baudelaire describes, if not similar feelings, at least a similar relationship between a kind of existential intensity and the conditions—internal or external—which might make it intelligible. The resemblance lies in an indifference to possible correlations between modes of being and what can be known about the self and the world. And this indifference both changes the psychological content of literature (by undoing the notion of coherent character) and makes literature less dependent on psychology (since the imagination can apparently invent in extravagant excess of what environment or a personal past can provide).

An overcast day in Paris sets off the fantastic depression of a famous "Spleen" poem:

> Quand le ciel bas et lourd pèse comme un couvercle
> Sur l'esprit gémissant en proie aux longs ennuis,
> Et que de l'horizon embrassant tout le cercle
> Il nous verse un jour noir plus triste que les nuits;
>
> Quand la terre est changée en un cachot humide,
> Où l'Espérance, comme une chauve-souris,
> S'en va battant les murs de son aile timide
> Et se cognant la tête à des plafonds pourris;
>
> Quand la pluie étalant ses immenses traînées
> D'une vaste prison imite les barreaux,
> Et qu'un peuple muet d'infâmes araignées
> Vient tendre ses filets au fond de nos cerveaux,
>
> Des cloches tout à coup sautent avec furie
> Et lancent vers le ciel un affreux hurlement,
> Ainsi que des esprits errants et sans patrie
> Qui se mettent à geindre opiniâtrément.
>
> —Et de longs corbillards, sans tambours ni musique,
> Défilent lentement dans mon âme; l'Espoir,

Vaincu, pleure, et l'Angoisse atroce, despotique,
Sur mon crâne incliné plante son drapeau noir.[9]

The anguished terror Baudelaire describes is, in the poem, less
interesting psychologically than rhetorically, although it may be
just the inflated rhetoric which at first puts us off. There is nothing more to "understand" about the depression than the ways in
which it lends itself to exaggeration, to the outrageously theatrical. To *explain* this type of anxiety, we would have to explain
Baudelaire, who, in a sense, is not the subject of the poem. He
is the subject of the life Sartre analyzes or of the dream Michel
Butor studies,[10] but in the poem the only autobiographical element is a day of bad weather. And, inasmuch as we can speak of
realistic poetry, Hugo's "Tristesse d'Olympio" and Lamartine's
"Isolement" are much more realistic than the "Spleen" piece in
that they make melancholy intelligible in plausibly biographical
terms (and it would not matter if the biography were invented).
The artificiality of Baudelaire's poetry, on the other hand, has
less to do with his interest in the drugs evoked in *Les Paradis
artificiels* than with the deliberate severance of the poetic state
from any plausible history. Indeed, the fabulous past conjured up
in so many poems of *Les Fleurs du mal* simply emphasizes this
break with the past, since it redefines memory as the sport rather
than the source of imagination.

The tone of "Quand le ciel bas et lourd . . ." is melodramatic
but somehow not serious. While we could hardly call the poem
comical, its solemnity seems to me implicitly mocked by the poet's
overindulgence in devices used to create an atmosphere excessively solemn. Allegory in Baudelaire, curiously enough, serves
the same function as his use of prosaic language: while they often
work in opposite directions in a single poem (the one deflating
what the other inflates), they both violently upset that natural-

9. Charles Baudelaire, *Œuvres complètes*, ed. Y.-G. Le Dantec and
Claude Pichois (Paris, 1961), p. 70.
10. See Sartre, *Baudelaire*, in *Les Essais*, XXIV (Paris, 1947), and Butor,
Histoire extraordinaire/Essai sur un rêve de Baudelaire (Paris, 1961).

istic seriousness which romantic eloquence was rarely willing to
forego. Eliot recognized something artificial in Baudelaire's suffering, and he spoke of Baudelaire's confusion of evil with its
theatrical representations, the "theater" being the "Byronic paternity and Satanic fraternity" behind many of his poems. But
this paraphernalia is, for Eliot, "redeemed by *meaning something
else*"; Baudelaire has, finally, a "fundamental sincerity" which
Eliot defines as his concern "with the real problem of good and
evil." Understandably, Eliot preferred the man to the poet; it is
easier for him to admire Baudelaire's remark that civilization consists in the "diminution of the traces of original sin" than to find
anything in his poetry that expresses such a message in unambiguously sincere—and poetically successful—terms.[11] For evil
and suffering in Baudelaire's poems may *not* be serious, although
the moral duplicities which Sartre finds (rightly, I think) more
characteristic of Baudelaire's life than the sincerity Eliot praises
is perhaps the source of Baudelaire's strength as a poet. We might
even say that in *Les Fleurs du mal* a certain frivolity is perhaps
the most serious Baudelairean note. On the one hand, inauthen-
ticity can be considered as an esthetic category as well as an ethical one; and in that case it may mean nothing more than a refusal
to impose certain forms of censorship (deriving, say, from notions
of psychological probability or of taste) on verbal play. But while
Baudelaire pulls out all the stops in letting his melodramatic
imagination transform internal and external realities into a single
allegorical scene (by the third stanza the poet no longer perceives
any difference between his mind and the world), he also manages
to suggest some detachment from the often tasteless artifices
(Hope knocking its head against rotten ceilings, Anguish pound-
ing its flag into the poet's head) which melodramatize this despair.
We are encouraged to see some self-mockery in these excesses by
the sophisticated, highly controlled contexts in which they occur.
The elaborate single-sentence structure of the first four stanzas

11. T. S. Eliot, "Baudelaire," *Selected Essays* (New York, 1932, 1936,
1950), pp. 378–81.

of the poem quoted, designed to get a maximum shock effect from the contrast between the silence or near-silence of stanzas 1–3, and the sudden, nerve-shattering clanging of bells in line 13, precludes any sense of the macabre as a "natural" expression of feeling. That is, Baudelaire's loudly advertised indifference to illusions of spontaneity or of nature provides the surest index to his special kind of seriousness: his continual emphasis on the richly theatrical possibilities of art.

In the marvelous "Spleen" poem beginning: "J'ai plus de souvenirs que si j'avais mille ans," the combination of weighty abstraction ("L'ennui, fruit de la morne curiosité,/Prend les proportions de l'immortalité") and of a trivial concreteness ("Je suis un vieux boudoir plein de roses fanées") emphasizes the virtuosity with which the poet plays with a paralyzing past rather than the sphinxlike inertia which is the apparent subject of the poem. He is self-consciously juxtaposing the most incongruous images to describe himself (a piece of furniture, a cemetery, a boudoir, a pyramid), and the casual solemnity with which he does this creates the poem's elusive tone. Its richness comes from an unstable mixture of light and heavy elements, from a refusal to settle on one tone, to take this bizarrely heterogeneous self seriously, *or* to deny the *ennui* and *humeur farouche* which the poem describes.[12] A thematic analysis of images in *Les Fleurs du mal* could help to construct that type of self we find in contemporary French criticism: neither a biographical Baudelaire nor the Baudelaire of particular artistic achievements, but rather the coherent psychological skeleton under his work. But what strikes me as far more interesting in his best poems is the way he makes such structures irrelevant. His melodramatic self-exposures are really leisurely self-inventions, and Baudelaire's tone invites us to consider those inventions as the self-conscious defiance of the psychology they presumably express. He is free *because* he is so hopelessly oppressed; the enigma of *ennui* inspires the *feux d'artifice* which Baudelaire ironically offers as autobi-

12. *Œuvres completes,* p. 69.

ography. And this is the autonomy of art which he defends less originally in his critical writing: the inspirational value of a melancholy which, in the restricted space of poetry, ignores its causes in order to produce some dazzling effects.

It has perhaps been one of the ambiguous privileges of realistic prose fiction to deplore this autonomy of the imagination while dramatizing it. In his fantastic tale about Saint Julien, Flaubert seems comfortable in subverting psychological intelligibility by means of a compositional restraint which equalizes the pathological symptom and the supernatural detail. *Madame Bovary* provides us with a more extensive illustration of a psychological portrait which becomes a critique of explanatory analytic procedures themselves. But the critique is more ambiguous than in "Saint Julien," first of all because Emma, unlike Julien, explicitly confronts her experience with the same preoccupations with which Flaubert confronts her. And, as we shall see, Flaubert both condemns and approves of Emma's notion of literary representations as valid only if they refer to a reality which precedes and sanctions them, and makes them intelligible. Now it is her failure to find this reality which plunges Emma into states resembling those I have just been discussing, states which Flaubert and his heroine, unlike Diderot or Baudelaire, are incapable of treating as occasions of superior entertainment or of self-creation. They are occasions *only* of anxiety, and they crystallize the Flaubertian anguish about imagination in a deceptively modest portrait of the pathology of boredom.

I am thinking especially of chapters in the first half of the novel, before Emma's affair with Rodolphe, when it is simply the fact that nothing happens which creates in Emma a kind of continuous floating anxiety. This can be described most simply as Emma's boredom with a world inadequate to her dreams of romantic excitement. But in treating this state of mind, which at first glance would hardly seem to require a revolution in literary practice, Flaubert commits himself to a kind of sustained meaninglessness which justifies his title as the prophet of today's literature of boredom. He illustrates an imbalance between the self and the world which most of the romantics, for all their sense of being lost in a hostile or indifferent universe, were able to avoid by seeing the world—especially certain aspects of nature—almost entirely as a metaphor for their emotions. Thus literature, in the midst of crisis, could continue to represent adequate and intelligible correspondences between the self and the world. But while Emma is painfully aware of the unrelieved drabness and monotony of Tostes and Yonville, her dreams, absolutely unrepresentable in the world she inhabits, remain ideally abstract. And the unresponsiveness of Emma's environment to her dreams of glamor produces the symptoms which, while they superficially suggest a complex psychology, emphasize the highly original thinness of her character.

There are, early in the novel, two particularly agitated but empty periods in Emma's life: the year and a half between the ball at Vaubyessard and the Bovarys' decision to leave Tostes, and the time between Emma's realization that Léon loves her and Léon's departure from Yonville. At the beginning of each section, something thrilling has happened; at the end of both, we see Emma in a near catatonic stupor. But nothing has happened in the intervals; her sickness is purely imaginary. The excitement she felt at Vaubyessard keeps her busy for a while: she dreams of Paris and even begins to buy the clothes and luxury objects she has seen in the fashion magazines. But the vulgarity of Charles and of Tostes absorbs and trivializes these fragments from a more glamorous world, and we watch Emma slowly sink into discouraged passivity. She abandons music, drawing, and reading (" 'I have read everything,' she said to herself"), stares vacantly out of the window at the uneventful life on the streets of Tostes, becomes capricious, develops palpitations and a dry cough, and remains "without speaking, without moving" after equally inexplicable outbursts of feverish talk (40–49; 377–87). This instability is even more marked during the period following her discovery of Léon's love. Her immediate reaction is a voluptuous self-satisfaction which she enjoys by curious self-denials. She admires her economy in refusing the scarves and slippers Llheureux tempts her with, and she exasperates Léon by suddenly playing the role of the devoted wife. "[Full of covetous desires,] of rage, of hate," hoping for some catastrophe that would reveal her love to Léon, but held back by "idleness and fear," she consoles herself by taking "resigned poses" in front of a mirror and congratulating herself on her virtue. But the strain is too much, and instead of seeking an escape from her suffering, she forces herself to think of it, "urging herself to pain and seeking everywhere the opportunity to revive it." She abandons herself to wild adulterous fantasies, blames Charles for all her unhappiness and wishes that he would beat her so that she might hate him more intensely. When she thinks of running away with Léon, ". . . a dark shapeless chasm would open within her soul," and she finally seeks help from the town priest, who has no idea of what she is talking about. Her last hope gone, she returns home in a stupor, knocks down her daughter in a fit of irritation, frantically worries about the bruise on Berthe's cheek, but later that evening stares coldly at the sleeping child and thinks how strange it is that Berthe should be so ugly (72–83; 417–30).

The absence of events thus produces fairly rich psychological sequences. But these are merely incidental to what interests Flaubert most deeply in Emma's suffering. The most original passages in the first of the two sections I have been referring to are not analyses of Emma's feelings, but rather some coolly precise descriptions of Tostes. Emma watches, at an incalculable distance, the most ordinary events: "How sad she was on Sundays when vespers sounded! She listened with dull attention to each stroke of the cracked bell. A cat slowly walking over some roof put up his back in the pale rays of the sun. The wind on the highroad blew up clouds of dust. A dog sometimes howled in the distance; and the bell, keeping time, continued at regular intervals its monotonous ringing that died away over the fields" (45; 383).

And before the ball at Vaubyessard, Emma takes walks with her little greyhound, Djali, boringly eventless walks in the country which somehow end in panic:

> Occasionally there came gusts of wind, breezes from the sea rolling in one sweep over the whole plateau of the Caux country, which brought to these fields a salt freshness. The rushes, close to the ground, whistled; the branches of the beech trees trembled in a swift rustling, while their crowns, ceaselessly swaying, kept up a deep murmur. Emma drew her shawl round her shoulders and rose.
>
> In the avenue a green light dimmed by the leaves lit up the short moss that crackled softly beneath her feet. The sun was setting; the sky showed red between the branches, and the trunks of the trees, uniform, and planted in a straight line, seemed a brown colonnade standing out against a background of gold. A fear took hold of her; she called Djali, and hurriedly returned to Tostes by the highroad, threw herself into an armchair, and for the rest of the evening did not speak. (32; 366)

More than Emma's self-punishing or sadistic fantasies, this kind of thoughtless stupor in front of the world dramatizes the anxiety of a consciousness living entirely off itself. The symptoms result from Emma's contemplation of a world with which nothing in her fantasies connects. The ordinary, which Emma never *imagines,* becomes alien and inspires fear. And not only is the world foreign to Emma's dreams of romance; it also offers no images which she can use as a relatively appeasing spectacle of her anguish. When she returns from her fruitless visit to church, she is dumbfounded by the calm immobility of the objects in her house, "while within herself there was such tumult" (82; 430). Flaubert's detailed, literal descriptions deprive Emma of any metaphorical relief. Things simply *are there,* much more so than, say, in *La Nausée* or *Le Voyeur,* where the supposedly alien nature of objects is belied, in the first case, by the sickening richness of their metaphorical viscosity and, in the second, by a compulsive geometry—both of which are obviously projected on the world by very particularized psychologies.

Flaubert's descriptions give considerable novelistic space to a world in which the novel's heroine has no interest. Stendhal, as we have seen, does something similar in *La Chartreuse,* but Flaubert allows for no exception in the alienation of his heroine from her environment, and, more important, he would have us see in such alienation not so much the fate of the exceptional person, but rather the fate of the imaginative faculty itself, regardless of its quality in particular works of imagination. Jean-Pierre Richard has brilliantly traced the "history" of a terrifying fantasy of one-ness with the world in Flaubert's writing. Flaubert's search for principles of differentiation in language, Richard argues, is an attempt to overcome his fear of absorption, of drowning in a kind of undifferentiated liquid matter.[13] But literary solutions reverse the obsession; writing, which keeps the world at a distance, immediately creates a problem of being which can be accounted for only by the activity of writing itself, and which Flaubert drama-tizes through Madame Bovary's anxieties. The phenomenologi-cal obsession Richard speaks of is thus superseded, with the cre-ation of Emma, by an anguish about the distance (rather than about the nauseating indistinctness) between imagination and reality. And, as we shall see later, Emma's occasional illusions of oneness with the world, even when they are terrifying, are privi-leged moments of exception. The deeper horror in *Madame Bovary* is Flaubert's stunning achievement of describing a world which represents nothing. For in the anxiety Emma feels in front of the most banal aspects of an astonishingly banal environment, Flaubert indicates the more profound mystery of a totally abstract sickness, that is, of an agony and a death whose insignificant cause is merely the exercise of imagination.

The interest of Emma Bovary as a figure in literature has been obscured by her intellectual and psychological triviality as a

13. See "La Création de la forme chez Flaubert," *Littérature et sensation* (Paris, 1954).

"character." I would associate that profundity first of all with
what may seem like a sign of her imaginative mediocrity: her
indifference to and curious irritability over occasions which seem
to realize her dreams. For, even in this mortally boring province,
occasions do present themselves: there are, after all, the adventures with Léon and Rodolphe. But, significantly, Emma is never
more exasperated than during her love affairs. The love affair
with Rodolphe could, one imagines, have gone on indefinitely;
it is *Emma* who ends it with her frantic insistence on transporting
it to other, more suitable climates. And Léon doesn't really break
with her; with docility and terror, he plays the pathetic game of
an extravagant, brutal sexuality meant to deaden Emma's constant sense of love's inadequacy. With no betrayal on Léon's part,
and before the crisis of her debts, Emma lucidly condemns her
love as another proof of life's "lies" and "insufficiency," of the
instant rotting of everything she leans on (206; 584). Even during their discreet, unavowed love at Yonville earlier in the novel,
Léon's presence destroys the pleasure of thinking of him. "Emma
thrilled at the sound of his step; then in his presence the emotion
subsided, and afterwards there remained in her only an immense
astonishment that ended in sorrow" (77; 423). What are the reasons for that sorrow? Superficially, they are obvious enough:
Rodolphe and Léon are hopelessly mediocre, and Emma's dreams
of romance are so absurd that no lover could help her to realize
them. But the sickness of imagination from which Emma suffers
is linked, most profoundly, to her interest in literature—and we
can understand this only by looking more closely at Emma the
reader of novels.

To what extent is *Madame Bovary* a critique of romanticism?
In a sense, the mediocrity of Emma's mind provides the best case
for admiring Flaubert's novel as an exercise in sociological realism. Flaubert cannot be said to be satirizing or even confronting
nineteenth-century romantic myths, which are simply not the
subject of *Madame Bovary*. What he dramatizes is the effect of

a mystique of heroism and love on an average sensibility. Emma can hardly bear the burden of a critique of romanticism; *any* cultural or spiritual style can be made to appear absurd if it is "studied" through someone who does not understand it. To the extent that Flaubert would in fact like Emma's triviality to reflect on romantic literature in general, he is, in part, trying to pull the same kind of trick Voltaire brilliantly gets away with in *Candide*. Neither Leibniz nor even Pope is really taken to task by Voltaire, although, in his profound intellectual (if not emotional) indifference to metaphysics, he is quite willing to let Pangloss pass as a sufficient demonstration of the absurdity of Leibnizian philosophy. The metaphysical, esthetic, and social revolution which we call romanticism is equally shortchanged in *Madame Bovary*. Or rather, Flaubert is more interested in some of its concretely revolutionary aspects than in anatomizing a particular cultural style in its most distinguished and abstractly typical form. What we see almost exclusively in *Madame Bovary* are the trivial but pervasive ways in which a powerful style of being comes to affect the expectations about life of the most unremarkable people.

Emma's romanticism is that of the fashion magazines, of keepsakes, of the novels which the old woman who works in the laundry of the convent lends to the girls: "They were all about love, lovers, sweethearts, persecuted ladies fainting in lonely pavilions, postilions killed at every relay, horses ridden to death on every page, sombre forests, heartaches, vows, sobs, tears and kisses, little boatrides by moonlight, nightingales in shady groves, gentlemen brave as lions, gentle as lambs, virtuous as no one ever was, always well dressed, and weeping like fountains" (26; 358–59). Who is the author of these adventures? Obviously, no one; the great romantic talents have been filtered through a process which leaves only a sediment of anonymous, parodically simplified images. Originality has become a popular commodity and therefore resembles the conventional; good literature has not disappeared, but the interest people take in it is determined by the images it has inspired in women's magazines. Emma reads novels for the descriptions of furniture advertised in journals of fashion. She knows Balzac, and at the convent she heard passages from *Le Génie du christianisme,* but her taste for art is determined by the pictures from the *Corbeille* and the *Sylphe des salons.* As in all popularization, literature is finally judged by its success: the forms in which it effectively penetrates ordinary social life provide the standards it has to "live up to."

Of course, today we are used to the instant popularization of art. This is partly because TV and the press have become our *avant-garde;* they are, in their hunger for the new, ahead of all experimental art, emptily ready to advertise anything that may be imagined. As a result, the time between original art and the public awareness of it has been reversed. Instead of the artist having to wait for recognition, recognition seems almost to precede his work. Furthermore, this voracious willingness on the part of the public to recognize anything is necessarily more daring and more advanced than any specific performance. Art, however explosive or spontaneous it may be, can never be ahead of that which anticipates it. But, as *Madame Bovary* shows, all art eventually becomes, if not pop art, at least popularized art. The process was of course slower in Emma's day than it is today, and so there *was* a gap between the diffusion of romantic themes and their treatment (or invention) in the great works of romantic literature. And because of that gap, the mental style of an Emma Bovary is probably a better index of the cultural atmosphere of her period than the romantic art we still admire. For, like most interesting art of the past, those works have too strong a personal signature to be spoken of primarily as representative. We would be more likely to find something like "the spirit of the age" in the pages of the fashion magazines Emma reads than in works where that problematic spirit is obscured by the idiosyncrasies of individual talent. Some current efforts to erase the personal signature in art will perhaps make such distinctions unnecessary in the future. Theatrical happenings, chance music and painting, and some literary collages conveniently make of art a palely prestigious exercise in tautology: such art simply emphasizes the fact that we live, and it does this by ritualizing events, by advertising them as spectacles. But that may be a fair if inadequate definition of what art has always done, although we have usually preferred ways of talking about its imitations of life's processes which make art seem more special, more distinguished than life and which thus disguise an essential and even stimulating banality.

It is precisely that "special" quality of art which Flaubert attacks in *Madame Bovary*, and he does this by deliberately ignoring the most intellectually respectable aspects of romanticism. The content of Emma's thought is crucial, not so much because it allows Flaubert to satirize the best expressions of romantic sensibility, but rather because those trivialized romantic fantasies provide the ideal content for a demonstration of the unreality of *all* art. Flaubert's antiromantic posture in *Madame Bovary* is, essentially, anti-artistic, for he seems to recognize in romantic art an exemplary if hyperbolic version of all imaginative activity. The literary fantasies which Emma feeds on combine the two qualities which fascinated and exasperated Flaubert in art as well as in life: the exceptional and the cliché. And, for Flaubert, the immense advantage of the third-rate literature which Emma reads is that, being such a radical "condensation" of art, it makes its arbitrary and artificial nature unmistakably clear. It exposes the equivalence between the exceptional and the cliché as a fundamental truth about imagination.

Now the romantic attitudes which have, at some distance, corrupted Emma were both aristocratic and revolutionary. On the one hand, the romantics emphasized the difference between ordinary consciousness and a tragic or heroic consciousness. And in this way they belong to a tradition which at times would seem to accommodate them rather poorly. Romanticism in the broadest sense is a cultivation of the rare, the extreme. There is in French literature, for example—from the courtly romances to Maurice Blanchot—a current which, far from promoting the illusion of literature as the mirror of social life, seems deliberately to explore and create kinds of experience which could *not* be recognized as representative, or as socially representable. (The importance of an analogous adventure in American literature has been impressively argued by Richard Poirier in *A World Elsewhere*.[14]) Such experiments may, as they did in the nineteenth century, take the form of an exaltation of the personal, even of the idiosyncratic. The hero, in this most familiar version of what I am calling romanticism, has a unique, generally tragic destiny which sets him apart from other men, although, as I suggested earlier, the rhetoric of much nineteenth-century romanticism in France assumes at least the possibility of genuine communication with others. But the superior or at least irreducibly different individual is, historically, only one of several dramatic metaphors for a sense of literature which, in its most extreme form, may express itself as a quest for the *im*personal. Thus, behind the radically different attitudes toward the *value* of personality in, say, Rousseau and Georges Bataille or Blanchot, there is perhaps a similar willingness to exacerbate it—whether it be for the sake of exalting it or of destroying it. Literature in both cases is an exercise of the spiritually elite; it implies a daring, aristocratic indifference to the psychological definitions and limits legislated by the ordinary uses of language.

Blanchot alludes to the impersonal, anonymous nature of language, and Bataille would violate the self, escape through some "rip" of being, some *déchirure*, into an ecstatic communication with the world. But in a sense it matters little whether or not one has the cult of personality when the very escape from it involves such a superior (and ultimately private) sense of its possibilities. Our contemporary proponents of the psychologically neutral have as fine a sense of the irrelevance of the probable to the possible as the most flamboyantly self-dramatizing figures of historical romanticism. And the step from the privately hyperbolic

14. *A World Elsewhere/The Place of Style in American Literature* (New York, 1966).

to the publicly prophetic is of course an easy one to take. Romantic writers from Hugo to Breton could be social revolutionaries because—the case is especially clear in the shaky alliance between surrealism and Marxism—they felt that the world could *objectively* be made adequate to their representation of the world. Historical progress is the social myth which corresponds to the conviction that reality can be coerced into the shapes of our personal fictions. And the conviction, needless to say, can have a power sufficient to produce fantastic material changes in our environment, to create the real effects engendered by a myth of permanent revolution.

Flaubert is aware of and fundamentally hostile to the power of such beliefs and myths. His work is an anguished condemnation of the idea of correspondence between reality and what the imagination invents. Flaubert's realism is both democratic and conservative. The novel has so often lent itself to explicit social protests that we like to think of it as more subversive, at least potentially, than its principal conventions may actually allow it to be. Realistic fiction, which by Flaubert's time had pretty well settled structurally as a conflict between an exceptional individual and an unexceptional environment, provided an ideal form for the reduction of the exceptional to the ordinary. The novel democratizes the heroic by making it subsist, as well as it can, in a context antagonistic to heroism. However great the realistic writer's admiration for his hero may be, he makes him a somewhat comical figure by allowing both the quality and time of ordinary social life to erode his ambitious projects, and by giving so much novelistic space to the resistances of an already established world. The alternative in realistic fiction to some adjustment to society, on the hero's part, is often self-destruction. It is in this sense that the novel can be both conservative and democratic: the unresponsiveness of the world to the hero's visions may (as we have seen in Stendhal) imply some irony about his superiority just as easily as it does a critique of social life. And we conclude from such confrontations that, however angry and interesting the protest may be, reality has a weight which makes it essentially unchangeable. Thus we can see the profound links between realism, comedy—and, finally, classicism. French classical literature addresses itself to a small, aristocratic audience, but its psychology is far from aristocratic, and its political ethic is of course conservative. Its "universality" is a pessimistically democratic fiction: Hermione the princess has the same passions as Arnolphe the bourgeois, and spiritual grandeur is merely an illusion supported by the factitious glamor of social position. In contrast to an authentically aristocratic notion of the radical and original nature of imagination, French classical writers skeptically offer their noble rhetoric as a transparent sublimation of uncontrollable appetites.

If, as it has often been said, Flaubert holds a privileged place in the history of modern literature's self-awareness, we should not forget how massive and aggressive an attack he mounts against literature in his investigation of its nature. In terms of the paradigm of realistic fiction which I have just outlined, the heroic or the exceptional in *Madame Bovary* is the literary; the resistance to imagination is provided by the prosaic, inert, self-satisfied communities of Tostes and Yonville. Flaubert's originality is to present the conflict as a secret complicity. His heroine is destroyed not only by the unresponsiveness of her world, but also by *our* sense of how easily her superiority can be reduced to the mediocrity of her antagonists. Early in the novel, Flaubert writes that after trying unsuccessfully to make Charles a more exciting lover by reciting "passionate rhymes" and "melancholy adagios" to him in the moonlight, Emma convinces herself that his love "was no longer very ardent." Her infatuation with the imaginary excludes sympathy, a more humane imagination: she is "incapable . . . of understanding what she did not experience or of believing anything that did not take on a conventional form" (31; 364–65). Flaubert runs the gamut of "formes convenues" in *Madame Bovary*; from the italicized clichés to Emma's most extravagant dreams, the novel continuously illustrates both the unreality and the tempting availability of formulas as a ready-made explication of life.

Now the cliché condenses both the appeal and the dangers of imagination. Imagination can, ideally, as both Emma and Flaubert know, *produce anything*, and that is its horror. In *La Tentation de Saint Antoine,* Hilarion conjures up all the ancient faiths as a way of weakening the saint's attachment to Christianity. "Don't you find," he asks Antoine after all the "false gods" have disappeared, "that . . . sometimes . . . they rather resemble the true one?" [15] In Flaubert, such a statement proceeds less from historical skepticism than from an intuition of the deplorable richness of imagination. The religions Hilarion evokes create a chain of similarities which, instead of inspiring epistemological confidence, suspends reality in an imaginary series with no objective beginning or end. Some of Blanchot's reflections strike me as pertinent to what seems to be Flaubert's fundamental anguish about metaphor: no link in a metaphorical chain is truer, more "original" than any other. For in the imagination supposed points of departure have a no more privileged status than any other moment in a time (or, more exactly, a space) of theoretically endless comparisons. What we assumed to be the real *serves* the imaginary by providing just another metaphorical resource in the development of similarities. The images of reality thus make reality doubtful, for the images are equal and interchangeable in a mental activity which can use the same term indifferently as vehicle or as tenor. As resemblances multiply, "priority" becomes a nostalgia for chimerical fact.

The imagination can accommodate anything, and Flaubert exploits its naturally fantastic nature in what we call his romantic works. The most naïve and extreme example of the free-floating imagination in Flaubert is *Saint Antoine.* At the end of the story, the most extravagant fables of the mind make a physical appearance. Antoine is surrounded by the fabulous beasts, such as the

15. I, 160.

griffin and the unicorn, by which men have combined and extended the beasts of nature into a new nature of limitless combinations, and finally animals are confused with vegetables, pebbles resemble brains, stalactites are like udders, and plants can no longer be distinguished from stones. It is as if the imaginative capacity to see resemblances had *acted* on the world, which vacillates among the various fancies of the mind. External reality becomes as rich as men's fantasies about it have ever been. Antoine both sees a monstrous proliferation of being and feels with exhilaration his inability to make forms settle into any definitive version of the real. "In fragments of ice, he makes out efflorescences, imprints of bushes and of shells—to the point of not being able to tell if he is seeing the imprints of those things, or the things themselves." [16] It is as if he were present at the birth of being, at the passage from the potential to the real, and in his final temptation he speaks of wanting to penetrate forms, to become matter itself. The sin of his dream can be easily explained in theological terms; more interestingly for us, that wish is the temptation of the imagination itself, the dream of being all forms and of making all forms be.

Flaubert's realistic works express his nausea at the unreality of such dreams. Emma Bovary and Frédéric Moreau of course illustrate the exhaustion and the dangers of these confusions between the imaginary and the real. They also illustrate something more important, for Flaubert, about the nature of imagination: it is, essentially, always a cliché, since it articulates the real by impoverishing it—however rich or extravagant its articulations may be. It is enough to view the splendors of *La Tentation* and of *Salammbô* as *purely imaginary* in order to make them appear comical and trite. And so perhaps the most striking fact of character in *Madame Bovary* is the similarity between Emma and Homais. On the one hand, she is as cliché-ridden as the druggist; on the other hand, he is as seduced by imagination as Emma. Homais is, in fact, throughout the novel, torn between his ambi-

16. I, 198.

tion, his shrewd sense of fact, and what can only be called
his artistic extravagance. Interestingly enough, the community,
Flaubert tells us, is suspicious of him. Few people come to his
Sunday soirées, "his scandal-mongering and his political opinions
having . . . alienated, [one after the other,] various [respect-
able] persons" (70; 414). Homais's monumental banality is not
exactly conformity, and he risks being ostracized because he cannot resist the pleasure of distinguishing himself through speech.
And his speech reveals and parodies the essential stupidity of
imagination. A "realist" like Homais, once he begins to express
(what?—the verb, applied to Flaubert, should be intransitive),
is as insubstantial as the most extravagant dreamer.

For Flaubert, only silence testifies to a sense of reality, for
reality is inexpressible. The most marvelous inventions of art
therefore imply a certain insensitivity to the real, and to inhabit
the world of words is the sign of an epistemological vulgarity
which Homais epitomizes and to which genius and originality are
perhaps irrelevant. Homais's stupidity is his capacity for the life
of the mind,[17] although that important fact is obscured by the discipline which his ambition imposes on his imagination. Because
of that discipline, his extravagances finally coincide with the
clichés of those in power—and he receives the cross of the Legion
of Honor. Homais's complicated meaninglessness is both comical
and dangerous: we laugh at his invulnerability to self-doubt, but
at the same time his immense confidence in his own eloquence
makes him, eventually, a man of power: the state rewards him
for a virtuosity both uncontrollably self-promoting and yet politically safe.

The triteness of imagination embodied in Homais (and, more
generally, in the bourgeois communities of Tostes and Yonville)
is not only compatible with imaginative extravagance; it is also

17. Albert Thibaudet, whose study was first published in 1922, had
already spoken of Homais's intelligence (Gustave Flaubert [Paris, 1935],
p. 113), and Sartre develops the idea in "La Conscience de classe chez
Flaubert," Les Temps modernes, XXI (May and June 1966), 2147–49.

morally dangerous. The inventions of language lend themselves easily to the rhetoric of tyranny. In the agricultural fair scene, the most spectacular example of what Albert Thibaudet called Flaubert's *vision binoculaire* (a simultaneous perception of opposite poles of a subject which cancel each other out),[18] Flaubert's collage of fragments from Rodolphe's praise of passion and of fragments from Lieuvain's praise of agriculture would be a rather uninteresting tour de force if we saw only incongruities in the juxtaposition. The most striking fact about the passage is the similarities between the two speeches: both men are using the familiar rhetorical devices of public eloquence to seduce their audiences into obedience. It hardly matters that the obedience would be political in the one case and sexual in the other, for the language being used is neither "about" politics nor "about" sex. It rather illustrates the serviceability, even the promiscuity, of language. The techniques of seduction are abstract but nonetheless effective: the audience is hypnotized by the rhythms of language into an indifference to its sense. And it is precisely because Flaubert, like Emma, is tortured by the emptiness of language that he is so sensitive to its deliberate use as a tool for domination. Language doesn't signify, it excites—and nothing suits Rodolphe and Lieuvain better, for "what they have to say" would alienate their victims.

Flaubert's humaneness is peculiarly—and perhaps exclusively—linguistic: cruelty is an eager willingness to use the empty forms of language to satisfy an appetite for control. The best people in Flaubert are the most awkward verbally: his most admirable characters are the inarticulate Dussardier in *L'Education sentimentale* and the almost mute Félicité of "Un Cœur simple." True, Flaubert cannot find much more interesting ways to designate them than as "pauvre" and "brave," but that's enough; their principal merit is that they are not adept at talking, and, in a sense, that makes them uninteresting enough to be good. For perhaps no speech is "truer" than any other, and in his

18. *Gustave Flaubert*, pp. 83–84.

polemical mistrust of *all* fictive versions of reality, Flaubert re-
serves his deepest sympathy for the dumb.

It is therefore not surprising that Flaubert should come to
Emma's defense when she fails to express herself effectively.
Rodolphe, Flaubert harshly notes, stupidly doubts Emma's love
because he has heard the same language of passion from his other
mistresses, "as though the abundance of one's soul did not sometimes overflow with empty metaphors, since no one has ever been
able to give the exact measure of his needs, his concepts, or his
sorrows. The human tongue is like a cracked cauldron on which
we beat out tunes to set a bear dancing when we would make the
stars weep with our melodies." It is not that Rodolphe fails to
see what is personal or original in Emma's language, for she *does*
speak like all the other women who have loved him. "Emma was
like all his mistresses; and the charm of novelty, gradually falling
away like a garment, laid bare the eternal monotony of passion,
that has always the same shape and the same language." Rodolphe's coarseness consists in not recognizing "the [dissimilarity]
of feelings hidden within the same expressions" (138; 500). That
is, he really listens to Emma too closely; he condemns her style.
But since no style can ever give "the exact measure" of the self,
since language is by definition a failure of expression, there is
something stupid and cruel in taking someone's style seriously.
The ground between words and meaning, which is for Henry
James the exhilarating space where human beings invent themselves most freely, is for Flaubert the tragic space which makes
the self inexpressible and unknowable.

But in spite of this apparent austerity, Flaubert shares both
Homais's taste for eloquence and Emma's longing for extravagant romance. In one of his numerous complaints to Louise Colet
during the writing of *Madame Bovary*, he notes that while a
few readers will find in his work "some truth of detail and observation," he himself is suffering from a lack of "air" in composing
a book "made up entirely of calculations and stylistic tricks."
"The grand and eloquent turns of phrase, bold sweeping periods

rolling like rivers, the teeming metaphors, the dazzling effects
of style, in short, everything I love, will be absent." [19] Such out-
cries from the correspondence are certainly to be taken with a
grain of salt. Composition, regardless of the subject, was always
a torture for Flaubert, and his letters, written late at night after
a day of agonizing stylistic asceticism, were an occasion for letting
off steam, for enjoying the irresponsibility of undisciplined ex-
clamation. Nevertheless, Flaubert's work contradicts neither the
preferences he flamboyantly announces in the letters nor the
mistrust with which he just as frequently refers to those preferences.

He had only to experience some ease in writing in order to
stop writing, to recoil in fear from the dangers of facility. In an
extraordinary letter to Louise, he starts by saying that "one must
write more *coldly*. Let us beware of that overheated state called
inspiration, in which there is often more nervous emotion than
muscular strength." The observation, we learn, has been provoked by the fact that Flaubert has been feeling exceptionally
productive: "Right now, for example, I feel at the top of my
form, my forehead is burning, sentences are coming to me. I have
wanted to write to you for the past two hours and I keep being
drawn back to my work. Instead of one idea I have six, and where
I need the simplest exposition my mind comes up with a comparison. I am sure I could go on until noon tomorrow without feeling
tired." The letter, we may suppose, is written at one of those
significant moments when Flaubert is actually experiencing the
cancerous possibilities of imagination, its frighteningly proliferating nature. "But I am well acquainted with those masked
balls of the imagination from which one returns with death in
the heart, worn out, having seen nothing but falsity and uttered
only nonsense. Everything must be done coolly, deliberately." [20]

The false and the stupid: these are the qualities of the free
imagination. And so, curiously enough, it could be said that for

19. *Correspondance de Flaubert*, 9 vols. (Paris, 1926–33), III, 201–2.
20. *Correspondance de Flaubert*, III, 104–5.

Flaubert the highest artistic integrity consists in a profound *re-luctance to produce,* in resisting the seductiveness of the arbitrary and the unreal. Flaubert's whole career supports such a view. The subject of all his fiction, in spite of the obvious but superficial distinction between the realistic and the nonrealistic works, is the excesses of imagination. He both reveled in and mistrusted those excesses. *Madame Bovary, L'Education sentimentale,* and *Bouvard et Pécuchet* are analogous in Flaubert's career to that familiar stylistic fall, which, in so many of his sentences, deflates an eloquent fantasy with a prosaic detail. Emma, Frédéric, and Bouvard and Pécuchet are the scapegoats through whom Flaubert does penance for *La Tentation de Saint Antoine* and *Salammbô.* Scrupulously masochistic, Flaubert sadistically punishes those inferior versions of himself for his own intoxicating inventions.

The cliché is the lowest form of imagination's debauchery. On the one hand, it underlines the distance between the imaginary and the real: it is the most easily recognizable way of using language to violate the richness of experience. But we may also find it attractive for that very reason. We know that Flaubert's horror of cliché was equaled only by his fascination with it. The cliché is the enemy of style, but the great stylist's most cherished project was simply a compilation of clichés: the *Dictionnaire des idées reçues.* The epic of stupidity Flaubert spent his life trying to write was of course partly conceived as an act of rage; he dreamed of a preface to the *Dictionnaire* in which tradition and order would be defended in such a way that ". . . the reader would not know whether or not he is being made a fool of . . . ," [21] and he confided to Louise Colet his ambition to write some long novel in which he would be able to give full vent to his "awful itch to give hell to the human race." [22] But the appeal of cliché was not simply as the most dramatic evidence in the misanthrope's case. I think that Flaubert recognized the cliché as the ideal form of expression. It is, in a sense, the purest art of intelligibility, the

21. *Correspondance de Flaubert,* II, 237–38.
22. *Correspondance de Flaubert,* III, 66.

product of an anonymous imagination enviably indifferent to experience. "Yes," Flaubert wrote to Louis Bouilhet, "stupidity consists in wanting to conclude" [23]—but the cliché nevertheless provides the relaxing illusion that in the life of the imagination it is possible to conclude. It checks the drifting of the mind among its unaccountable fancies (or among its six ideas instead of one) not by the adherence of words to reality, but by the ideal *un*reality of a language which disciplines the mind by making it merely predictable. The cliché corresponds to little else than its own gratuitous clarity. For the writer who spent weeks trying to adjust the rhythms of a single paragraph to the contours of the real, the cliché was bound to be a desirable if also hateful way of "covering" experience by totally ignoring it. And if the most original creations of the mind are judged only by their distance from the real, there is perhaps no epistemological justification for preferring them to the most worn out of language's "formes convenues." The cliché parodies the exercise of imagination, but it also exposes its profound nature.

The objective realism which Flaubert outlines in his letters is a struggle against both the temptation of the cliché and the interminable flow of a language which never stops coming. But the theoretical program suggested in the correspondence (especially in the letters written during the composition of *Madame Bovary*) reduces the problem of representing reality in art to the comparatively uninteresting question of authorial intrusions. The writer's personality is the stumbling block to what Flaubert thought of as the scientific literature of the future: *"The less we feel a thing, the better qualified we are to express it as it is* (as it *always* is intrinsically, in its generality and freed from everything ephemeral and accidental about it)." [24] Writers would be merely catalysts who convert reality, without changing its nature, into language. More exactly, they would be gods: Flaubert's ideal

23. *Correspondance de Flaubert*, II, 239.
24. *Correspondance de Flaubert*, II, 462.

artist is a man without a point of view, whose work expresses not
a vision of the world but objective knowledge of it. As Eric
Auerbach said of Flaubert's esthetic ambition: ". . . the perfect
expression, which at once entirely comprehends the momentary
subject and impartially judges it, comes of itself; subjects are
seen as God sees them, in their true essence." [25]

While the possibility of exact correspondences between imagination and reality is, as we have seen, the major issue of Flaubert's fiction, his theoretical notions of how to achieve such correspondences are surprisingly superficial. Irritated by confessional
literature, by sociological or philosophical digressions, and by the
dear-reader chattiness of earlier novelists, Flaubert confuses a
judgmental and analytical reticence on the part of the narrator
with the total absence of the author from his work. Proust rightly
saw the irrelevance of that reticence to the *presence* of the author
in his work. He found Flaubert interesting precisely because of
what Flaubert was, theoretically, most anxious to avoid. In contrast to Balzac who, Proust felt, "does not think of a sentence as
made of a special substance in which everything that was once an
object of conversation, of knowledge, etc., must be eliminated and
unrecognizable," Flaubert transforms all the different parts of
reality "into a single substance, made of vast, uniformly shimmering surfaces [une même substance, aux vastes surfaces, d'un
miroitement monotone]. No impurity has remained. Surfaces
have become like mirrors, in which everything can be portrayed,
but by reflection, without changing their homogeneous substance.
Everything that was once different has been transformed and
absorbed." [26] As a result of what Proust called the "subjectivism"
of Flaubert's novels,[27] the most diversified material—from *Saint
Antoine* to "Un Cœur simple"—is converted into a continuously

25. *Mimesis/The Representation of Reality in Western Literature,* tr.
Willard R. Trask (Princeton, New Jersey, 1953), p. 487.
26. Marcel Proust, *Contre Sainte-Beuve, suivi de Nouveaux mélanges*
(Paris, 1954), pp. 207–9.
27. "A propos du 'style' de Flaubert," *Chroniques* (Paris, 1927), p. 197.

recognizable voice, into the "notes fondamentales" of the writer's personality.[28]

I shall come back to the question of the "voice" we consistently hear throughout Flaubert's work. First, however, I want to emphasize how little his most famous letters help us to discuss the kind of impersonality most profoundly implied in his fiction. Flaubert's cult of impassivity[29] is the least original aspect of his rigorous but impossible realistic faith. While Flaubert's correspondence might lead us to think that a temptingly easy but undesirable self-expression is the major obstacle to realism in art, *Madame Bovary* presents a much profounder—and more pessimistic—statement of the Flaubertian dilemma. As Flaubert indicates when he sympathizes with Emma for not being able to find the words adequate to her love for Rodolphe, *self*-expression is at least as problematical as an accurate representation of external reality. Contrary to what the letters suggest, it is not subjectivity which prevents us from seeing "nature as it is." [30] Rather, language itself, for Flaubert, may separate us from both nature (or the external world) *and* the self. We can therefore neglect what seem to me the misleading clues of Flaubert's correspondence in looking at some of the consequences for his work of his obsession with a supposed gap between the imaginary and the real. What are the conditions, for Emma and for her creator, in which that gap might be closed, and, finally, how does Flaubert's very concern with such questions affect our critical response to his art?

A few privileged moments in Emma's experience provide a testing ground for the success of Flaubert's project. The distance

28. *A la Recherche du temps perdu*, ed. Pierre Clarac and André Ferré, 3 vols. (Paris, 1954), III, 626.
29. For some useful distinctions among "impersonal," "impassive," and "impartial" as applied to Flaubert, and for a discussion of how he tries to appear "impassive," see Marianne Bonwit, *Gustave Flaubert et le principe de l'impassibilité*, in University of California Publications in Modern Philology, Vol. 33, No. 4 (Berkeley and Los Angeles, 1950).
30. *Correspondance de Flaubert*, III, 158.

between Emma's fantasies and her experience is abolished at certain exceptional moments in the novel, moments when sensation is strong enough to create an illusion of continuity between the mind and the world. Such illusions can be occasions of terror. When Emma is tempted to jump from the attic window after reading Rodolphe's letter of good-by, "the ground of the village square seemed to tilt over and climb up the walls, the floor to pitch forward like in a tossing boat." The light from below "drew the weight of her body toward the abyss . . . ; the blue of the sky invaded her, the air was whirling in her hollow head . . ." (148; 513). Reality is hallucinated into a kind of complicity with her pain; an habitually inert world momentarily corresponds to the tumult in Emma's mind. Such correspondences are, of course, the dubious benefits of suicidal despair or insanity. In her stupor after Rodolphe refuses to give her money (a few minutes before she takes the poison), Emma experiences a similar confusion—this time, between her frantic mind and a suddenly spinning countryside. She thinks she hears the beating in her arteries "burst forth like a deafening music filling all the fields," all her thoughts and memories "seemed to explode at once like a thousand pieces of fireworks," and the air is filled with "fiery spheres," each of which contains the image of Rodolphe's face (228; 611).

The nightmarish visions of Emma's despair thus bring the world alive as her bookish fantasies of romance are never able to do.[31] But occasionally the experience of romance has effects similar to those of hysterical anguish. The dream of love is realized as an ecstatic synchronization of Emma's body with the rhythms and sounds of nature when Rodolphe makes love to her for the first time in the forest:

31. For an analysis of some hallucinatory visions in Flaubert, see John C. Lapp, "Art and Hallucination in Flaubert," *French Studies*, X (October 1956), 322–34. Charles Du Bos wrote many years ago about "an intensity of stupor" in Flaubert (in "Sur le 'milieu intérieur' chez Flaubert," *Approximations*, Première série (Paris, 1922), pp. 158–78.

The shades of night were falling; the horizontal sun passing between the branches dazzled the eyes. Here and there around her, in the leaves or on the ground, trembled luminous patches, as if humming-birds flying about had scattered their feathers. Silence was everywhere; something sweet seemed to come forth from the trees. She felt her heartbeat return, and the blood coursing through her flesh like a river of milk. Then far away, beyond the wood, on the other hills, she heard a vague prolonged cry, a voice which lingered, and in silence she heard it mingling like music with the last pulsations of her throbbing nerves. Rodolphe, a cigar between his lips, was mending with his penknife one of the two broken bridles. (116; 472)

The world becomes responsive only at moments of sensations so enveloping that imagination can no longer function. Absorbed in her first completely satisfying sexual experience, Emma naturally makes none of her usual comparisons—which condemn both imagination and reality—between experience and mental scenarios. Dreams of romance are realized in the banal but intense particularity of sensations which merge with the chance occasions of a real setting: "something sweet seemed to come forth from the trees," and the "vague prolonged cry" gives a meaningless but appropriate extension to the vibrations of Emma's nerves. Furthermore, Flaubert stylistically supports her peacefully mindless harmony with the world.[32] He contributes to that harmony by the solemn preparation for the scene in the first sentence, by the delicate comparison of the patches of light to the colorful, scattered feathers of hummingbirds, and by the attenuation of a possibly ominous note in the cry Emma hears by allowing it to "carry" her trembling nerves like a piece of music. Such privileged moments naturally depend on Emma's receptiveness to sensations: only the strongest sensual stimulations

32. Thibaudet refers to the "delicate and almost religious emotion" with which Flaubert speaks of Emma whenever she is "purely sensual" (*Gustave Flaubert*, p. 94).

deaden the mind and allow Flaubert, as it were, to fill in Emma's
mental blankness with a rhetoric which authenticates rather than
deflates her illusions about life's possibilities.

Rare as these moments are in Flaubert's fiction, we come to
recognize how carefully they are cultivated, how they are even
signaled (perhaps somewhat mechanically) by key scenes and
expressions. I'm thinking of the Flaubertian countryside with its
long lines of trees, and especially of those shadows which prolong the shapes of things and which, metaphorically, express the
extension of the present into the past, of perception into memory
and imagination. ". . . Speech," Flaubert pessimistically notes,
"is like a rolling machine that always stretches the sentiment it
expresses" (169; 539); and, by the time she goes to the opera
in Rouen, Emma herself has learned "how small the passions
were that art magnified" (162; 331). But occasionally a sort of
happy torpor provides those sentimental intensities and extensions which language promises but never delivers. As if in compassionate anticipation of Emma's suffering, Flaubert emphasizes
an extraordinary concordance between sensations and memory,
as well as between the lovers and their surroundings, on the
last night Emma and Rodolphe spend together outside her house.
"The tenderness of the old days came back to their hearts, full
and silent as the flowing river, with the soft perfume of the
syringas, and threw across their memories shadows more immense and more sombre than those of the still willows that
lengthened out over the grass" (143; 507). The setting materializes a tenderness both Emma and Rodolphe have reason
enough to doubt now. That lost feeling is actually smelled in the
odor of the syringas, seen in the willows' shadows, and felt as
abundantly present in the river's silent flowing. Generally, the
past in *Madame Bovary* is as inaccessible as the adventures with
which Emma glamorizes her future. But on her last evening with
Rodolphe, the past is no longer just a distant and seductive
tableau. The tenderness of the past, having penetrated the world
Emma and Rodolphe now perceive, "returns" to the mind and

makes history the projected shadow of a richly substantial present.

A similar sensualizing of memory—and, inversely, an enrichening of perception with the unsatisfied longings and dreams of the past—takes place when, alone with Rodolphe in the council-room of the town hall on the day of the agricultural fair, Emma abandons herself to a pleasantly dizzying *mollesse* as the odor of Rodolphe's pomade reminds her of the vanilla and lemon smell of the viscount's beard at the Vaubyessard ball, and the sight of the *Hirondelle* in the distance revives her old tenderness for Léon. "The sweetness of this sensation revived her past desires, and like grains of sand under a gust of wind, they swirled around in the subtle breath of the perfume that diffused over her soul" (106; 459). This poetry of torpor, of *engourdissement*, is an interlude in the comedy of language. Flaubert, unlike Emma, who will merely suffer from not perceiving the difference, sharply distinguishes between Rodolphe's rhetoric of seduction, which is pitilessly juxtaposed with the superficially antagonistic speech of the councillor, and the smell of his hair, which is at least the occasion—however incongruous—for a brief sensual gratification of past longings. In the same way, alone with Léon in a Rouen hotel room for the first time since he left Yonville, Emma goes along with all the banalities and lies with which Léon tries to invent a romantic past which will help him to profit from the present occasion. Their language tricks them into believing in that "sentimental immensity" which Emma eagerly grabs at. But Flaubert is much less indulgent toward the bad faith and calculation of their cliché-ridden attempt to create "an ideal to which they were now trying to adapt their past life" than he is toward a moment when they are no longer speaking. Once again, an authentic confusion of the sensual and the imaginary produces an "ecstasy" which Flaubert frames in a harmoniously restful tableau: ". . . as they looked upon each other, they felt their heads whirl, as if waves of sound had escaped from their fixed glances. They were hand in hand now,

and the past, the future, reminiscences and dreams, all were
confounded in the sweetness of this ecstasy. Night was darken-
ing over the walls, leaving visible only, half hidden in the shade,
the coarse colours of four bills representing [four] scenes from
La Tour de Nesle, with Spanish and French captions under-
neath. Through the sash-window they could see a patch of [dark]
sky between the pointed roofs" (170; 540–41).

These languors exist beneath, or in the intervals of language,
and it is at such privileged moments that Flaubert celebrates an
ironic realization of dreams of ecstasy by their very extinction in
an absorbing sensuality. And he saves his most poetic effects for
the dismissal of words, for affirming the "more serious speech"
which silently supports the trivialities of Emma and Léon's
conversation on their walk back to Yonville from the wet-nurse's:

> Had they nothing else to say to one another? Yet their eyes
> were full of more serious speech, and while they forced them-
> selves to find trivial phrases, they felt the same languor stealing
> over them both; it was like the deep, continuous murmur of the
> soul dominating that of their voices. Surprised with wonder at
> this strange sweetness, they did not think of speaking of the
> sensation or of seeking its cause. Future joys, [like tropical shores,
> extend to the immense inland world of past experience their
> innate softness, a fragrant breeze, and we are lulled by this
> intoxication, without even worrying about the unseen horizons
> beyond]. (68; 411–12)

There is, then, in *Madame Bovary* the ecstatic silence of sensation, of being carried away by the "fragrant breeze" of tropical
shores which do not necessarily have to exist, but which provide
the glamorous images with which literature "explains" certain
rare pleasures of the body. Brunetière, who judged Emma as
vulgar and commonplace in all other respects, acutely saw in
her "something extreme, and therefore rare: the delicate sharp-
ness of her senses." [33] To this we can add that Emma's dreams

33. Ferdinand Brunetière, *Le Roman naturaliste* (Paris, 1893), p. 195.

are the natural but disastrous extension of her sensuality. The countries of romance are an *image* for sensual torpor; they are the fables of our sensations, the fabulous but intelligible translations of a private physical life into social sentimentality.

The difference between Emma and Flaubert is one of literary sophistication or propriety: what we see him using as an expressive resource (the comparison of a languorous anticipation of physical pleasure to the odorous breezes of a tropical shore) is for Emma a sequence from dream to reality. She would like to *go* where the pleasing images are, as if the appeal of the language of romance came from the reality it literally describes rather than from the kind of abstract sensuality we enjoy by verbalizing sensations. Flaubert exploits Emma for precisely those abstract pleasures: the only legitimate romantic talk in the novel is when he fills in her silences with the images she has momentarily forgotten. He indulges in her dreams in order to describe the indescribable sensation, allowing her the world of romance in its only "realistic" form: as a verbal luxury. In his characteristic alternation between withdrawal and identification, Flaubert coldly exposes the unreality of Emma's dreams by repeatedly demonstrating the fragility of their purely mental life; but at the same time, when the dreams are both drowned and substantiated by particular, intense sensations, he sympathetically uses the literature of romance to illustrate how poetry is made from the life of the senses.

At such moments imagination does, so to speak, proceed from the real. But, significantly, the condition for demonstrating the propriety of imagination is a halt in the action of the story, a moment when a blank in the characters' consciousness leaves the narrative open for a stylistic performance on the part of Flaubert. The blank may be due to an ecstatic sense of oneness with the world or to a stupor in which the world appears hopelessly alien to the self. In both cases—and in spite of their opposite emotional values for Emma—the narrator *continues speaking* in a dramatically gratuitous way. The poetry he then creates is a luxury in an absolute sense: it promotes nothing in the story, and no one in the novel profits from it. If Flaubert, unlike Emma, realizes that the countries of romance are not "behind" the literature of romance, he is also unable to imagine any novelistic use for such literary fictions apart from rearranging them as self-contained descriptive displays. And many of Flaubert's characters are ideally suitable for a suspension of our interest in them. Flaubert often has to fill in for them, thus reminding us of a deficiency or absence of life, and of the predominance of verbal performance. Emma's anxiety in a world unresponsive to her dreams, her sensual intensities and visual fantasies (both of which must be verbally translated), Félicité's simplicity, and Frédéric Moreau's passivity all create situations of little dramatic pressure, situations in which stylistic virtuosity seems almost necessary to sustain the narrative. A poverty of event and of psychological interest provides occasions in which language justifies Flaubert's distrust of language by demonstrating its independence from the life which fiction presumably reflects.

Such occasions are what several of today's best French critics invite us to admire most in Flaubert. For Jean Rousset, "the most beautiful" things in *Madame Bovary* are those "great vacant spaces" of boredom and inaction, passages where we have "a void rather than a presence." [34] Gérard Genette has written brilliantly of the descriptive passages in Flaubert which break the dramatic tension of his stories, which immobilize the narrative by their "admirable gratuitousness." "But language itself," Genette writes, "becomes literature at the cost of its own death, since it must lose its significance in order to enter into the silence of the Work." Flaubert is the first writer to undertake this "renvoi du discours à son envers silencieux"—this enterprise of returning

34. "*Madame Bovary* ou le 'livre sur rien'. Un aspect de l'art du roman chez Flaubert: le point de vue," *Forme et Signification/Essais sur les structures littéraires de Corneille à Claudel* (Paris, 1962), p. 207.

speech to its silent origins which, Genette asserts, we now recognize as the "place" of literature itself.[35]

In the face of such claims, it is easy to forget or dismiss our
first impressions of Flaubert's immobilizing descriptions. They
deserve to be looked at closely once again. We find most frequently the kind of congealing moment I'm thinking of in
L'Education sentimentale. On the one hand, the novel does have
a conventional subject, and its originality can in fact be assimi-
lated to a realistic view of the nature of fiction. In L'Education
sentimentale, Flaubert treats the pathos of postponement; the
novel dramatizes the banal but nonetheless overwhelming fact
that to wait for life is finally to lose life. Frédéric, like Emma, is
a person of expectations, a vain dreamer, but he does not have
her energy, and while Flaubert obviously shares his disgust with
the stupidity and duplicity of others, he also dismisses him much
more brutally than he does Emma. The world in which Frédéric
lives is mediocre enough, but the weakness of desire in Frédéric
is even more mediocre. He does not even have the energetic,
remorseless egotism which makes Emma greedily seize every
occasion for pleasure and which Flaubert cannot help but admire. Frédéric the velléitaire, tempted by everything, does nothing; he is a failure in literature, in politics, and in love, and the
essential thing to be said about his life at the end of the novel
is just that it has gone by. Unlike Emma, Frédéric survives, and
his survival undoubtedly frightens Flaubert more than Emma's
suicide, for it suggests how easy and unremarkable it can be
to give in to a will-less languor which Flaubert glamorizes in
Madame Bovary by giving it the form of an attractive woman's
sensuality. Emma is foolish, and nothing in life may be worth
doing anyway, but the alternative to Emma's frantic effort to
love—and to the martyrdom of Flaubert's daily efforts to write—
is the strangely embarrassing spectacle, which Flaubert gives us
in the last two chapters of L'Education sentimentale, of a middle-

35. "Silences de Flaubert," Figures (Paris, 1966), pp. 234 and 242.

aged attempt to sentimentalize the boring and the insignificant.

But because the idle hero of *L'Education sentimentale* wanders so aimlessly through life, he gives Flaubert the chance to arrange his world as a succession of pictures undisturbed by any energetic projects. Frédéric's passivity provides an appropriate point of view from which the world can be taken in with a leisurely esthetic perception. The only affirmation in the novel is descriptive. A kind of superfluous compositional beauty is offered to the reader as the *narrator's* achievement with a life in which his hero has achieved nothing. For example, as Frédéric walks through Paris dreaming of Madame Arnoux, Flaubert uses the situation almost as a scholastic exercise in "doing a scene," and we have some of those polished, excessively written descriptions which are the main "events" of the novel:

> But the sun was setting, and the cold wind stirred up whirling circles of dust. The coachmen thrust their chins into their scarves, the wheels began to turn more quickly, the pavement grated; and all the carriages went at a brisk trot down the long avenue, brushing up against one another, overtaking and pulling away from one another, then, at the Place de la Concorde, they dispersed. Behind the Tuileries, the sky took on the hue of the slate roofs. The trees in the garden formed two enormous masses, tinged with purple at the top. The gas lamps were being turned on; and the vast greenish expanse of the Seine broke into myriads of tiny silvery clouds against the pilings of the bridges.[36]

> *   *   *

> The street lamps blazed in two straight lines, as far as one could see, and long red flames quivered in the depths of the water. The water was the color of slate, while the sky, which was clearer, seemed supported by the great masses of shadow which rose from each side of the river. Invisible buildings intensified the darkness. [Des édifices, que l'on n'apercevait pas, faisaient des redoublements d'obscurité.] Beyond, over the roof tops,

36. II, 55.

a luminous haze was floating; all noises melted into a single hum; a light wind was blowing.[37]

Nothing in Stendhal or Balzac (in spite of the latter's sermons and digressions) is as self-contained as such passages in Flaubert. I'm thinking especially of these and of other descriptions of Parisian scenes during Frédéric's walks, of the images of Versailles during his stay there with Rosanette, of the crowd scenes when they are at the races, and of the extraordinary pictorial fragments which Flaubert gives us of masses in movement during the political upheaval of 1848. To a certain extent, these passages give us an impression of naturalness. With his characteristic economy and attention to detail, Flaubert avoids the Balzacian comprehensiveness which reminds us that what we have is a literary study of a scene rather than an immediate impression of it. Flaubert does, it would appear, give us the immediate impression: colors, reflections, shadows, and sounds rather than a systematic survey and definition of all the scene's elements. But this calculated immediacy suggests artificiality much more than Balzac's frankly omniscient, detached, and encyclopedic view of things. It is as if an excessive concern with the realistic immediacy of impressions led, finally, to the reduction of the real to some transparent mechanical tricks. The connection, in literature, is clearest in the Goncourt brothers, in whose work the desire to render life directly is realized mainly by a life-killing artiness. We naturally find Flaubert immeasurably more interesting, but part of his interest lies in the fact that he illustrates more brilliantly and more profoundly the very connection which we find rather comically confirmed in the Goncourts. The tortuous care with which Flaubert seeks to make language transparent to reality consecrates the very opaqueness of language which he dreaded. For his realism entails a kind of attention to words which can only make them appear heavy and unmanageable. Tirelessly worked over, they finally settle into

37. II, 81.

combinations which represent a difficult but curiously unimpressive victory over verbal incoherence. Flaubert develops, clings
to formal procedures which replace the real as an object of literary imitation. Because the terror of art in the name of life
seems to be the death of life in art, style comes to be a solemn
reference to its own achievements and to *express* little more than
an inflexible model of linguistic coherence.

Flaubert is extraordinarily repetitious. The *miroitement mono-
tone* which Proust generously saw as the multiple reflections of
Flaubert's deepest self can rather easily be analyzed as the effect
of a few relentlessly repeated devices. *Miroitement,* at any rate,
is a happy find: Flaubert seems incapable of missing the possibilities of light reflections in any scene he describes. Shimmering
points of light are perhaps even more recurrent in his writing
than those immense, often purple shadows which, like the reflections, are in the two passages I have quoted from *L'Education
sentimentale.* A small anthology of reflections and of tableaux
spotted with bright colors could be gleaned from *Madame
Bovary.* Llheureux tempts Emma with some Algerian scarves:
"From time to time, as if to remove some dust, he flicked his nail
against the silk of the scarves spread out at full length, and they
rustled with a little noise, making the gold spangles of the
material sparkle like stars in the greenish twilight" (74; 419).
In the Rouen cathedral: "The nave was reflected in the full
fonts together with the base of the arches and some fragments
of the stained glass windows. But the reflections of the painted
glass, broken by the marble rim, were continued farther on
upon the pavement, like a many-coloured carpet" (173; 544).
And when Rodolphe sees Emma again toward the end of the
novel: "He had drawn her upon his knees, and with the back of
his hand was caressing her smooth hair; a last ray of the sun
was mirrored there, like a golden arrow [il caressait du revers
de la main ses bandeaux lisses, où, dans la clarté du crépuscule,
miroitait comme une flèche d'or un dernier rayon du soleil]"
(226; 609). At best, such passages are merely pretty; at worst,
the obsessiveness with which Flaubert sees reflections every-

where becomes ridiculous. Thus, to describe Arnoux, in *L'Edu-cation sentimentale,* dozing behind his counter, he writes: "He had aged enormously; he even had round his temples a crown of pink pimples, on which the gold crosses, shining in the sun, cast their reflections [une couronne de boutons roses, et le reflet des croix d'or frappées par le soleil tombait dessus]." [38] Finally, the light from the fire in the *Lion d'or* not only covers Emma's body, "[penetrating with] its harsh light . . . the [weave] of her gown," but it also filters through "the fine pores of her [white] skin" and even—for that, apparently, is not enough— "her eyelids [which] she blinked from time to time" (56; 397).

It is tempting to think of all these luminous reflections as symptomatic of Flaubert's sense of the elusive, teasing nature of the real. Shimmering points of light and color partially demate-rialize objects; the preponderance of luminosity over substance would seem to be the descriptive equivalent of the insubstantial-ity to which language reduces reality. But this insubstantiality strikes me as the result of the very effort to circumvent it. Rather than a descriptive metaphor for Flaubert's feelings about the relation between the imaginary and the real, it is, I think, a consequence of the discipline Flaubert embraced in order to change that relation. The recurrent reflections, the shimmering points of light are less significant as thematic images than as one of the short cuts by which Flaubert substitutes the repetition of a few patterns or formulas of perception and expression for the development of a personal style.

Nothing could be more ambiguous than Flaubert's attitude toward style. On the one hand, style is irrelevant in the realistic program: language has merely to verbalize the nonverbal nature of each subject. But in a famous, and rather obscure, passage from the letters, Flaubert suggests an entirely different view of style:

> What I find beautiful, what I would like to write, is a book about nothing, a book without any external support, which

38. II, 425.

would be held together by the inner strength of its style, as the earth hangs by itself suspended in space, a book that would have almost no subject or at least in which the subject would be almost invisible, if that is possible. The most beautiful works are those in which there is the least matter; the closer the expression comes to the thought, the more adequately the word adheres to the thought and disappears, the more beautiful the result. I think that the future of Art lies in these directions. I see Art, as it has developed over the years, becoming as ethereal as possible, from the Egyptian pylons to the Gothic lancets, and from the twenty-thousand verse poems of the Indians to the brief flights of Byron. Form, as it becomes more skillful, is attenuated; it abandons all liturgy, all rules, all measure; it deserts the epic for the novel, verse for prose; it no longer recognizes any orthodoxy and is as free as the individual will that produces it. This liberation from materiality can be found in everything, for example in the evolution of governments from the Oriental despotisms to the socialist states of the future.

That is why there are neither beautiful nor ugly subjects and why one could almost establish as an axiom, from the point of view of pure Art, that there is no such thing as subject, style being in itself an absolute way of seeing things.[39]

Now the "absolute way of seeing things" might mean that objective view of reality which Flaubert speaks of elsewhere, but— and I feel this is more likely here—it can also be an attempt to define style as completely autonomous. That is, "pure Art" could take anything as its subject or—even better—dispense entirely with inferior occasions, with stories, with characters, with words. There is something admirable in the impossible rigor of this passage: Flaubert's dream, however fantastic we may find it, is, after all, the democratization of literature. A free form, a classless society: everyone, as we say, would simply be himself. But what can that "liberation from materiality" really mean? It can only be an ethic and an esthetic of the ineffable, for we both live and write by some "rules" or "measure," however liberal

39. *Correspondance de Flaubert*, II, 345–46.

they may be, and the ideal of a form without measure is a dream of the disappearance not just of subjects, but of form itself. The dangers of that dream are shown clearly enough by Flaubert himself. His hope is to escape from a dilemma familiar enough to us by now. An ineffable self, an ineffable reality outside the self; "between" the two, words which do not adhere to either, a language indifferent to everything but its own seductive suggestiveness. To solve this unsolvable problem there is only silence—or, as a kind of mocking compromise, a mechanically disciplined language in which form is merely the security of cliché. Nothing is stranger—and more inevitable—than that Flaubert should come to consider pure art as a question of managing obvious literary effects, of reducing form to prosodic virtuosity. "Divorce yourself more and more, as you write," he advises Louise Colet, "from everything that is not pure Art. Always keep your eye on your model, and on nothing else. . . . Have faith, have faith. I want (and I am determined) to see you get enthusiastic about a caesura, a sentence, an enjambment, in short about form itself, considered apart from the subject as you used to get enthusiastic about feeling, the heart, the passions." [40] Flaubert's prose, far from being "free," inflicts upon us the eternal ternary rhythm, the frozen tableaux in the *style indirect libre*, the nonconnective *et* to introduce a final clause, the adverb at the end of a sentence, and the deadening *c'était* at the beginning of descriptions. The high priest of style is the master of the rhythmical tic. By an irony which should now be clear, the fear of exaggeration, of "unnatural" hyperbole in the self and in literature, can be the triumph of an artificiality which just parodies inventive artifice.

Perhaps the only way to prevent words from appearing as nonhuman inhabitants of the mind or as cancers of reality is to treat them as metaphorical entertainments, or as therapeutic metaphors. But the death of metaphor is the search for an original link—the "real cause"—in a metaphorical chain. Proust

40. *Correspondance de Flaubert*, III, 21.

claimed, with some exaggeration, that he could not find a single beautiful metaphor in Flaubert's work.[41] It would be a thankless task to list many of Flaubert's unsuccessful metaphors; these examples from *Madame Bovary* should suffice:

> On Emma's suffering after Léon's departure from Yonville: "Henceforth the memory of Léon was the center of her boredom; it burnt there more brightly than the fires left by travellers on the snow of a Russian steppe." (88; 438)

> On Emma's enslavement to Rodolphe: "It was an idiotic sort of attachment, full of admiration on his side and voluptuousness on hers, a beatitude which left her numb; and her soul sunk deep into this intoxication and drowned in it, all shrivelled up, like the duke of Clarence in his butt of malmsey." (138; 500)

> And on Rodolphe's blasé attitude toward love: ". . . pleasures, like schoolboys, in a school courtyard, had so trampled upon his heart that [nothing green grew in it anymore, and] whatever entered there, more heedless than children, did not even, like them, leave a name carved upon the wall." (145; 510)

To be sure, these famous images are among Flaubert's worst; they do not, however, give a very unfair picture of the majority of his comparisons. Banal, awkward, farfetched; Flaubert's metaphors are the "fall" of his style, and they give the impression of a literary chore done conscientiously and unenthusiastically. It is ingenious to defend them, as Don L. Demorest has done, as dramatically representative of the mediocre imagination of Flaubert's characters.[42] But such attributions are by no means easy to make in Flaubert: a continuously recognizable manner of writing dominates and assimilates the individual styles of all his characters. It seems to me impossible to decide to whom these metaphors "belong," and even when we have finished

41. "A propos du 'style' de Flaubert," pp. 193–94.
42. See *L'Expression figurée et symbolique dans l'œuvre de Gustave Flaubert* (Paris, 1931).

explaining their origins within the story, we have still to explain why Flaubert creates people who not only think in vulgar metaphors but who have extraordinary difficulty in *connecting* things at all. But that is the very deficiency I have been speaking of all along. These startlingly clumsy similes express Flaubert's impatience with the epistemologically approximative nature of metaphor. Things are not to be *like* other things, but each expression is meant to cover and absorb its hypothetically real subject with literal precision. Like Emma, Flaubert seeks a perfect fit between reality and words; neither he nor Madame Bovary is willing to admit that mental fictions may *generate* the realities of life and of literature at least as much as they reflect them, or that those realities are any less livable because they cannot be tested against some chimerical, nonverbal self or experience which precedes them.

We must look to Proust for a greater indulgence toward imaginative versions of reality. His extraordinarily successful artifice is to subvert the credibility of his characters as "real" people and to demonstrate the kind of livable cohesion possible within a strictly personal labyrinth of metaphorical correspondences. Unlike Flaubert, Proust never had to cripple his inventiveness in the hope of making his work a transparent, intelligible tableau of the real world; and nothing could be further from *A la Recherche du temps perdu* than the Flaubertian art of retrenchment. To subordinate our imaginative excesses to autobiographical or external sources is inevitably to cripple imagination *and* to see a world as poverty-stricken as Homais's Yonville. What we like to think of as living in harmony with reality may be simply a knack for multiplying fictions, for accommodating new versions of experience to older ones so that we may impose a personal if always tentative unity on the inexplicable richness of being. The alternative to this submissiveness to our far-out states of consciousness, to the suggestiveness of imagination, is the Flaubertian panic at the mind's deceptive inventions, and the torture of trying to be realistic.

IV

PROUST AND THE ART
OF INCOMPLETION

For Flaubert, the success of art depends on its ability to provide a definitive image of a reality anterior to art. Although the end of *Madame Bovary* gives to the novel a dimension it cannot explore but merely points to—that of a social order best characterized by the place it allows for Homais—this open-endedness is more apparent than real within the structure of the work. In its references to social history, *Madame Bovary* is deliberately incomplete, but formally its ending is an authentic conclusion, closing the work by helping, like the beginning, to enclose Emma's life within a larger and less analytically detailed picture of French provincial life. The intended finality of the work is indirectly reflected in Flaubert's awkward transitions from paragraph to paragraph and from chapter to chapter. His notion of style imprisons him in isolated, drawn-out battles with each narrative unit. And between the perfect and perfectly self-contained sentences and paragraphs, there is—ideally, we might almost say—nothing but the creative void in which the novelist's work (his novel and his struggle) has simply ceased to exist.

But what happens if the very impossibility of writing definitive sentences and definitive works—or, more radically, the
refusal to do so—is recognized as the most interesting fact about
artistic creation? Proust is the first major novelist to consider
what we recognize as a still somewhat enigmatic but central
proposition of contemporary art. But he formulates this proposition in a hesitant and even contradictory way, and much of the
richness or the weakness (depending on how we feel about such
hesitancies) of *A la Recherche du temps perdu* depends on just
this ambiguity in his commitment to changing the literary expectations and interests of his readers. Proust's characteristically
qualified and almost subverted audacity is well illustrated in a
passage from *La Prisonnière* on what the narrator calls the incomplete character of nineteenth-century masterpieces. Marcel
has been praising Wagner; but ". . . I thought how markedly,
all the same, [his] works participate in that quality of being—
albeit marvellously—always incomplete, which is the peculiarity
of all the great works of the nineteenth century, [a century
marked by the literary miscarriages of its greatest writers, who,
however,] watching themselves at work as though they were at
once author and critic, have derived from this self-contemplation
a novel beauty, exterior and superior to the work itself, imposing
upon it retrospectively a unity, a greatness which it does not
possess." [1]

1. Marcel Proust, *Remembrance of Things Past*, tr. C. K. Scott Moncrieff
and (for *Le Temps retrouvé*) Frederick A. Blossom, 2 vols. (New York,
copyright 1924, 1925, 1927, 1930, 1932 and renewed by Random House,
Inc.), II, 490. *A la Recherche du temps perdu*, ed. Pierre Clarac and
André Ferré, 3 vols. (Paris, 1954), III, 160. Subsequent page references
to *A la Recherche* will be given in the text; the first reference in each
case will be to the Moncrieff-Blossom translation, the second to the Pléiade
edition in French. All other translations are my own. Moncrieff and
Blossom worked with the Nouvelle Revue Française text published from
1919 to 1927; when it has been necessary in the passages I quote from
A la Recherche du temps perdu, I have changed their translation to
make the English correspond more closely to the most recent French
edition.

If, as Ionesco has suggested, it is superfluous to speak of crises in art because interesting art is always an expression of crisis,[2] we can nevertheless speak of a specifically modern type of crisis in which artistic importance is identified with failure. It is true that Proust's narrator does not go so far as to say that the artists he mentions later on in this passage—Wagner, Hugo, Michelet, and Balzac—are great *because* they failed; in France, the necessity of failure in art will be argued and illustrated most explicitly by Blanchot and, as we shall see, by Beckett. Furthermore, the passage from *La Prisonnière* contains several shifts of tone and position. On the one hand, the narrator has suggested the irrelevance to modern art of centuries of esthetic theory. He implicitly defines "unity" and "greatness," which had traditionally been thought of as attributes belonging to the work itself, as myths of criticism—myths, we might add, engendered by certain cultural assumptions about the nature and function of art. But then what is there to admire in art? Having recognized and even praised the "literary miscarriages" of the nineteenth-century's "greatest writers," Proust's narrator is nevertheless tempted to turn from their art to the unifying—and falsifying—summaries of their art, summaries which announce intentions made obsolete by the works themselves. The prefaces to the *Histoire de France* and the *Histoire de la Révolution*—"prefaces, that is to say pages written after the books themselves"—are where we should look to find "the greatest beauties in Michelet" (II, 490; III, 160). Committed to humanistic canons of artistic appreciation at the same time that he is aware of how modern art undermines those canons, the Proustian narrator seems almost inclined to transform what he judges to be inaccurate description of art into the work of art itself. This implied promotion of criticism to the status of an activity as creative as art is not uncongenial to some of our views about the inventive rather than the purely descriptive nature of criticism. But in *La Prisonnière*, the narrator is

2. Eugène Ionesco, *Notes et contre-notes,* in Collection Pratique du Théâtre (Paris, 1962), p. 207.

attracted to the essentially *conservative* nature of Michelet's prefaces or Balzac's *Avant-propos*: the latter "recompose" the writer's work in a traditional language, and instead of suggesting intentions which might open and expand the works they consider, such summaries have only the ambiguous appeal of any pose or attitude sufficiently strong or blind or stubborn to ignore the experience which surrounds it.

The narrator's remarks raise other difficulties. He is both vague about the nature of incompleteness in nineteenth-century art and uncertain about the retroactive effect of such critical attributes as unity. We find a shift in the passage from "a unity, a greatness" which the works in question do not have to a unity which is apparently real and which the artist's enthusiastic appreciation just belatedly discovers. Wagner "perceiving all of a sudden that he had written a tetralogy," and Balzac deciding that the books he has already written would be more beautiful "brought together in a cycle in which the same characters would reappear" have not, we are now told, created a new beauty "exterior and superior to the work itself," but have merely articulated a design and a coherence already present *in* the works.

A unity that was ulterior, not artificial, otherwise it would have crumbled into dust like [so many] systematisations of mediocre writers who with the elaborate assistance of titles and sub-titles give themselves the appearance of having pursued a single and transcendent design. Not [artificial,] perhaps indeed all the more real for being ulterior, for being born of a moment of enthusiasm when it is discovered to exist among fragments which need only to be joined together. A unity that has been unaware of itself, therefore vital and not logical, that has not banned variety, chilled execution.

But it is immediately after these sentences that Marcel confesses how uneasy Wagner's "Vulcan-like craftsmanship" makes him. When he notes that "the melancholy of the poet" in Wagner "is consoled, surpassed—that is, [alas, partially destroyed]—by the delight of the craftsman," he is complaining about the happy

ingenuity by which the composer gives a definitive significance
to what had been merely fragments of melodic inspiration by
finding a place for them in an opera for which they had originally not been composed. Wagner's joyful intuition that a certain melody ("the half-forgotten air of a shepherd's pipe") could
be harmoniously fitted into the larger operatic structure of
Tristan and Isolde is, for Proust's narrator, a source of disappointment. It is as if Wagner were *not* discovering that "real"
unity "among fragments which need only to be joined together,"
but had instead, by a piece of superior trickery, obscured the real
lack of unity in his music, the incompleteness which Marcel
began by finding "marvelous" in nineteenth-century art (II, 491;
III, 161).

As these shifts of attitude show, two very different things
appeal to the Proustian narrator: the fragmentary nature of major artistic productions in the nineteenth century, and the notion
that great art, by definition, has a "vital" unity and completeness
which critical recognition can make explicit but does not create.
I think that the latter expresses a nostalgic view of the relation
of art to the world and to the self which the narrator's experience—psychological, social, and esthetic—tends most profoundly
to undermine. If the quality of completeness is recognized as a
cultural imperative rather than an attribute inherent to art, art
runs the risk of losing the privileged status it has always been
granted among life's activities. If, like other processes in life, it
can never be thought of as "completed," its relation to the rest
of our experience can no longer be defined as that of a kind of
epistemological monument which reassures us about the intelligible significance of reality, extracts its hidden meanings. The
real is no longer the *object* of art any more than it is the object
of any other activity—like making love or playing chess—which
simply coexists with all the other activities we call reality. What
Proust's narrator finds moving in nineteenth-century art is, it
seems to me, the transparency of its lifelike incompleteness. It
then naturally becomes much more difficult than ever before to

define what is specifically "artistic" about the activity of art, and the attempt to do so has, in the modern period, given us works which have become more and more open-ended and purely interrogative. Is art *about* anything? Is there a subject "behind" the work? Do we have to discard an esthetic of imitation or expressiveness?

The incompleteness which the narrator of *A la Recherche* sees in nineteenth-century art is, I think, the sign of this problematic self-reflection. And the insecurities and failures are all the more impressive in those grandiose enterprises of nineteenth-century art—for example, Hugo's *Légende des siecles,* Balzac's *Comédie humaine,* and Wagner's tetralogy—which make a last-ditch stand for a securely comprehensive art, for works which might be an adequate, cohesive, perhaps definitive *Summa* of human experience. These enterprises tempt Proust's narrator at the same time that he recognizes their moving and "marvelous" failure. Proust himself worked all his life perfecting a single work, dreaming of a book which would be finally and completely expressive, which, when finished, would have that "vital" unity he both attributes to the art he mentions and yet recognizes as factitious.

We find a similar ambivalence in the narrator's attitude toward his own work—or, more exactly, in the hints given to the reader about both the relation between the narrator's book and his past life, and the relation between the narrator's life and Proust's life. Now the subject of *A la Recherche* is precisely the relation between a writer's life and his work. The main character is the author of the book we are reading, and the reason he plays such an important role in his own work is, apparently, to demonstrate the equivalence between literature and history or autobiography. He has been unable to write as long as he has thought of art as anything *but* self-expression, as revealing the essence or truth of realities external to the artist himself. What Marcel discovers in the Guermantes library toward the end of *Le Temps retrouvé* is that art simply expresses "our true life, reality as we have felt it," and, more significantly, that "we are not at all free in the presence of the work of art to be created," for ". . . it existed prior to us and we should seek to discover it as we would a natural law because it is both necessary and hidden" (II, 1002; III, 881). In a sense, then, the kind of criticism in which *A la Recherche* is meant to educate us might appear to be biographical. The artist translates a self already there ("The duty and the task of a writer are those of translator" [II, 1009; III, 890]), and here we seem to be close to the Flaubertian idea of the writer as the fundamentally inactive catalyst in the verbalizing of a preexistent reality. He may extract significance from events, but he neither changes their nature nor promotes new events. The pretense of impersonality has been dropped, but the self would seem to be as objective for the Proustian narrator as Flaubert's Platonic novelistic subjects.

Even more: the work invites us to confuse the fictional autobiography of Marcel with the real autobiography of Proust. The trap of biographical reference is particularly well set in the novel. There are enough similarities between the narrator's experience and what we know of Proust's life to make the reader think of the work as a disguised autobiography. Also, the very notion of disguised autobiography seems to justify the interpretive method which consists in removing the disguise—that is, in correcting the work by an appeal to its supposed sources in order to fill the gaps between the fictions of art and the supposed facts of biography. In the crudest version of this, it is argued that Albertine is "really" a man, or that Marcel is "really" a snob, or that he is "really" more hostile to his parents than he admits.[3]

3. See Justin O'Brien, "Albertine the Ambiguous: Notes on Proust's Transposition of Sexes," *PMLA*, LXIV (December 1949), 933–52. Harry Levin, in a brief comment on this article in "Proust, Gide, and the Sexes," *PMLA*, LXV (June 1950), 648–52, points out that a change in Albertine's sex introduces more difficulties than it settles, and that, in any case, the effect of narrative art depends on our accepting the novelist's characters and situations as he presents them.

George D. Painter's Biography of Proust (*Proust: The Early Years*

But *any* biographical argument, however careful and sophisticated it may be, tends to deaden the work by assuming that it transposes the writer's self instead of re-creating it. To emphasize re-creation rather than transposition is not to deny any continuity between the book and the writer's experience. But it does mean that we recognize the book as a self-constituting activity sufficiently energetic to create, to try out and explore, a self different from the selves experienced and explored before the experience of writing the book.

The peculiarity of *A la Recherche,* however, is that it makes us wary of such obvious distinctions. Written into the novel itself is an autobiographical intention which encourages us to identify the narrator and Proust much more effectively than any anecdotal similarities between their lives. Proust almost seems willing, within the work, to be taken for Marcel. His willingness is hesitant, since he avoids naming his narrator for more than two thousand pages. But on two occasions he finally does allow him to call himself Marcel, although he stops short of adding a last name which would commit Proust more definitely to the project of autobiography or to the rejection of autobiography. The way in which the name is given in *La Prisonnière* expresses this indecision. The description is of how Albertine wakes up in the narrator's room: "As soon as she was able to speak she said: 'My—' or 'My dearest—' followed by my Christian name, which, if we give to the narrator the same name as the author of this book, [would have made for] 'My Marcel,' or 'My dearest Marcel' " (II, 429; III, 75). Until now, much of the novel's

and *Proust: The Later Years* [Boston and Toronto, 1959 and 1965]), is, on the positive side, exhaustively informative about Proust's schedule. But, far from telling us anything about "the workings of [Proust's] imagination at the very moment of creation" (I, xiii), Painter's work merely juxtaposes aspects or "passages" from the life and passages from the work. It is further vitiated by Painter's nostalgia for the heyday of the French aristocracy, his tendentious manipulation of the available material, and his curious determination to rehabilitate Proust sexually. For a sharp review of Painter's first volume, see Elaine Marks, "The Relevance of Literary Biography" *The Massachusetts Review,* VII (Autumn 1966), 815–23.

interest has depended on our willingness to think of the narrator *as* the author. The Proustian view of the relation between an artist's life and his work can be convincingly dramatized only if the writer of the work we are reading and the man who has spent years wondering about the relevance of his life to literature are the same person. Only the present literary accomplishment of the narrator provides a possible resolution of the most urgent concerns in the past he evokes. The questions about art become pointless and merely pathetic if the recollection of asking them cannot be considered as a helpful experiment in answering them. The unexpected reference to *another* author in the passage just quoted advertises an indisputable fact of literary history (Marcel Proust wrote *A la Recherche du temps perdu*), but within the novel this fact is dramatically inadmissible. We know that Proust created the narrator, but how can the narrator know it? Proust's presence in the novel can be recognized only by the audience outside the novel. But if the main character begins to talk about the author, we wonder where the author is in the narrative—and of course he cannot be anywhere, since (from the first page to the last) we hear only the voice of the character who, mysteriously, suddenly refers to him.

The narrator is a superficially simple but profoundly important discovery: he allows Proust to connect as well as to distinguish between life and art because both are constantly contained within the work of art. Experience and literary expression, thanks to this discovery, are now comparable terms; the former exists nowhere outside of the narrator's literary effort. This trick of genius finally does send us back to Proust and to "life," but only because the narrator has convincingly shown how literary activity penetrated his life long before he began to write. And the demonstration is possible only if his life is entirely within the book. Proust is reluctant, and for good reason, to allow his narrator to suggest that *Proust's* life is behind the work. Although later on in *La Prisonnière* Albertine again refers to "Marcel," this time without any narrative reservations accompanying the reference (II, 488; III, 157), in the earlier passage we are teased with a "Marcel" only conditionally proposed: Albertine uses the narrator's Christian name, "ce qui, en donnant au narrateur le même prénom qu'à l'auteur de ce livre, eût fait: 'Mon Marcel,' 'Mon chéri Marcel.' " [4]

I have insisted on this passage because it is a striking example of an indecision important for the whole novel. It is connected to Proust's ambivalent feelings about "incomplete" art, and "Marcel" as a compromise between a purely fictional narrator and Proust can help us further to define the notion of incompleteness. The adherence to the narrator or Marcel not as Proust but as the principal character *and* author of this work reveals an aspect of literary creation which Proust hesitates to accept unreservedly: its self-inventiveness. To prevent us from thinking of the fictionalized narrator as a negligible convention, to force us to take him literally as the author of the book we are reading, and to make his vocation as a writer the subject of that book are to make impossible certain conclusions about art which I think Proust clings to in spite of his artistic experience.

The most essential (if unavowed) of these conclusions is that literature is a strategy for the enjoyment of death in life. This peculiar and terrible hope is expressed theoretically by the notion that writing is the psychologically passive activity of merely translating into language a life already lived. Dramatically, it is expressed with the greatest power in the final pages of *A la Recherche,* where we see the narrator settling down to his work as to a duty made stale and joyless by an unrelenting obsession with death. It seems at first that he feels only the ["reasoned fear"] of not having the time to finish his book (III, 1037), but after a mysterious accident one evening when he almost falls three times while going down a staircase, he becomes "indifferent" to his work itself, which he finds an "irksome" chore to get done before "the long rest that would eventually come." "Since that day on the staircase, nothing concerning the social

4. The italics are mine.

world, no happiness, whether it came from [people's friendship,]
the progress of my work, the hope of fame, any longer penetrated to my consciousness except as such a pale ray of sunlight
that it no longer had the power to warm me, put life into me,
give me any desire whatsoever; and even at that, wan though
it was, it was still too dazzling for my eyes and I preferred to
close them and turn my head toward the wall." He hates death,
but he speaks of it as lodging itself definitively within him with
the power and pervasiveness of a love. The thought of death
"adhered to the deepest stratum of my brain so completely that
I could not turn my attention to anything without first relating
it to the idea of death and, even if I was not occupied with
anything but was in a state of complete repose, the idea of death
was with me as continuously as the idea of myself" (II, 1119–20;
III, 1041–42). As a result, the literary transcription of the narrator's past is begun in a state of terror: the resurrection of lost
time is the condition for writing, but to carry the weight of the
past is also felt as an immense task which finally destroys a man.
With ["a feeling of fatigue and fright,"] the narrator has a sense
of being "perched on [the] dizzying summit" of time, thinks of
all men as engaged in a difficult and perilous walk on the stilts
of their pasts, and wonders with anguish whether or not he will
be able to keep his balance long enough to describe this fantastic
extension of men in Time (II, 1123–24; III, 1047–48).

No life, it would therefore seem, is created by the work. Life
is the oppressive burden of the work; the somber task of literature is to describe a paralyzing continuity in men's lives which
is equivalent to death, since it leaves no psychic space for any
future. There is something shocking in these final passages of
Proust's novel, shocking in that we have just read over three
thousand pages which demonstrate exactly the reverse of what
is implied at the end. The novel has in fact shown—I will return
to this—the astonishing lightness of the past, its almost negligible
weight in the enterprise of recording it. We have seen in dra-

matic detail a process by which temporal continuity is made continuously re-creative. In each disappointment of the past, the narrator has exploited the liberating inventiveness he had failed to see at the time; and it is only while writing his book that he realizes how permeable each unhappy event might have been to his desires. In fact, we could even say that *because* everything that happens in *A la Recherche* is in Marcel's past, he has never in his life enjoyed more freedom than now. The final, definitive quality of events is felt at the moment we live them. It is then that we experience most concretely the impoverishing limitations and exclusions implicit in each emotion we have, each spectacle we see, each decision we make. It is only in memory that the future of each moment appears promisingly uncertain, and therefore open to possibility. For in memory we can profit from a larger notion of consequences than we can afford to use at the "first" or present version of each experience. Retrospectively, the immediate effects of events can be subverted by an interpretive will. At the actual time of those events, we were too busily engaged in their first consequences to see those consequences as anything but necessary and final. Proust's novel constantly illustrates this distinction. It is a literary dramatization of the psychoanalytic assumption that in certain conditions a restatement of the past creates new possibilities for the future.

We will, of course, have to look more closely at the conditions and the strategies, but for the moment it is enough to point out that for all its apparent backward-looking, *A la Recherche du temps perdu* is a more projective novel than *La Chartreuse de Parme*. Fabrice only rushes forward in time, and the pathos of his life is that his experience creates an irreversible destiny. Life narrows the range of his projects until, with unattackable logic, he has nothing more to do but die. When he returns to his past it is to rest, not to re-create. Proust's narrator, in a characteristic gesture of false surrender, turns his back on life in order to make some extraordinary claims for the future of his life. Aggressively active and self-revising, he remakes a once disappointing and uninteresting past into the field of an extravagant exercise in self-expansion.

But this openness also frightens the narrator. It is as if, after the Guermantes *matinée*, he had to punish himself with the thought of death in order to obscure the fantastic amount of new life he has set out to invent. And the punishment is also an advantage: death would protect Marcel from the uncertainty of the new, and the attempt to write his work under the sign of death suggests an effort to find in art an escape from the anguish of the unexpected. The novel documents this ambivalent attitude toward the new in Marcel's shifting feelings about habit. Habit is secure but deadening; when it is broken we enter what Beckett describes as "the perilous zone in the life of the individual, dangerous, precarious, painful, mysterious and fertile, when for a moment the boredom of living is replaced by the suffering of being."[5] The narrator knows that the destruction of habit is the condition for art, for any original perception of life; but he is also tempted by the security of the familiar, the effortless repetition of habitual, definitive versions of experience. And by almost allowing us to confuse the narrator with himself, Proust exposes this temptation as his own. It would be even easier for us to think of the writer as the mere "translator" of his life if we were to think of that life as the external, unknowable origin of the book. Nothing in the work could then be used as an argument against the psychologically passive nature of writing. The translation may be a difficult job, and we may also be able to list innumerable differences between Proust's life and his work; but neither of these possibilities would permit us to question the work's uniquely retrospective orientation. Its only project would be to fix the past; at the very most, it would distill the essence of a life already lived.

Psychologically, the function of art, if it is thought of in this way, is to consecrate a whole life as habit; esthetically, art can

5. Samuel Beckett, *Proust* (New York, 1931), p. 8.

then be defined as closed, definitively expressive documents. Incompleteness, on the other hand, means most profoundly that literature can never be final or finished because each of its statements brings forth a new project in the very process of attempting to express an old one. The alternative to a full recognition of the "marvelous miscarriages" Marcel praises in *La Prisonnière* is to prolong the fiction of art as the lifeless if instructive museum where we enter, in the "pauses" of experience, to replenish ourselves with the dead significance of safely immutable trophies of life.

A la Recherche du temps perdu is largely an account of the superficially nonliterary experience which explains the Proustian hesitation between two different kinds of literature. The issues I have raised so far—the difference between "complete" and "incomplete" art, the importance of accepting the fictional narrator (rather than Proust) as the author of the work we are reading, and the narrator's inclination to think of literature as a mere translation of lives already lived—are far from being specialized problems concerning novelistic form. Nothing illustrates more convincingly the intimate connections between art and the rest of life in *A la Recherche* than the fact that these problems are not raised in the novel in exclusively esthetic terms; instead, they are made to seem dramatically implicit in every aspect of Marcel's experience. The work itself accounts for the tension we find between two different kinds of art by a history much more personal than the literary history to which Proust naturally belongs and of which he was more than moderately aware. We can see the urgency of the literary choices which have been outlined only if we trace their formulation in contexts other than that of a specific program for literature. The revolutionary aspects of *A la Recherche du temps perdu* in the history of the novel coincide with courageous self-renewals on the part of a very particular, and very peculiar, personality; and the conservative elements in Proust's novel correspond to the lingering nostalgia in Marcel's personality for the security of certain enthusiasms and anxieties which he has, in large part, learned to judge and transcend.

A Flaubertian preoccupation with the correspondences between language and reality would seem also to characterize Marcel in *A la Recherche du temps perdu*. But the problem is posed in a way which brings Proust's work, in spite of its bleak analyses of human possibilities, closer to the most optimistic Stendhalian assertions of human freedom than to the nihilistic conclusions of *Madame Bovary* and *L'Education sentimentale*. For Flaubert, the experience of dealing novelistically with the question of how expressive words are of reality does nothing to change the way in which he asks the question. Emma's tragedy is the result of what we might call her uncritical dependence on Flaubert's formulation of the novelistic dilemma. Apparently, nothing that happened in the writing of *Madame Bovary* led Flaubert to suspect that he had perhaps created an unnecessary dead end in thinking that art must be a perfect fit between expression and a preexistent reality. And Emma does nothing but reenact the same assumptions from, as it were, the other direction. Flaubert dreams of a style adequate to the independent reality of his subject; Emma searches for the reality adequate to the vocabulary of romantic clichés. Because Flaubert immediately equates having experience with a problem of verbal designation, language blocks Flaubert's interest in discriminating among the choices by which we experiment with different ways of defining the self and the world. The very fact that language has to be used in making such choices leads Flaubert to a tortured weighing of the instruments available to describe them. He is, as Sartre has argued, indifferent to the commitments which a *use* of language creates,[6] and because he thus isolates language from the activities it inspires and accompanies, words naturally

6. And Flaubert can identify these word-objects, as Sartre says, with stupidity (Jean-Paul Sartre, "La Conscience de classe chez Flaubert," *Les Temps modernes*, XXI [May and June 1966], 2125–26).

appear to have a frighteningly impersonal life of their own. In one sense, Flaubert's disgust with life could be explained by his never having *reached* life in his epistemological investigations. And his choice of art as an alternative to life is, as the progress of his fiction from *Madame Bovary* to *Bouvard et Pécuchet* suggests, just as much a rejection of art as it is of life. His activity in both is paralyzed by his reluctance to examine the consequences of different uses of language and his obsession with its supposed essence.

Superficially, Proust's narrator is as concerned as Flaubert and Emma with the problem of what words designate. Marcel's life, like Emma's, appears to be structured by a series of hopeful fantasies and "falls": Madame de Guermantes does not provide the reality needed to make the notion of Merovingian mysteries come alive, Balbec does not embody the idea of nature's glamorously violent life, and Berma's acting, at first, cannot be fitted to the notion of dramatic talent. During his adolescence, Marcel, a little like Emma, waits for life to bring what he vaguely but passionately expects from it. Fascinated by words—the names of people and of places, and moral abstractions—he strains anxiously to receive "the secret of Truth and Beauty, things half-felt by me, half-incomprehensible, the full understanding of which was the vague but permanent object of my thoughts" (I, 64; I, 84). The disappointments Marcel suffers are of course important, but, interestingly enough, they do not provoke an obsessive mistrust of thought and language. And this, I think, is because his sense of self is so dependent on the shape of his expectations that their destruction literally *empties* his imagination. As a result, the Flaubertian rhythm of illusion and disillusion is redefined by Proust as a discordance between the self and the world rather than as an imbalance between inexhaustible, impersonal fictions and a reality which is always either hypothetical and beyond language (Flaubert's Platonic subject) or flatly material and inferior to language (Tostes and Yonville).

Marcel never has the psychological leisure to be tortured by the impersonality of words. Significantly, the Flaubertian way of defining correspondences between language and reality is dismissed as a false problem in *A la Recherche* long before the narrator feels confirmed in his literary vocation. The second time that Marcel sees Berma act, his impression, "though more pleasant than on the earlier occasion," is not really different. "Only, I no longer put it to the test of a pre-existent, abstract and false idea of dramatic genius, and I understood now that dramatic genius was precisely this." He realizes the uselessness of returning to the *words* "dramatic genius" to wonder what they mean, since in fact they mean nothing apart from particular occasions which they name but do not describe.

> The impression given us by a person or a work (or a rendering, for that matter) of marked individuality is peculiar to that person or work. We have brought to it the ideas of "beauty," "breadth of style," "pathos" and so forth which we might, failing anything better, have had the illusion of discovering in the commonplace show of a "correct" face or talent, but our critical spirit has before it the insistent challenge of a form of which it possesses no intellectual equivalent, in which it must detect and isolate the unknown element. It hears a shrill sound, an oddly interrogative intonation. It asks itself: "Is that good? Is what I am feeling just now admiration? Is that richness of colouring, nobility, strength?" And what answers it again is a shrill voice, a curiously questioning tone, the despotic impression caused by a person whom one does not know, wholly material, in which there is no room left for "breadth of interpretation." And for this reason it is the really beautiful works that, if we listen to them with sincerity, must disappoint us most keenly, because in the storehouse of our ideas there is none that corresponds to an individual impression. (I, 748; II, 49)

There is, the narrator goes on to say, an "interval" between the world in which we feel and the world in which we think and give names to things. If we can establish a certain correspondence or harmony between the two, we cannot really bridge the gap that separates them (I, 749; II, 50). Emma tries to live up to the world of names. And while Flaubert condemns her for this, his own hatred of life was perhaps the result of a similar inability to experience impressions strong enough to compete with the abstract glamor of words. It is as if a fundamental passivity in Flaubert and in his heroine both protected them from the shocks of experience and created a kind of psychological idleness in which they could be precisely what Flaubert aspired to be as a writer: impersonal. Nothing could be more different from the way Marcel in *A la Recherche* is victimized by particular impressions. In destroying the world of names, they make imperative a reorganization of personality in which imaginative creation, far from "floating" among inaccessible realities, must actually sustain and even make the reality of the self and the world.

The fragility of Marcel's sense of self will be recognized by readers of Proust as the principal "theme" of Marcel's life.[7] It is the source of an anguish from which there seemed no escape at Combray and which only literature can provide a way of circumventing or, more exactly, of transforming into a creative exhilaration. *A la Recherche* is punctuated by crucial episodes which dramatize a spectacular loss of being: the description at the beginning of "Combray" of the narrator's dizzying flights from one bedroom to another—and from one identity to another—when he awakes at night not knowing where, and therefore who, he is; the child's panic when he is separated from his mother at night; Marcel's horror at being surrounded, in the Balbec hotel room, by "enemies," by "things which did not know me" (I, 506–7; I, 666–67); and the emptiness of personality (". . . I was nothing more than a heart that throbbed . . .") which prevents Marcel from recognizing the city of Venice when his mother angrily leaves without him for the railway station (II, 837–38; III, 652–53). In none of these cases is it a question

7. From here to the end of this section, I condense and develop aspects of ideas proposed in Chapters One and Two of my book on Proust (*Marcel Proust: The Fictions of Life and of Art* [New York, 1965]).

of the Flaubertian excess of designation which removes the individual from the world and imprisons him in a rich but objectless imagination. Rather, the failure to recognize a place is experienced as a failure of all designation—most profoundly, as a failure of self-recognition. Such incidents melodramatize the Proustian narrator's peculiar *lack* of imagination: at certain moments he is unable, as it were, to domesticate the strangeness, the menacing otherness of the world by finding analogies between a present spectacle and a familiar personal past.

The opening pages of *A la Recherche* and the Balbec and Venice episodes could be thought of as a satire of Flaubert's literary dream. For that dream involved the chimerical project of eliminating recognition from cognition. And in the passages just mentioned, Proust simply places a kind of impersonal and objective consciousness in front of the world and shows the resulting chaos and panic. All knowledge, as Marcel at first painfully and finally exuberantly realizes, is self-knowledge, and the inability to project the self on the world makes for the perfect and terrifying realism of Marcel's perception of Venice as merely heaps of solid and liquid matter. Any workable or coherent knowledge necessarily involves making analogies, and we have seen how uncomfortable Flaubert felt with analogies. Not only can the second term of an analogy be provided only by the experience which constitutes a personal history; there can also never be an exact equivalence between the two terms. Even the most recent memory of an object which we bring to the object in order to identify it is bound to differ somewhat from our present perception. The most habitual identifications are, therefore, analogies, and the abundance of metaphors in *A la Recherche* rightly emphasizes the approximative nature of all knowledge and, conversely, the epistemological function of metaphor. Finally, the analogy itself is a new event. When Marcel does succeed in finding images that make objects familiar to him, the juxtaposition of the image and the object is a creation of the moment when it is made. The passage in which the narrator remembers comparing the "action" of the hawthorn's "blossoming" in the Combray church to the movement of a young girl's head (I, 85–6; I, 112) illustrates particularly well the inventiveness of metaphorical knowledge. Neither the hawthorns nor the image of the girl "disappears" in this act of recognition, but the activity of making a relation between the two creates something which did not exist before it was *expressed*.[8]

The full importance of such creative analogies, while they are the continuous achievement of the book we are reading, is not recognized by Marcel himself until late in his life. Indeed, his helplessness rather than his strength is emphasized most explicitly throughout a work which is of course a massive demonstration of his strength. Now the panicky sense of emptiness Marcel feels in Venice goes back to the *drame du coucher* at Combray. To be separated from his mother at night is for the child to be separated from himself: the message which Françoise agrees to bring to his mother appeases Marcel because it renews his own existence. An image of himself will penetrate his mother's attention as she reads his letter. And it is not only as a child that Marcel depends on his mother's readiness to provide an image of himself which serves as a guarantee of his identity. The sequence of events in the Venice incident makes it clear that what his mother has done in leaving for the station without him is, actually, to take him with her. She has, as it were, stolen his being, and he is reduced to the psychological anonymity of a "throbbing heart." As the narrator confesses at the end of *Le Temps retrouvé*, after describing how the guests at the Guermantes *matinée* laugh at his reference to himself as a young man: "I realised that the remark which had made them laugh was one that my mother, to whom I was always a child, might have made in speaking of

8. Georges Poulet has a good analysis of this passage (in terms of the internalization of a material object) in *Etudes sur le temps humain* (Paris, 1950), pp. 385–86.

me. From which I noticed that, when I wished to form an opinion of myself, I took the same point of view as she" (II, 1039; III, 931).

Marcel's relation to his mother suggests not only the historical origin of these crises, but also the reasons for it and, most profoundly, its convenience. "Combray" is not simply the record of the child's weakness and anguished dependence on his mother. The period the narrator describes is one of a great physical and intellectual awakening for Marcel. Not only does he feel himself on the threshold of discovering "the secret of Truth and Beauty" in art, nature, and history; he also experiences the exhilarating if undirected strength of his own body and, more specifically, of his sexual energies. Impressions of nature and of literature and the wish to find a peasant girl on the Méséglise way feed and intensify one another, ". . . and, my imagination drawing strength from contact with my sensuality, my sensuality expanding through all the realms of my imagination, my desire had no longer any bounds." But, crucially and mysteriously, this complex of immense energies becomes, to use the word in another sense, a debilitating complex. The peasant girl does not appear, Marcel can express his enthusiasm for nature only with an inarticulate "Zut, zut, zut, zut," and, deprived of other outlets and other kinds of expression, his energies are partially spent in what he imagines as the dangerous pleasures of masturbation. Enraged at the world for not satisfying his desires (he furiously strikes out at the trees in the Roussainville forest), he discovers the world as merely the "conventional framework," the unreal setting ("which from now onwards lost all its charm and significance") for desires which themselves are simply "the purely subjective, impotent, illusory creatures of my temperament." And masturbation seems to be experienced not so much as an expression of energy but rather as a fantasy-strategy to dissipate it: it is the "untrodden path which, I believed, might lead me to my death" and which Marcel sets out on "with the heroic scruples of a traveller setting forth for unknown climes, or of a desperate wretch hesitating on the verge of self-destruction" (I, 120–22; I, 156–59).

In a sense, when night comes Marcel *is* dead: the strength of the day is gone, and he is nothing more than a "throbbing heart" waiting for the kiss from his mother which will bring him back to life. What connection can there be between the exuberantly active boy of the afternoon and the helpless, defeated child at night? These alternating states of strength and weakness provide the first evidence the narrator remembers for his shocked view of time as discontinuous, spatial units of experience, and for his view of personality as a series of deaths and resurrections: "And so it was from the 'Guermantes way' that I learned to distinguish between these states which [reign] alternately in my mind, during certain periods, going so far as to divide every day between them, each one returning to dispossess the other with the regularity of a fever and ague: contiguous, and yet so foreign to one another, so devoid of means of communication, that I [can] no longer understand, or even picture to myself, in one state what I had desired or dreaded or even done in the other" (I, 140–41; I, 183).

The "Combray" section does not present these different states or activities—Marcel's enthusiasm, his masturbating, and his nightly anxiety—in any causal sequence. Indeed, the passage just quoted expresses the narrator's feeling that there are no connections between the states which frequently divide his life. He is tracing his view of the self as discontinuous back to his boyhood at Combray, but he says nothing to suggest that the sense of discontinuity hides certain transitions from one state to another. There is, however, a psychological logic in what happens at Combray, although it is never spelled out in the text. But I think it is implied in the nature of the different feelings and incidents which the narrator merely juxtaposes without providing any links to connect them. What he describes—and the pattern is similar to one I have described in Balzac—is an overpowering

sense of strength and energy followed by a loss of all strength
and energy. Or, to put it another way, we see a state of aggressive
desire toward the world followed by a state in which Marcel feels
defenseless and victimized by everything around him. The
energy turned on the world is turned back on himself, first of all
when he makes himself the object of desire in masturbation, and
in a more hallucinated version of this switch, when the world,
apparently dismissed as a dead, "conventional framework" unresponsive to Marcel's desires, suddenly comes alive in the evening
and threatens to overwhelm him with *its* hostile energies.

Masturbation could be thought of as a mediating stage for
Marcel between aggression and passivity. On the one hand, it is
a direct expense of energy; on the other hand, it contains the
punishment for this physical self-assertion by seeming to promise
death, to be the suicide of desire. It therefore satisfies desire while
controlling and atoning for it. And in Marcel that combination
seems particularly significant. It is as if he were unable to enjoy
desire or aggressiveness without feeling guilty about it, without
having to punish himself for it. The world is condemned with
precipitation for failing to produce objects to satisfy Marcel's desires; but this condemnation can perhaps be explained by the
effect it has of allowing Marcel to think of his desires themselves
as "impotent, illusory creatures of my temperament." The Venice
incident dramatizes the relation between aggression and helplessness: it is immediately after defying his mother and thinking with
feverish excitement of having sexual relations with the Baronne
de Putbus's chambermaid that Marcel can no longer even find
the energy to project enough of himself on the city so that he
could recognize it as Venice.

But what, specifically, is the sinfulness of desire? The answer,
I think, has to do with the individualizing nature of desire, that
is, with the fact that it separates Marcel from his mother, makes
him distinct from her. There is a guilt about individuality which
seems to be passed from his mother to Marcel: she herself attempts to erase all signs of her own personality after her mother's

death, as if anything purely self-expressive were a blasphemous violation of Marcel's grandmother's memory. And while artistic creation itself will come to be defined in *A la Recherche du temps perdu* as the expression of the most unique accent of the artist's personality, the narrator shares this view of individuality as sin. The "original sin" of the women we love, he remarks in *La Prisonnière*, is simply what makes them different from ourselves: ". . . even more than their misdeeds while we are in love with them, there are their misdeeds before we made their acquaintance, and first and foremost: their nature" (II, 483; III, 150–51).

The connection between sexual desire and the essence of personality is explicitly made in *La Prisonnière* and *La Fugitive*. The narrator emphasizes that in seeking to find out if Albertine had sexual relations with other women at the baths in Balbec, he is not asking "subordinate, immaterial questions, questions of detail," but is rather probing into "the uttermost depths" of her being (II, 745; III, 516). Marcel's detective-like investigations into Albertine's activities have led Jean-François Revel to insist that Proust sees no real mystery in other people's personalities, that what is unknowable in someone else's life in *A la Recherche* is simply his or her "schedule." [9] But such a judgment brings into the work notions of personality foreign to it. For Marcel, to get the schedule right, to satisfy "the painful, or wearying curiosity that I felt as to the places in which Albertine had stayed, as to what she might have been doing on a particular evening, her smiles, the expression in her eyes, the words that she had uttered, the kisses that she had received" (II, 649; III, 385)—all that *is* to penetrate another person's uniqueness, for the uniqueness consists in precisely those desires which do not have Marcel as their object.

9. *Sur Proust: Remarques sur "A la Recherche du temps perdu"* (Paris, 1960), p. 198. Marcel Muller echoes this idea: "Rather than an impression of a fundamental mystery of being, we have the impression of a lack of knowledge which could be remedied by some more information" (*Les Voix narratives dans La Recherche du Temps perdu* [Geneva, 1965], p. 128).

There is no reason to condemn such a view of individuality as trivial, for the only way we concretely experience other people's individuality may indeed be in our puzzled sense of their consciousness not being entirely occupied by the familiar image of ourselves. *Any* desire directed somewhere else (the loved one's sexual interest in other people is the most dramatic version of this) expresses a project for independence. It threatens the fantasy of a tranquil, really deathlike coincidence of being between two people in which each one merely receives, is wholly contained within, and sends back the image of the other. This is the security Marcel yearns for between himself and his mother and grandmother, and the two women seem to encourage this cult of love as self-sacrificial and yet all-devouring. To desire a peasant girl from Méséglise or the Baronne de Putbus's chambermaid is to *be* someone different from *maman*; and, perhaps most profoundly, desire is felt—with guilt—as dangerously aggressive because Marcel knows that in fact it is an aggression against those who would fix and limit his own being in their love. To immolate desire is to immolate the self; it is the payment he has to make in order not to escape from his mother's attention, in order to continue "receiving himself" from her.

And yet the temptation to be—which is the temptation of freedom—is painfully strong. Marcel yields to it with such intense excitement and such intense fright that his desire seems almost to have the magic power to destroy both the world and the self. What conquest could compare with that extraordinary assault on the universe which Marcel feels he is making the evening he tries to kiss Albertine in the hotel at Balbec? He approaches her room with "a strange feeling of absolute power"; the very idea of the world surviving his death becomes incredible, since ". . . it was it that was enclosed in me, in me whom it went a long way short of filling, in me, where, feeling that there was room to store so many other treasures, I flung contemptuously into a corner sky, sea and cliffs." Nothing could be more different from Marcel's usual complaint that the world is out of reach and impenetrable. The exhilaration of desire makes the world an insignificant, inadequate field for his infinitely expansive appetite for absorption:

> The sight of Albertine's bare throat, of those strangely vivid cheeks, had so intoxicated me (that is to say had placed the reality of the world for me no longer in nature, but in the torrent of my sensations which it was all I could do to keep within bounds), as to have destroyed the balance between the life, immense and indestructible, which circulated in my being, and the life of the universe, so puny in comparison. The sea, which was visible through the windows as well as the valley, the swelling breasts of the first of the Maineville cliffs, the sky in which the moon had not yet climbed to the zenith, all of these seemed less than a featherweight on my eyeballs, which between their lids I could feel dilated, resisting, ready to bear very different burdens, all the mountains of the world upon their fragile surface. Their orbit no longer found even the sphere of the horizon adequate to fill it. And everything that nature could have brought me of life would have seemed wretchedly meagre, the sigh of the waves far too short a sound to express the enormous aspiration that was surging in my breast.

At the time he remembers this incident, the narrator can of course exaggerate his intoxication; and this makes for a humorous contrast between Marcel's excitement and the deflating effect of the "precipitous, prolonged, shrill" sound when Albertine angrily rings the bell for help (I, 698–99; I, 933–34). But the feelings being remembered are no less important for lending themselves to a comic effect here. The intense exhilaration we find in this passage recurs, moreover, throughout the novel: it resembles Marcel's intellectual and sexual appetites at Combray, his excitement about meeting Madame de Guermantes, and his feverish need to possess the Baronne de Putbus's maid in Venice. There are, then, immensely powerful energies drawing Marcel out of himself. And they are the energies which define his self, which express his designs on the world and give to his history its personal shape.

Because he seems to condemn these passionate projects and desires as a betrayal of his mother, and because the resulting conflict over them increases their potency while limiting their frequency of expression, Marcel comes to fear them, without, however, renouncing the independent identity they create. If the loss of self is the punishment for desire—that is, for energetic designs on the world—some new form of self-assertion becomes necessary in order to protect Marcel from the consequences of self-assertion. The very extremity to which Marcel is reduced—his emptiness, his loss of memory, the discontinuity of being from which he suffers—authorizes the most thoroughgoing investigation of ways to construct and possess a self which could no longer be lost. The punishment, we might say, legitimizes the crime. Literature in *A la Recherche du temps perdu* is Marcel's indulgence in the "crime" of his own individuality as well as his subtle strategy for imprisoning others within the designs of his own desires. But in the enactment of what can easily be seen in Proust as an ungenerous solution to this problem of being, the project of imprisoning the self and the world in a document of ontological security is transformed into the courageous exercise of making the self as indefinite and indefinable as possible, and even of protecting the freedom of others.

We can easily see the continuity between the drastic self-depletions from which Marcel suffers and the narrator's ambivalent attitude toward "incomplete" art. The dream of art as a way of achieving a deathlike fixity of self in life, for example, has the appeal of promising a kind of sculptural organization of the self and the world into immutably intelligible patterns. To salvage the self from the dissipation it suffers at moments of passionate desire, Marcel, while he never really considers the renunciation of desire, is tempted by the possibility of satisfying desires by de-energizing them. A certain self-petrification would seem to be the compromise between an uninhibited appetitive attack on the world and the probably expiatory victimizing of a "throbbing heart" by a world hostilely different from the self. And the perspective of memory allows for just this sort of passionless reenactment of Marcel's desires, although, as I suggested earlier, it also permits a manipulating of the past for the sake of a richer future. In part, Proust's novel illustrates the truth of Sartre's claim that only in reflection can we posit affectivity for itself, that is, in terms of mental *states* which make for a psychology of the inert.[10] Cut off from the objects which inspired and defined them, Marcel's desires, so to speak, now have nowhere to go. They no longer "move" toward the world, but only around one another, creating those peculiar inner constellations which encourage the narrator to speak of mental life as if it were organized into clearly delimited conflicting states, and enacted as allegorical confrontations. Thus the narrator can at last live according to his desires, or, more exactly, *within* his desires. The retrospective expression of desire coincides with self-expression. Indeed, it belatedly constructs a self shaped by projects now transformed into abstractions. The psychology of states in *A la Recherche du temps perdu*, like the general laws about human behavior, allows Marcel to think of literature as the reassuring completion of life. Both are maneuvers for placing art in the privileged position of giving permanent forms and significance to experience; as a distiller of psychological essences, the narrator's work defines and closes his life.

But Marcel discovers another possibility of self-identification (as well as of contact with the world), a possibility which allows for a richly incomplete life and a richly incomplete work. Marcel's jealousy can provide a first illustration of how this discovery is made. In *La Fugitive*, the narrator speaks of a certain "com-

10. "La Transcendance de l'ego," *Recherches philosophiques*, VI (1936–37), 102–3.

pensation" in the suffering which the lies of "insensitive and inferior women" inflict on sensitive and intellectual men:

> And so these men feel that they are being betrayed without quite knowing why. Wherefore the mediocre woman with whom we were surprised to see them fall in love enriches the universe for them far more than an intelligent woman would have done. Behind each of her words, they feel that a lie is lurking, behind each house to which she says that she has gone, another house, behind each action, each person, another action, another person. Doubtless they do not know what or whom, have not the energy, would not perhaps find it possible to discover. A lying woman, by an extremely simple trick, can beguile, without taking the trouble to change her method, any number of people, and, what is more, the very person who ought to have discovered the trick. All this creates, in front of the sensitive and intelligent man, a universe all in depths which his jealousy would fain plumb and which is not without interest to his intelligence. (II, 814–15; III, 616–17)

Any statement recognized or felt as a lie evokes the possibly truthful statements to which it could be compared. But if the lover cannot fix on any one house or action or person as the reality behind the lie, the lie itself can never be eliminated from the attempt to know the truth. The fictive version of her behavior proposed by Albertine or Odette becomes the center around which Marcel and Swann organize a group of conjectures. The pain of not being able to eliminate that center—it is necessary to inspire the different conjectures whose greater or lesser probability it also helps to determine—is somewhat "compensated" for by the variety and depth which the lover's searching and unsatisfied imagination gives to the world. The need for truth stimulates the novelistic impulse, and the impossibility of truth makes of experience an infinitely expandable novel. The narrator explicitly makes the connection between his jealousy and his art in Le Temps retrouvé. The former is a good recruiter when there is a gap in the novelist's picture; if his jealousy of a woman to whom he has now become indifferent is momentarily reawakened, his frantic imagination supplies the material he needed for his work: "The brushes, drunk with infuriated love, paint and paint!" (II, 1028; III, 916–17)

The psychological crises of emptiness in *A la Recherche* are moments when Marcel can no longer relate one image to another, when he cannot find a "second term." What saves him is not a sudden ability to describe reality accurately, but rather the discovery of *other* phenomena to which present phenomena can be compared and thereby made intelligible. As it has often been pointed out, affirmations of joy in *A la Recherche du temps perdu* generally occur in the context of occasions which give birth to analogies in Marcel's imagination. Even the torture of jealousy, as we have just seen, is alleviated by the pleasure of imagining relationships between various "truths" and the lies which distort them. The disappointments of going into society are somewhat compensated for by the historical allusiveness of the aristocracy's names. The garrulous and vain Duc de Guermantes holds Marcel's attention by partially disappearing from Marcel's field of vision: he merges into his family's past, into a harmonious set of associations among the names of different regions in France and among different periods of time. And Marcel's interest at the Verdurins' home on the Quai Conti in Paris is awakened only when Brichot tells him that the room they are in can give him an idea of the Verdurins' drawing room twenty-five years ago in the Rue Montalivet. "A certain common air of family life, a permanent identity" which Brichot sees between the Quai Conti and the Rue Montalivet, and which Marcel himself recognizes between the Quai Conti and the drawing room at La Raspelière, gives to the present room "a sort of profundity," a "patina" ("velouté") which things acquire when their ["spiritual counterpart"] has been added to them. And that spiritual counterpart is an image from the past which helps to dematerialize the present by relocating it in the "general element" it shares with another place and another time (II, 577–79; III, 284–86).

Involuntary memories have a similar function. Numerous commentators have rightly emphasized their importance in *A la Recherche du temps perdu*, but it seems to me that the crucial role they play in the novel derives from what most of Proust's readers have been unwilling to admit: their extremely modest significance. Involuntary memory is a brief coincidence between a present moment and a past one: a sensation now (such as the taste of the *madeleine*) accidentally awakens the full sensory memory of a past experience, and, "for the duration of a lightning flash," Marcel appears to exist "between" the present and the past, that is, in the similarity between the two—a similarity which is actually an abstraction from experience but which the senses fleetingly live (II, 996; III, 872). Now these memories *create* nothing. The extratemporal essence which the narrator claims they disengage from a present sensation and a past sensation may not have been previously felt as such, but it is nonetheless a truth about Marcel's *history* of sensations and in itself it contains nothing to inspire a future. In this respect, as we shall presently see more clearly, involuntary memory is unlike metaphor, although, as Robert Brasillach pointed out, Marcel's temporal illusion when he tastes the *madeleine* does resemble the optical illusions which are the metaphors of Elstir's painting.[11] We could perhaps say that involuntary memory is a kind of metaphor *of* metaphor: it provides a sensory analogy for the contiguity and conjoining of two separate terms which characterize metaphor.

The greatest interest of the so-called essences which involuntary memories reveal is that they make impossible any definitive self-formulations. The napkin with which Marcel wipes his mouth in the Guermantes library, having "precisely the same sort of starchy stiffness as the towel with which I had had so much trouble drying myself before the window the first day of my stay at Balbec," evokes a vision of "azure blue," spreads out, "in its various folds and creases, like a peacock's tail, the plumage of a green and blue ocean. And I drew enjoyment, not only from

11. *Portraits* (Paris, 1935), pp. 99 and 113.

those colours, but from a whole moment of my life which had brought them into being and had no doubt been an aspiration toward them, but which perhaps some feeling of fatigue or sadness had prevented me from enjoying at Balbec and which now, pure and disembodied, freed from all the imperfections of objective perception, filled me with joy" (II, 993; III, 868–69). This remark from Le Temps retrouvé implies nothing less than a reorganization of the hierarchy of interests and projects by which we rationally, and most habitually, recognize and define ourselves. It would be banal merely to point out that we are never completely aware of all our interests in any given situation. But, first of all, involuntary memory is a particularly powerful proof of this. Furthermore, Marcel's "return" to Balbec in the Guermantes library undermines the anxiety he felt at the time. It suggests that at least as strong as his fears was an aspiration toward certain colors, a thirst for sensation which complicates his arrival at Balbec by making it impossible for us—and for him—to settle on any one characterization of his feelings. Proust's exceptionally strong sensuality is revealed in a more continuously explicit way in Jean Santeuil, where the narrator insists over and over again on a richly cozy contentment of the senses, especially in nature and in scenes of quiet domesticity. We find this in A la Recherche, especially in the "Combray" section, but the narrator is now less interested in detailing the joys of the senses than in profiting from the psychological and literary implications of occasions which reconfirm his sensuality. Involuntary memory, while it appears to offer evidence of "an individual, identical and permanent self" and thus appeases Marcel's fear of psychological discontinuity (II, 800; III, 594), also dislocates self-definitions by illustrating how incomplete they always are.

The importance of this is somewhat obscured by the narrator's emphatic distinctions between loss of self and self-possession; but the strategies for self-possession are by no means strategies for permanent self-immobilizations. An involuntary memory "returns" Marcel to himself at the same time that it demolishes the

coherent views of his past which, in spite of the crises in which
he seems to lose his past, he of course possesses all the time in
his voluntary or intellectual memory. The taste of the *madeleine*
and the sensations in the Guermantes library are trivial and tentative self-possessions, and this is exactly why they point the way
to a literature of inventive autobiography. The essence liberated
by an involuntary memory is, therefore, first of all personal: it
is not in things, but in the particular analogies or identities which
Marcel's sensory apparatus establishes among sensations. And it is
in no sense the essence of his personality; it is, instead, just the
essence of a particular relation in his history. Finally, by relocating or at least raising doubts about what was most important to
him at a past moment, Marcel's involuntary memories legitimize
an open-ended view of personality which informs the psychologically re-creative activity of writing *A la Recherche du temps
perdu.*

"Informs" in what way, exactly? How is the view of the self
which I find implicit in Marcel's involuntary memories expressed
and confirmed by style and novelistic structure in *A la Recherche?*
If what the narrator calls the ["fundamental notes"] of personality (III, 626) is inadequately rendered in the language we
ordinarily use in our attempts to be recognized by others as belonging to a life already familiar to them, he must find a language which contains his most personal accent without, however,
sacrificing the signs by which that accent may be communicated
to others. The solution to this problem depends on the literary
exploitation of what we might call experimental knowledge
through self-disguises. Now the disguises of personality have both
a positive and a negative value in *A la Recherche*. The narrator
insists so often on the pain caused by such disguises that he
somewhat obscures his own indulgence in a liberating art of disguise. Sexuality—especially homosexuality—is presented in the
novel as the field in which the Proustian ["creatures of flight"]
can most effectively conceal their personalities by "dressing" them
in desires inconceivable to the pursuing and possessive lover (II,

441; III, 93). Marcel cannot understand the "play" of Albertine's lesbianism because he fails to imagine what "role" she plays in it. Her love of women is an impenetrable disguise of his own love of women; she has his desires, but since she is a woman he cannot recognize himself in them. The connection between complicated sexual roles and the wilful elusiveness of personality is most strikingly dramatized in the scene at Rachel's theater in *Le Côté de Guermantes*. Rachel's flirtation with a young male dancer who reminds her of another woman and to whom she speaks of having "a wonderful time" with him "and a girl I know" plunges Saint-Loup's jealous imagination into a labyrinth of psychological disguises. Images of desire become inextricably embroiled in a costume play in which the man would presumably be playing the role of a woman for Rachel or her friend, or for both, and they might be taking the role of a man with a man looking like a woman. (See I, 841–44; II, 177–80.) Finally, the most baroque costumes of sexual desire are evoked in the letter Charlus accidentally reads from the lesbian actress Léa to Morel. In it Léa uses an expression about Morel which Charlus has always associated with homosexuality ("'. . . Toi tu en es au moins, etc.'"), but homosexuality here seems to mean that Morel has "the same taste as certain women for other women." Poor Charlus finds himself confronted with "the sudden inadequacy of a definition," and the letter sets up an unsolvable problem for the baron's imagination: by what images and identifications can the homosexual man calm his jealousy of another homosexual man who finds his pleasure with lesbians? "Where" is Morel in such pleasures? What is it like to be a man being treated like a woman who desires women acting like men? (II, 529–30; III, 214–15)[12]

Such are the disguises of escape from others, disguises which, as we see in Rachel's treatment of Saint-Loup, can be sadistically adopted in order to make the lover suffer from a spectacularly mysterious assertion of otherness. But in the literary work which

12. For a longer discussion of these complicated roles, see my book, *Marcel Proust: The Fictions of Life and of Art*, pp. 63–75.

devotes so much space to the anguished documentation of this
sinister art of self-concealment, the narrator discovers other techniques of self-diffusion, techniques which transform the accidental and infrequent "airing" of personality which involuntary
memory provides into a willed and continuous process of self-
renewal. I'm thinking mainly of the therapeutical diffusiveness
of metaphorical representation in art. Analogy in *A la Recherche*
is often humorous. This is especially evident when the narrator
compares some prosaic aspect of his past to an illustrious historical
event. Françoise's passionate and fearful commentary of Léonie's
slightest change of mood, of the way she gets up in the morning
or has a meal, reminds the narrator of the nobility's anxious at-
tentiveness to almost imperceptible signs of favor or disfavor in
Louis XIV (I, 90–91; I, 118–19). The cruelty with which
Françoise strangles the chickens she serves to Marcel's family at
Combray changes the boy's view of her moral merits and makes
him think of all the brutality hidden behind the official piety
with which royal figures from the past are represented to us: "I
began gradually to realise that Françoise's kindness, her compunc-
tion, the sum total of her virtues concealed many of those back-
kitchen tragedies, just as history reveals to us that the reigns of
the kings and queens who are portrayed as kneeling with clasped
hands in the windows of churches, were stained by oppression
and bloodshed" (I, 93; I, 122). Finally, the water lily ceaselessly
carried from one bank of the Vivonne to the other by the water's
currents fascinates Marcel, who watches it thinking of the
"strange, ineluctable, fatal daily round" in the habits of "certain
victims of neurasthenia," and then expands his analogy to include an illustrious literary precedent which, by a final humorous
twist, brings him back to his own staring at the "possessed" plant:
"Such as these [the victims of neurasthenia] was the water-lily,
and also like one of those wretches whose peculiar torments, repeated indefinitely throughout eternity, aroused the curiosity of
Dante, who would have inquired of them at greater length and
in fuller detail from the victims themselves, had not Virgil, strid-

ing on ahead, obliged him to hasten after him at full speed, as I must hasten after my parents" (I, 129–30; I, 167–68).

On the one hand, such analogies make fun of Françoise, Léonie, and Marcel; they give a mock-heroic importance to the most unremarkable events or habits in their lives. But they also trivialize life at Versailles and Dante's trip through hell. From both points of view, the uniqueness of each element in the metaphor is undermined by its availability for an unexpected comparison. The analogies clarify, but they are also reductive, and they easily serve intentions of mockery. Historical repetition may be instructive, but it also parodies individuality. Or, perhaps more exactly, it makes us skeptical about or indifferent to individuality since the quality which two incidents have in common is detached from the historical existence of each incident. Life at Versailles is an episodic illustration of a *type* of life reincarnated in a scene from French provincial life at the end of the nineteenth century.

Such historical continuities are what the narrator finds, or invents, as he writes the story of his own life. But the repetitions of autobiography are of course *self*-repetitions. And in the purely verbal organization of a literary work, the chronological sequences of events can be thought of as "spatialized" in constellations of literary metaphors. From his perspective of re-creative memories, the narrator constantly anticipates future events by "trying them out" metaphorically before they happen. Poulet has spoken of a "reciprocal intelligibility" among originally distinct episodes in Marcel's life; analogies establish patterns that bring together apparently isolated moments.[13] Each aspect of life Marcel has encountered becomes an inner resource for understanding other aspects of life; images that are first used to describe certain incidents may become later on real incidents in Marcel's life. Military tactics, for example, are used metaphorically to describe Marcel's servants' shrewd strategies for dealing with his character

13. *L'Espace proustien* (Paris, 1963), p. 133. From here to the end of this paragraph, I have used a passage from *Marcel Proust: The Fictions of Life and of Art*, pp. 236–37.

before we see Marcel at Doncières. But with Saint-Loup and his
friends at Doncières, it is military strategy itself that Marcel has
to understand with the aid of other analogies (provided, for example, by painting and surgery). Finally, the art with which Marcel
becomes familiar at Doncières will be useful later on in helping
him to understand the psychology of his pursuit of Albertine.
Works of art help him to appreciate aristocratic genealogies; certain observations of nature provide a language in which to describe both Madame de Guermantes's beauty and the chance
meeting between Jupien and Charlus; and the discontinuities in
Marcel's own memory make intelligible the forgetfulness of those
people who, at the last Guermantes *matinée*, think that Bloch
has always been received in the highest society or praise a man
they detested twenty years before during the Dreyfus Affair.
These analogies both evoke what has already been written and
point to what is yet to be written. As Georges Piroué has said,
the memory of the work tends to be substituted for direct experience of the world; the narrator's book provides him with the
comparisons he needs to finish the book.[14]

In returning to these remarks made in my book-length study of
Proust, I now find the patterns of metaphorical *renvois* in *A la
Recherche* interesting above all for their psychologically disinte-
grating and therefore psychologically creative consequences. This
network of metaphorical correspondences does give to the work
what at first appears to be a self-contained unity. But, more originally, they also have the effect of drawing us away from any
fixed *center* of the self from which all its images might proceed.
It has often been said that the narrator has little personality compared to the other characters of *A la Recherche*. And this is
usually meant as an adverse judgment of the novel. As B. G.
Rogers puts it: ". . . the absence of a real hero in Marcel is hard
to reconcile with the massive emotional and spiritual emphasis
placed upon him in *Le Temps retrouvé*."[15] This impression is

14. *Proust et la musique du devenir* (Paris, 1960), p. 256.
15. *Proust's Narrative Techniques* (Geneva, 1965), p. 191.

particularly interesting in view of the fact that no reader can be unaware of the psychological repetitiveness in *A la Recherche du temps perdu*. And the narrator does tell us enough about himself so that we easily recognize the psychological patterns repeated throughout the novel as belonging to *his* personality. It is nonetheless true that he tends to disappear as the visible and sharply defined source of those patterns. But I take this to be the sign of the narrator's most impressive achievement. The vagueness of Marcel as the center of his world can be the basis of a reproach only if we impose on the work notions of what it means "to have personality" which the work is engaged in discarding. I think that even a critic as astute as Robert Champigny fails to realize this when he writes that ". . . the man of Proust can create, but cannot create himself"; as Roger Shattuck has appropriately answered, the narrator's role in *A la Recherche du temps perdu* is one of constant self-renewal.[16] What we might call the narrator's scattering of self is the technique of an often humorous and always liberating displacement of his most crippling fantasies. There is no one version of these fantasies more authoritative than other versions, and the self therefore has the freedom of *being* the variety of its disguises.

The various uses of metaphor in *A la Recherche* have, fundamentally, the function of entertaining as many interpretive extensions of experience as possible. There is, for example, a certain type of social life which we recognize as the narrator's particular sense of society. The continuities among different social images in the novel are often astonishingly transparent. The Verdurin receptions repeat details from the Guermantes receptions. La Patronne, like Oriane, boasts of the paintings Elstir did for her. An annoyance with illness and death because they spoil dinner

16. Champigny, "Temps et reconnaissance chez Proust et quelques philosophes," *PMLA*, LXXIII (March 1958), 131; and Shattuck, *Proust's Binoculars/A Study of Memory, Time, and Recognition in "A la Recherche du temps perdu"* (New York, 1963), p. 152.

parties and dances is repeated in progressively more shocking (and more improbable) versions: in the Duc de Guermantes's refusal to be told that his cousin is dead at the end of *Le Côté de Guermantes*; in Monsieur Verdurin insisting, one day at La Raspelière, that no one speak of Dechambre's death to Madame Verdurin; and in the latter's nervy denial—during the party at the Quai Conti in Paris—that she feels any sorrow over the Princesse Sherbatoff's death. We might say either that the narrator describes three different social events in a surprisingly similar manner, or that he finds impressively different disguises for a rather simple and bitter view of social life. But the various disguises of that view make it difficult to fix the exact quality of the pessimism. There is a greater tolerance of emotional callousness in the presentation of Oriane's inability to decide if she should give up her parties after Swann tells her he is going to die than in the image of Madame Verdurin's defiant advertising of her indifference to the princess's death. The second incident enacts a pessimistic view of social life in a manner more likely to shock the narrator out of social life. Each repetition of a radical skepticism about human feeling allows for different consequences, broadens or narrows the range of possible response to an essentially unchanged but nonetheless flexible conviction.

Furthermore, the world Marcel is presumably remembering strikes us in many respects as a projection of his own psychology and history. In the process of remembering an impenetrable world, and while documenting with somber lucidity the hopelessness of seeking to know the lives of others, Marcel has both illustrated his thesis and partially refuted it by now drawing the world of his past into the orbit of a single, recognizably continuous personality: his own. What might be called the creative space between the narrator and the world he describes—the actual work of self-dramatization which Balzac and Stendhal hide by suggesting that the decisions of writing are decisions of point of view toward a world already there—becomes a principal object of our attention in *A la Recherche du temps perdu*. The novel provokes the drama of our own unsettled feelings about the exact sense in which these people and events belong to Marcel's past. And they seem to "belong" to *him* in an allegorical sense. The narrator appears to be illustrating, more or less transparently and in spite of his explicit claims that he is reporting on the real world of his past, the processes by which a novelist invents a world of fiction and, more specifically, the degree of differentiation possible within a group of self-projective images.

The very inability to differentiate others from the self is dramatized within the novel as the anguish of love, at the same time that it defines the limits of characterization in a novel about love. Albertine is largely an unembodied name. She does have a distinct physical presence, and she is drawn clearly enough so that we certainly do not confuse her with Gilberte or Madame de Guermantes. But much of her personality is literally nothing but Marcel's jealous fantasies about her. As a character, she is fascinatingly unrealized; and we do not feel that Proust has failed in *his* attempt to make her come alive for us, but rather that the very vagueness of her image is necessary to authenticate Marcel's anguished jealousy. She is, as it were, a successful creation because she fails to become a definite character. By being so embroiled in Marcel's tortured doubts about her real personality, Albertine dramatizes an abortive attempt to disguise novelistic conjecture as a clear and fixed image of the external world.

Saint-Loup and Madame de Guermantes, on the other hand, are so sharply individualized that they do seem to exist, so to speak, independently of the narrator's inventiveness. The handsome, gregarious, self-consciously intellectual Saint-Loup provides an apparently complete temperamental contrast to Marcel. But his love for Rachel parallels Marcel's possessively jealous love for Albertine; and, less obviously but even more revealingly, Saint-Loup's "shift" to homosexuality in *Le Temps retrouvé* is part of that peculiar psychological and social return to self-images which announces the narrator's imminent discovery of his literary vocation as one of self-exploration. Even Oriane seems partly a projection of Marcel. Her anxious reluctance (common to all the Guermantes) to let her guests leave at the end of a party reminds us of Marcel's terror at being separated from his mother. The fear of being alone, of an inner emptiness or lack of personality in solitude, is shared by the duchess, Charlus, and Marcel. But with Charlus and especially with Oriane, the psychological parallel with Marcel may strike us as less important than the effectiveness of a *social* comment. Because of their idle lives, the Guermantes's inner richness is "unemployed"; it seeks an outlet "in a sort of fugitive effusion, all the more [nervously excited,]" which, while it is part of their charm, also expresses the sterility of their lives (I, 1105; II, 545). The duchess's anxious self-expense at the end of an evening is, then, a characteristic which both reminds us of the hypersensitive child at Combray and also provides a nicely condensed image of the aristocracy's unproductivity. Since the life of the *salon* fails to produce anything in which the Guermantes might continuously recognize and identify themselves, they hold on to the guests in whom they find temporary and intermittent guarantees of their own being. They are nowhere except in their public's appreciation.

But simply by summarizing Proustian social life in these terms, we find ourselves once again in the vocabulary of Marcel's particular psychology. The assumption that there is no purely inner evidence of personality, the need to arrange and control the world so that it gives a reliable and permanent assurance of the self's existence, and the inability to imagine any interesting life unless this condition is fulfilled: the pattern is of course Marcel's, and the brilliant social satire depends partly on our willingness to believe that his own anxieties about the self provide adequate criteria for judging the value of any form of social life. Indeed, the assumptions which we find so idiosyncratic and even pathological in "Combray" are sufficiently disguised, take into account enough variety of experience in *Le Côté de Guermantes* so that they appear to be intelligent conclusions about life rather than the given limitations with which Marcel approaches life. Every incident and every character in *A la Recherche* could be placed on a range of self-projection, a range extending from the most transparent versions of Marcel's psychology to those complexly particularized images in which allegory and observation appear to coincide. The world of Marcel's past becomes, in the process of writing, a fiction dramatizing Marcel himself, but the very self-dramatization is such a liberal and inclusive one that it strikes us as a viable or livable framework in which to place the world.

Viable, and therefore capable of development. What Marcel gives us is by no means a final, limiting version of experience. The fact that in describing the world he shapes it into an almost allegorical reflection of his own imagination diminishes the constraints of reality on his life. Superficially, this psychological repetitiousness in his work would seem to testify to the narrowness of his responses. More profoundly, by illustrating the power of his self-projections, it subverts the impoverishing authority of reality in whatever he says. No fact is strong enough to expel Marcel's fantasies from his report of it, which means that nothing in his life, short of death, can prevent him from using fact for a continuous revision of fantasy. He is as free as his imagination can make him precisely because, when he is most faithful to his experience, he has no illusion of being able to make statements about reality from which his imagination would be absent. The inconclusiveness of "knowledge" allows for the theoretically limitless use of the world as a testing-ground for fictions.

Flaubert's superstition of the real naturally led him to a process of constant deletion in his writing: how could he ever be sure that each sentence or each metaphor was not saying too much about reality, and therefore violating it? Proust, on the other hand, can add endlessly to his work, for it is as if he discovered, through his narrator's self-re-creative memory, that even the most oppressively narrow experience can be interpreted into a constantly open-ended view of the world. And there is nothing naïve in this. Objects and other people are present; they impinge on Marcel's consciousness and they make him suffer. But in the process of admitting his inability to possess and control them, he finds that the barrier of his subjectivity gives him another kind of power: the power to invent and revise the significance of events and, by the excesses of experimental revision, to coerce reality into the field of his desires. Furthermore, nothing in the novel has to "stand for" reality in order for the operations of fiction to be both meaningful and disciplined. The astonishing magnetism which draws the most diversified experience into an expanding but always recognizable individual psychology is an adequate exposure of Marcel's massive fictionalizing of his past. His fantasies can be measured and checked by their own history within the work. An unqualified commitment to fiction creates a kind of hierarchy of fictional viability, the standards which both control and encourage the self-transcending inspirations of fiction in art and in life.

Repetition in *A la Recherche* is therefore a mode of freedom. And while the freedom which the narrator enjoys throughout his work is self-creative, it also coincides with a kind of impersonality. The narrator's metaphorical style allows him to repeat himself at the same time that it raises the contents of self-definitions above any one embodiment of them. "In anyone we love," the narrator writes in *Le Temps retrouvé*, "there is always present some dream that we cannot always discern but which we constantly seek to attain. It was my faith in Bergotte and Swann which had made me love Gilberte, just as it was my belief in Gilbert the Bad which had made me love Mme de Guermantes. And what a wide expanse of unfathomable ocean was set apart in my love for Albertine, painful, jealous and individual though that love was! Moreover, just on account of this individual quality which we pursue with such eagerness, our love for someone else is already somewhat of an aberration." Our loves are most deeply characterized by a "persistent, unconscious dream" which seeks to incarnate itself in various persons (II, 972; III, 839–40). The dream is a specific type of desire; *it expresses an individuality more general than individuals.* And that individuality is what the Proustian narrator calls an "essence"; it belongs to "the world of differences" which only art reveals (II, 572; III, 277).

Gilles Deleuze has brilliantly analyzed the Proustian notion of essences. An essence revealed in art is "a difference, the ultimate and absolute Difference." As in Leibniz, essences in *A la Recherche* "are veritable monads, each one being defined by the point of view from which it expresses the world, each point of view itself referring to an ultimate quality within the monad." Most important, the world thus expressed "does not exist outside of the subject which expresses it, but it is expressed as the essence, not of the subject itself, but of Being, or of the region of Being which is revealed to the subject." [17] This is the "lost country" which the artist does not remember but with which he nonetheless remains unconsciously in harmony; and ". . . he is wild with joy when he is singing the airs of his native land . . . ," when his work renders "externally visible in the colours of the spectrum that intimate composition of those worlds which we call individual persons and which, without the aid of art, we should never know" (II, 559; III, 257–58).

In spite of a certain ambiguity at the end of this passage, it seems probable that what Marcel means by the "lost country" of Vinteuil's music is not exactly equivalent to Vinteuil's personal existence. The individuality of a point of view embodied in but not dependent on the existence of an individual person: this is what the narrator comes to recognize as the source of the pleasure he experiences in front of great art. And this identification of the absolutely individual with a region of Being transcending individuals saves the Proustian narrator from the despair of feeling that language can never communicate the "fundamental notes" of an artist's personality. By distinguishing between individuality and what we ordinarily think of as subjectivity, he can entrust the expression of individuality to a system of communication in which meanings are always *shared* meanings. Only an esthetic of

17. *Marcel Proust et les signes* (Paris, 1964), pp. 36–38.

the ineffably personal rejects words because of their inescapably generalizing nature. Nothing could be further from the kind of personality which *A la Recherche du temps perdu* seeks to express. Its austere drama consists in the narrator's effort to *abstract* an individual style from a life in which style is constantly threatened by the obsessions of a particular existence.

The narrative texture of *A la Recherche* is open-endedly metaphorical, which is one of the ways in which it differs most strikingly from *Jean Santeuil*. Metaphor in *Jean Santeuil* is ornamental and psychologically distracting. In a sense, it is a far more "literary" or "written" work than *A la Recherche*. It has an uninteresting stylistic complexity which makes each of its sections a self-contained, carefully wrought—overwrought—"piece." Proust could not, I think, have changed the intrinsic discontinuity of *Jean Santeuil* by providing more links from one episode to another; to make smoother transitions would not have changed the underlying conception of style as an exercise of verbally enshrining disconnected experience. As a result of this conception, incidents in *Jean Santeuil* often have a kind of depth which is largely eliminated from the later work. In *A la Recherche*, on the one hand, metaphors enrich specific incidents without completely "covering" them; on the other hand, the freedom of the metaphors themselves is protected by their extensions into other parts of the novel, by their being containers always larger than whatever they contain at any given moment. There is no network of multiple interpretations in *Jean Santeuil*, and, consequently, we frequently *see through* episodes to a single, definite, and limiting significance. We may, for example, feel that Jean's overwhelmed reaction at the discovery that Charlotte is willing to give him certain erotic satisfactions is intelligible only if we think of the scene as a mask for an unexpected homosexual encounter.[18] There is nothing in Proust's treatment of the scene which lifts it above the peculiarity of its literal detail. As far as "content" goes, *A la Recherche* has equally peculiar episodes. But the style

18. See *Jean Santeuil*, 3 vols. (Paris, 1952), III, 256–62.

now has a centrifugal energy which prevents us from considering such content as the transparent sign of something unsaid, of a hidden reality. Incidents no longer extend "behind" themselves into the author's veiled psychology; instead, they are now coerced by metaphor into extensions leading to other metaphorical inventions throughout the novel. They are, as it were, horizontally rather than vertically transcendent. The significance of each passage is limited only by the amount of novelistic space which the narrator will have the time to fill in the process of self-enlargement which is his literary vocation.

Literature in Proust's world does involve a certain moving away from life. The image of the writer sealed up in his cork-lined room is a dramatic enough metaphor for that removal. But the narrator in his hermetic seclusion reveals the mechanisms of self-removal as operative throughout his life. As a result, we see the establishment of esthetic distances as the most creative and liberating activities within *all* life's occasions. To be the artist of one's life involves the possibility of living within styles rather than within obsessions—that is, the possibility of repeating ourselves in an entertaining variety of performances rather than in the stultifying monotony of fantasies which break through each play of the self to be revealed as the boring "truth" of the self. A profound commitment to disguise (to what might even be labeled duplicity in an ethos of sincerity) is therefore perhaps essential for an exuberantly expansive self. *A la Recherche du temps perdu* is certainly a novel about art, but it is not—as *Madame Bovary* is—a novel about the impossible distance between art and life; it is rather an inventory of techniques which make for a highly artful life.

Self-re-creation in Proust has two boundaries beyond which it ceases to work in the manner I have been describing, boundaries which help to define a hierarchy of psychological and moral values. On the one side, there are the thin, transparent surfaces of *Les Plaisirs et les jours* and *Jean Santeuil*. Narrative drama in these early efforts collapses under psychological pressures (for example, homosexuality and snobbery) which Proust seems to find more compelling than the stories which weakly mediate them. On the other side, there are the general laws, which merely sublimate those pressures by feebly mediating them as abstract universalities. The laws provide final conclusions about versions of experience we may find more interesting if we think of them as tentative. The narrator's maxims encourage us to think of his omniscience as that of the traditional realistic novelist: it is as if, in spite of all he has demonstrated to the contrary, the artist could confirm our ability to know the real with godlike objectivity. The general laws in Proust illustrate his sympathy with the Balzacian and Flaubertian impulse to deny novelistic processes as our only form of knowledge—that is, to use novelistic fiction as a way of promoting the belief that our perceptions of reality can go beyond the fictional. The laws are the Proustian equivalent of the "Vulcan-like craftsmanship" which we saw the narrator complaining about in Wagner. They obscure the incompleteness of his work, they deny its experimental nature. Their axiomatic finality suggests an ideal of art as vindicating the hope that reality is knowable and intelligible, and an image of the artist as the carrier of reality's "message" to other men—an ideal which Proust himself, in bearing witness to its disintegration in nineteenth-century art, was one of the first to expose as vainly nostalgic.

The proliferation of the general laws in the later volumes of *A la Recherche* is the touching evidence of Proust's vulnerability, as the time for his life and for his work drew to a close, to the non-Proustian ideal of finality. It is as if the effort to develop techniques to keep art and life permanently incomplete lost some of its energy as he felt the end of his life approach—as if the imminence of death intensified the nostalgia for finalizing life (for making its meaning definitive) before it could be overtaken by the only unattackable end we know. But within the self-limiting boundaries of both the general laws and reductive psychological depths is the major enterprise which Proust's narrator undertakes: that of always postponing all conclusions in order to welcome each moment of experience as an occasion for trying out new versions of the self and of the world. Literature in *A la Recherche* is the activity of moving *toward* a finished literary work. At the end of *Le Temps retrouvé*, we can therefore feel that the narrator has in fact already written the work he has just outlined, and yet we can perhaps also agree with Germaine Brée's contention that only now is the narrator ready to begin that work.[19] For nothing in what we have read *realizes* the narrator's literary ambitions, and everything that we have read suggests that what he might have gone on to write would have continued to illustrate the self's admirable talent for diversifying and multiplying its fictions. The inconclusiveness of *A la Recherche du temps perdu* is the narrator's—and Proust's—courageous gamble on the quality of life which this refusal to be defined and limited by the "lost time" of our past can produce.

19. See *Du Temps perdu au temps retrouvé: Introduction à l'œuvre de Marcel Proust*, in *Etudes françaises*, XLIV (Paris, 1950), 23–33.

V

TOWARD AN ESTHETIC
OF DISAPPEARANCE?

EPILOGUE AND PRELUDE

The Balzacian strategies of containment in *Le Lys dans la vallée* depend on a faith in both the reflecting and the creative powers of language. The word makes manifest psychic energies which threaten the stability of the self and of society. The drama of *Le Lys* consists in Félix and Henriette's attempt to recompose and tame those energies by imaginatively working on the language which expresses them. Their defeated hope is that their verbal and floral compositions will inspire milder passions, and the analogous—also defeated—hope implicit in Balzac's way of organizing novelistic material is that a tightly structured fiction will impose its order on (and therefore "convert") the devouring appetites which are the subject of that fiction. The failure of this experiment testifies to the strength of Balzac's realistic credo: because language corresponds so closely to a reality independent of it, the use of language accomplishes little more than another realization of the dynamic energies which are its model. Balzac's very desire to remain faithful to a given model (contemporary French society) seems to create in the novelist a disposition in which the self and the world are explored as fatalities.

Balzacian realism is fatalistic and tautological. It is, theoretically, an unnecessary repetition of life, just as the story, in a sense, is an unnecessary illustration of the exposition. In spite of its impressive range of illustration, the meanings and *dénouements* of *La Comédie humaine* are contained in the beginnings which the stories of *La Comédie humaine* somewhat superfluously elaborate. The Balzacian narrator disgresses, but his digressions lead us nowhere; contrary to what Proust complained about in Balzac,[1] it could be said—the superficially wayward writing notwithstanding—that the apparent irrelevancies are quickly reabsorbed into a centripetal movement which unfailingly unifies all material around the themes (in the self and in society) which inspire and never cease to control their novelistic demonstration.

This centripetal movement is much more effectively undermined by the narrator's casually ironic comments in *La Chartreuse de Parme*. Stendhal's dramatic metaphors polarize life into the antagonistic but complementary extremes of happiness and social repressiveness. But the development of these metaphors provides multiple occasions for a partial transcendence of the restrictive theme. The elusive, qualifying voice of the Stendhalian narrator can, happily, not be contained within the simple and fundamentally desperate alternatives available to the characters whose lives he is chronicling. The narrator's ironic wit suggests that *he* is not entirely responsible for the imagination which composes experience into a contrast between the Farnese tower and the court of Parma. Narrative configurations in *La Chartreuse* therefore hesitate between an opposition which reduces the exuberant playfulness of the main characters to an irrelevant and dangerous luxury in the dull seriousness of social life, and a centrifugal movement away from the fantasy of

1. Proust's objections to Balzac's style are in *Contre Sainte-Beuve, suivi de Nouveaux mélanges* (Paris, 1954), pp. 207–9.

happiness versus society toward attitudes poised, as it were, between or above *any* thematic definitions.

Irony in Stendhal raises the possibility of a self created through the accumulated solutions of local compositional pressures. The range of the self would be as great as the inventiveness with which a rigid psychological structure is subordinated to responses too particularized and diversified to be reduced to a single psychological pattern. The theoretically endless expansion of narrative surfaces as a technique for re-creating the self is, as we have just seen, the vocation which Proust's narrator makes visible in his art. And the demonstration, while it is of course a wholly literary one, implies the pertinence of speculative, experimental fictions for constructing a life as well as for the activity of organizing a work of art. Stendhal's characters are helpless victims of a fantasy whose inevitable destructiveness is prefigured in contrasts (between the French and the Italians, between The Happy Few at Grianta and the sour but powerful society of Fabrice's father) which are explicit as early as the *Avertissement* and the first couple of chapters of *La Chartreuse*. Only the narrator represents and profits from a fictive self which, in its sophisticated comprehensiveness and its affectionate but firm judgments, is superior to those contrasts. The narrator of *A la Recherche*, on the other hand, shapes an entire life and an entire society from the perspective of a freedom which Stendhal exploits only in order to maintain a necessary, prudent distance from his story. The autobiographical project allows the Proustian narrator to discover, in the process of recording his past, that the reenactment of the past need not be constrained by a reality prior to and more authoritative than the imaginative decisions taken *now*. Those decisions constitute not merely a reaction to experience but also the substance of his experience.

What I would call the freedom of the Stendhalian and Proustian novels implies the dismissal of an esthetic which posits the notion of correspondences between art and reality. That esthetic appears to haunt *A la Recherche du temps perdu*, but the narrator's interest in universal laws of behavior and in a mere "translation" of the "fundamental notes" of his personality is belied by the liberality with which he is obviously allowing his work (his document of self) simply to *grow*. And it grows according to a logic of metaphorical associations which are the creation of the work itself. It would seem that the contradictions I have discussed in Proust's work either escape his attention or do not interest him. At any rate, he has comparatively little to say about the realistic premises which he both clings to and—as his work becomes its own model and source of inspiration—ignores. Among the writers I have been speaking about, only Flaubert has an intense, indeed a tortured consciousness of the difficulties of being realistic and of the dangers of being nonrealistic. What I consider as his immensely interesting failure as a writer can be explained by his uncompromising commitment to finding exact equivalences between an available language and a reality inaccessible except through a language which can be measured only against itself. The testing of reality in art can only be a testing, among themselves, of the instrumentalities of art. But, for Flaubert, to use those instrumentalities is to risk betraying a reality distinct from them. He was, in spite of his theoretical program, much more skeptical than Balzac and Stendhal about the possibility of making art a copy of reality. On the other hand, Flaubert was unable to take the leap which would consist in treating the imaginary as seriously as the real, or, ultimately, in abandoning the notion of the real as a *prohibitive* criterion for condemning the imaginary. His stylistic asceticism was the way that criterion exercised its pressure. It made of his art, as I have said, an art of retrenchment, of calculated verbal denials for the sake of a more than verbal expressiveness.

Flaubert's skepticism about what language expresses does not, however, prevent him from writing novels whose structure and style seem to indicate greater optimism about the representational potentialities of literature. Emma's anguished doubts about the fidelity of novels to life could be thought of as merely the most interesting aspect of a faithful portrait of *mœurs de province* in nineteenth-century France. Only *Bouvard et Pécuchet* almost reaches the ideal monotony of a work about nothing more than the problematic relation between reality and *any* use of language. Now much of contemporary thought about fiction, especially in France, prolongs the Flaubertian meditation about the nonexpressive, nonreferential autonomy of language. But has anything really new been added to what we can already find in Flaubert? Polemical theorizing has always been a great consumer of French literary energies, and it is possible to feel that the period since World War II has been characterized mainly by belligerent promotions of the already achieved. The assumptions behind realistic fiction have undoubtedly been more effectively undermined by the works of Flaubert, Proust, and Joyce than by the *a posteriori* manifestos, from Sartre to the theoreticians of *Tel Quel* and the Ecole des Hautes Etudes, which announce the bankruptcy of these assumptions. The New Novel is a more glamorous label than it is an accurate one; and it could be argued that the writers rather haphazardly bunched together under that rubric have done more to demystify old forms of fiction than to create new ones.

Nonetheless, the very desire to be as explicit as possible about the kind of novel it is no longer possible to write—however naïve that may sound—has helped the best French novelists to explore their most radical creative possibilities. What is both irritating and exciting about recent French fiction cannot be separated from the kind of strained theoretical consciousness which seems, in part, to sustain it. It may be uncongenial to us that novelistic originality should depend so heavily on certain arguments about novelistic practice. But—as Robbe-Grillet, Beckett, and Pinget sufficiently demonstrate—the originality is there, and even the arguments themselves have been useful. They have helped us to see more clearly the different types of contracts or agreements we enter into when we participate in different kinds of literary experiments. They have defined, more explicitly than ever before, the assumptions about art and reality which we at least provisionally accept in our enjoyment of Balzacian and Flaubertian realistic fiction. And in so doing, contemporary critical reflection has invited us, most fundamentally, to revise the conditions (of thought, and ultimately of social life) on which inventive writing and inventive living depend.

The appeal, within art, to a determining experience outside art; the conviction that human behavior is intrinsically meaningful (Balzac's interest in the "sens caché" of events is consistent with the documentary ambitions of the *Avant-propos*); the faith in the logical structures of language as a guarantee of the coherence of experience; and the use of words as symbolic tokens to allude to actual depths in the self and in the world—these are the principal traits and assumptions by which the realistic novel has been recognized and judged, and which we no longer think of as *necessary*. But necessary for what?—merely for writing novels, or for all our experience? Sartre's praise of *L'Etranger* depends on his willingness to accept, in art, what he recognizes as Camus's *parti pris*. The work is based on the "analytical postulate" according to which every reality is reducible to a sum of distinct elements. For Sartre, we can admire the work derived from that postulate without accepting the postulate as a valid description of experience. *L'Etranger* exploits certain tricks and privileges of literary art which Sartre aptly compares to the conventions that allow for social satire in the eighteenth-century *conte*. Camus "lies—like all artists—because he claims to be restoring experience to its purest state and he has cunningly sifted out all the meaningful connections, which also belong to experience." [2]

The remark is shrewd, but it strikes me as "saving" Camus by missing the larger intentions discernible in *L'Etranger*. For the work—like the fiction of Robbe-Grillet and of Beckett, which I will also be considering—is obviously meant as more than a literary *divertissement*. The one thing Camus is unquestionably

2. "Explication de *L'Etranger*," *Situations I* (Paris, 1947), pp. 115–16.

claiming for Meursault is that he tells the truth about human experience. Sartre's allowance for literary "lies" typifies his condescending attitude toward a form of activity of which he has become more and more impatient, at the same time that his own theatrical and novelistic efforts show no such indulgence toward the supposedly artistic luxury of ignoring and denying philosophical "truth." The massive attempt, in contemporary literature, to make language "designify" is also an attempt to redefine the nature of mental and physical realities, as well as to test the nature of language as a reflector or creator of reality. To bestow the privilege of lying on literature is simply another version of the tendency, which I have been arguing against, to isolate it almost as a freakish monument irrelevant to experience, and it hardly matters whether it be isolated as a graceful lie or as the distiller of truth and form from the formless raw material of life.

The myths denounced by modern art are denounced as myths unnecessary for both art *and* life. We would, for example, be right to feel that the successful elimination of psychological consistency and depth from the writing of Camus, Robbe-Grillet, and Beckett could only mean that the imagination can function, anywhere, unconstrained by such psychological fictions. Certainly, life outside art includes pressures and necessities absent from the confrontation of a man with a (somewhat deceptively) inert typewriter or notebook, but it is hard to see why the *processes* of having and designing experience should be intrinsically different in the two cases. The creation of literary characters without what we ordinarily think of as personality, of characters whose only self would be a succession of logically incoherent or of indefinitely expandable surfaces, has obvious consequences for our views on human freedom. It at least suggests the possibility that the range of our being need not be limited by such assumptions as that of the unattackable power of a given psychology over the play of verbal fantasies.

The recent French fiction I will be interested in here is an impressive testing of that possibility. True, it announces the fictions it wishes to dispose of much more explicitly than the Proustian novel, and its often polemical commitment to radically new programs makes it vulnerable to certain shortcuts, to solutions which by-pass the problems to be solved. Furthermore, traditional notions of psychology and of language obviously persist in contemporary fiction. The changing of cultural mythologies turns out, not unexpectedly, to be a slow and ambiguous process, and much of contemporary art frankly appeals to our appreciation of the quality of its failures rather than to our admiration for the firmness of its achievements. The failures are complex. They can, in part, be accounted for by historically tenacious habits of thinking. Also, if one holds that the revision of our fictions about reality involves the destruction of the notion of self and consequently of all confidence in the psychological expressiveness of language, the failure to express can in itself be considered as the ultimate success. The most radical project in contemporary literature is the terroristic one of annihilating the self. Happily, however, if we hesitate to envisage silence or a wholly depersonalized language as a utopia for either literature or life, the French New Novel also offers us a limited but impressive repertory of techniques in self-contestation for the sake of perhaps limitless self-expansions.

1

THE STRANGER'S SECRETS

[Camus's *L'Etranger*]

To do justice to Camus requires an indifference to literary fashions in the light of which Camus is likely to appear quaintly archaic, as well as to the appeal of a life and a work pervaded by an apparently unattackable integrity. Tough-mindedness would seem to demand that we ignore those claims to sympathy which made Camus something of a moral hero to many of his

readers: the struggle against poverty and illness, Camus's tortured conscience, his suspicion of political theories and positions
which might promote or justify human suffering, the simplicity
and intensity of his attachment to life, and the accident which
brutally vindicated Camus's impressive and useless protest against
the unacceptable fact of death.

Camus's work has profited from the quietly glamorous nobility of his life. More than that: his urgently sincere tone has
obscured the presence in his work of some of the habits of
thought and of feeling against which he argued most eloquently.
He is the least interesting of the writers discussed in this study,
and the quality of his achievement is, for me, all the more vitiated
by an indulgence in abstraction, a secretly prideful reticence of
feeling, and an easy cynicism, all of which he constantly, and
rightly, attacked for their dehumanizing effects on life. I find
the *moraliste* of *Le Mythe de Sisyphe* and *L'Homme révolté* a
dull and vague thinker; as a playwright, Camus strikes me not
only as less inventive or radical than Beckett, Arrabal, and even
Ionesco, but also, within the conventions of a more traditional
theater of linguistic and psychological coherence, less successful
than the Sartre of *Huis clos* and *Les Séquestrés d'Altona*.
Camus's fiction, however—especially *L'Etranger* and a couple of
stories in *L'Exil et le royaume*—is another matter, and *L'Etranger*
deserves to be discussed as an impressive if flawed exercise in
a kind of writing promoted by the New Novelists of the 1950's
to the dignity, and occasionally narrow rigor, of doctrine. The
doctrine is not Camus's, but the refreshed novelistic techniques
we find in *L'Etranger* could nonetheless be thought of as an
example and an inspiration for what has now become an excessively theoretical determination to restructure the relation between language and psychology in fiction.

Camus's title has been, for criticism, an unfortunate challenge. What exactly is the quality which makes Meursault a
"stranger"? Some early readings of the novel inspired dozens of

essays in support of the idea that Camus's hero lives only by sensations, that he never synthesizes his experience into "feelings," that he is uncontaminated by any of the psychological and moral fictions by which society attempts to make life coherent and significant. For Sartre, Camus had eliminated all the "meaningful connections" which impose unity on the succession of instants in an individual's life; each sentence is a new and isolated present, a creation *ex nihilo* without any affective ties to the preceding, equally isolated "island" of sensory experience.[3] Maurice Blanchot hailed the "absence of thought and of subjective life" in *L'Etranger*. Meursault describes himself from the outside, as others might describe him, and in so doing he subverts the notion of the self and tends toward "an unsurpassable objectivity." Having gotten rid of all "false subjective explanations," Camus has, according to Blanchot, given us "the very image of human reality when one strips it of all psychological conventions."[4] Roger Quilliot, in the first book-length study of Camus, echoes these ideas when he speaks of Meursault as a man "without a face. No inner life reestablishes the character's unity."[5] And in a less radical version of this approach, John Cruickshank finds Meursault "bemused by experience": "His intellectual powers are unimpressive, his psychological insight is almost nonexistent. . . . He also lacks an accepted ethical sense and generally displays moral indifference."[6]

Camus himself might have helped to check this tendency in criticism when he remarked, in a 1945 interview for *Les Nouvelles littéraires*, that he had intended to describe in Meursault "un homme sans conscience apparente."[7] In many

3. "Explication de *L'Etranger*," *Situations I* (Paris, 1947), pp. 116–17. Sartre's essay is from February, 1943.
4. "Le Roman de *L'Etranger*," *Faux pas* (Paris, 1943), pp. 256–61.
5. *La Mer et les prisons/Essai sur Albert Camus* (Paris, 1956), p. 85.
6. *Albert Camus and the Literature of Revolt* (New York, 1960), p. 152.
7. Jeanine Delpech, " ' *Non, je ne suis pas existentialiste,*' nous dit Albert Camus," *Les Nouvelles littéraires*, No. 954 (November 15, 1945).

quarters, much has indeed been made of that "apparente." If one takes a favorable view of the novel, it could mean, for example, that Meursault has very good reasons for paying attention only to the surfaces of things, and that our most interesting experience in reading the book will be, precisely, to discover why his conscience and psychological consciousness are so seldom in evidence. Camus's sharpest readers have, however, been somewhat disappointed by all that consciousness lurking behind the stranger's deceptively blank prose. Nathalie Sarraute, in a few pages of *L'Ere du soupçon*, has acutely unmasked the intellectual behind Camus's sensualist; she speaks of Meursault's "desperate and lucid refusal" of social values and fictions, and shrewdly suggests that Camus intends his hero to be "an example and perhaps a lesson." [8] Madame Sarraute is, of course, by no means anxious to eliminate psychology from the novel, but the tone of her remarks about *L'Etranger* suggests a critical view of the strategies by which Camus obscures the conventional thinking and feeling which sustain the stranger's decision *not* to be intellectual or emotional. Disappointment is even franker in Robbe-Grillet, who points out that ". . . the book is not written in a language as *filtered* as the first pages may lead us to believe. In fact, only the objects already charged with a flagrant human content are carefully neutralized, and *for moral reasons*. . . ." The work is full of "the most revealing classical metaphors," Meursault's relations with objects "are not at all innocent" (his reactions imply "disappointment, withdrawal, rebellion"); in short, Camus the humanist "does not reject anthropomorphism, he utilizes it with economy and subtlety in order to give it more weight." [9]

Literary communities tend to "wait" for certain literary events; they know what they want, and, in their impatience to see it

8. *L'Ere du soupçon/Essais sur le roman*, in Les Essais, LXXX (Paris, 1956), 15–23.
9. Alain Robbe-Grillet, "Nature, humanisme, tragédie," *Pour un nouveau roman* (Paris, 1963), pp. 70–72.

appear, they may mistake false goods for the real thing. Sartre's tricky underemphasis of those "anthropomorphic" elements in *L'Etranger* which he recognizes perfectly well, and Blanchot's praise of a portrait without "false subjective explanations" certainly have something to do with their wish to free literature from the psychological schemes of *La Princesse de Clèves* and *La Cousine Bette*. But to anticipate is, happily, not entirely to renounce discriminations, and, to do Satre justice, it must be added that he never hailed the nonanthropomorphic novel in the fiction of François Mauriac. *L'Etranger*, in other words—however necessary Madame Sarraute's corrective view may have become—produced a shock, and if its innovations were exaggerated, the exaggerations testify to a certain originality in the work itself. To locate that originality now, however, requires a perhaps unattractively austere critique of what made *L'Etranger* an immediately appealing revelation.

The first paragraph of the novel is justly famous: "Today, *maman* died. Or maybe yesterday, I don't know. I received a telegram from the old people's home: 'Mother passed away. Burial tomorrow. *Sentiments distingués.*' That doesn't mean anything. Maybe it was yesterday." [10] The point of view is undeniably peculiar. But why? We are disoriented, quite simply, by the narrator's concern with time. His emotional originality appears to consist in his choosing to develop only the least emotionally charged element in the first sentence: "today." But is it enough to say that "*maman* died" awakens only his chronological consciousness? The words most strikingly devoid of the feelings conventionally associated with a mother's death are not Meursault's at all; they are in the telegram. And there is some ambiguity in Meursault's comment about the telegram. The last

10. Albert Camus, *Théâtre, Récits, Nouvelles*, ed. Roger Quilliot, preface by Jean Grenier (Paris, 1962), p. 1128. All other page references from *L'Etranger* will be from this edition, and will be given in the text. Other references to Camus's fiction and drama will be to this edition published by Gallimard in the Pléiade series. All the translations in this essay are my own.

sentence suggests that "that doesn't mean anything" refers only to the fact that the day of *maman's* death cannot be guessed from the temporally cryptic message, but we may have already read more than this in Meursault's judgment. Indeed, the telegram "doesn't mean anything" from the point of view of human emotions; its only response to the drily noted fact of death is a bit of practical information ("burial tomorrow") and a ready-made formula with which people fill the void of a nonrelation by appealing to an enigmatic class of "feelings" somehow "distinguished." Is Meursault's lingering over the question of when his mother died "stranger," more "alienated" than the socially acceptable formulas which announce her death?

We may in fact feel that Meursault's interest in dates is useful as a pretext for drawing our attention to the inadequacy, even the absurdity of the telegram. Instead of saying explicitly that such formulas are a mockery of the personal, solemn nature of death, Camus's hero reacts just peculiarly enough to justify his quoting the message he has received and, perhaps above all, to save himself from being charged with too obvious a comment about the insignificance of that message. The point has been made about the telegram—it is not a very interesting point, and it presupposes a normal sense of and respect for human feelings —but it has also been effectively underemphasized by being attributed to a mind apparently bizarre in its own right. In other words, a mildly mystifying concern with the aspect of death having the least obvious human appeal is the narrative medium through which Camus filters, and gives an air of originality to, a piece of social satire.

The satire, it could be objected, may be part of Camus's intention, but nothing tells us that the larger criticism implicit in "that doesn't mean anything" belongs to *Meursault's* point of view. Nothing, I would answer, except the rest of the novel, except the numerous passages where Meursault drops hints of all the attitudes and decisions behind a perspective on experience which only hints at such things as attitudes and decisions.

There is ample support for Nathalie Sarraute's remark about the intellectual *parti pris* discernible in Meursault's pointedly neutral descriptions of objects and behavior. He acts on some extremely definite, if teasingly presented ideas. When Marie asks him if he loves her, he tells her that her question doesn't "mean" anything (1151), and he opposes a pregnant "No" to her remark about marriage being "a serious matter" (1156). To his boss's suggestion that working in Paris would provide a welcome "change of life," Meursault sententiously answers "that one never changed his way of life, that anyway one life was as good as another and the one I led here wasn't at all unpleasant" (1155–56). Meursault doesn't believe in God (1175); he doesn't like policemen (1152); and he has observed others closely enough to regret not having told his lawyer that there is nothing strange or inhuman about him at all: "I wanted to make it clear to him that I was like everyone else, absolutely like everyone else" (1173). (Camus had considered *Un homme comme les autres* as a title for the novel.) And although he is "surprised" by the lawyer's asking him if he felt grief on the day his mother died, Meursault manages to come up with a comparatively sophisticated answer: "In all likelihood, I was fond of *maman,* but that didn't mean anything. All normal people had more or less desired the death of those they loved" (1172).

The principal interest of the portrait we have of Meursault is that it is undeveloped. Psychological or intellectual significance does not lead us any further in one direction than a question about whether *maman* died yesterday or today. Nothing arrests Meursault's attention longer than anything else, and the fact that he has judged ambition to be futile, or—to judge from the number of sympathetic allusions to her throughout the novel— that he loved his mother, makes all the more striking the equal attention he gives to everything. His nonanalytical sequences are peculiar because of their provocative denials of their own suggestiveness. And it is as if he were defying us to take up that suggestiveness. The style of *L'Etranger* is an exercise in setting traps: by his emphases and by his omissions, Meursault tempts us to make mistakes analogous to those the prosecuting attorney will make in the second half of the novel, to say more about him than he says about himself.

I am inclined even to think of Meursault's impressive sensitivity to visual detail as another element in Camus's strategy of provocation. What, for example, is the function of the exquisitely refined perceptions in the following passage? Meursault has spent much of the Sunday following his mother's death watching people come and go on the streets under his terrace:

> Then the street lights abruptly came on, and they dimmed the stars which were beginning to appear in the night sky. I felt my eyes grow tired from looking at the sidewalks laden with men and with lights [les trottoirs avec leur chargement d'hommes et de lumières]. The street lights made the wet pavements glisten, and, at regular intervals, the reflections from a trolley were caught by someone's glossy hair, a smile or a silver bracelet [les tramways, à intervalles réguliers, mettaient leurs reflects sur des cheveux brillants, un sourire ou un bracelet d'argent]. Shortly after, when there were fewer trolleys and the night sky was already black above the trees and the lights, the neighborhood, almost imperceptibly, grew empty, until finally the first cat slowly crossed the now deserted street. Then I thought that I should have dinner. My neck hurt a little because I had been leaning for a long time on the back of my chair. I went out to buy some bread and spaghetti. I made my meal and I ate standing up. I wanted to smoke a cigarette at the window, but the night had become chilly and I felt a little cold. I closed my windows and, as I came back into the room, I saw in the mirror part of a table with my alcohol lamp standing next to some pieces of bread. I said to myself that I had gotten through another Sunday, that *maman* was now buried, that I was going back to work and that, all things considered, nothing had changed. (1141–42)

The effects here are various and manipulated with great skill. From "then I thought I should have dinner" to the end of the paragraph, we have a monotony of structure (all the sentences and clauses beginning, in French, with "je" and a *passé composé*) and a succession of brief, unembellished notations which tend to counteract the ampler rhythms and the richer language of the first half of the paragraph. The style is rather abruptly simplified. The narrator checks a movement toward more eloquent phrasing, and by the end of the paragraph he has, I think, succeeded in partially smothering our sense of his having a taste and a capacity for verbal organizations more complex and more seductively lyrical than "I went to buy some bread and spaghetti" and "I closed my windows."

But he has nonetheless revealed a range of expressive resources which may make us wonder why, on the whole, he seems to be deliberately limiting that range. Can it really be the supposedly benumbed, average clerk Meursault who notices how "les tramways, à intervalles réguliers, mettaient leurs reflets sur des cheveux brillants, un sourire ou un bracelet d'argent"? The observation is improbable, to say the least; the imagination that makes it is not simply fanciful, but also rather painfully fancy. The still life toward the end of the paragraph is more successfully poetic—but what could be more peculiar than our making such discriminations among Meursault's more or less successful ventures into poetic prose? It is peculiar, of course, only because one strain of *L'Etranger*, beginning with "Today, *maman* died. Or maybe yesterday, I don't know," has been such a loud announcement that he is *not* a poet. If, on the other hand, we simply grant him his more eloquent strain, the Meursault of "I made my meal and I ate standing up" requires some explanation. Of course, the most urgent explanation is required by the Meursault who, apparently unaware of the peculiar sequence he thus makes, inserts "*maman* was buried" between "I had gotten through another Sunday" and "I was going back to work." Is the thinker, the feeler, the poet really convincing when he speaks as if those three thoughts were identical in their emotional neutrality? Meursault profits from the ambiguity of "nothing

had changed." If he means that he will go back to work on
Monday, he is right. Is that what the puzzling "all things considered" ("somme toute") is supposed to convey, or is his parenthetical remark a way of teasing us with a glimpse of some
withheld and perhaps complex wisdom? His sensitivity has been
amply demonstrated, and it is arbitrarily schematic to say that
he is sensitive only to appearances and surfaces. His failure to
see certain things is shocking because he in fact sees so much.
As a result, when he "closes up" we are mystified, and his sudden
insensitivities strike us as evidence of a purposeful reticence
rather than as examples of a "natural" ignorance of familiar emotional reactions. L'Etranger is a mystery story. What is the key
to Meursault's pose as a stranger?

The function of the crime in L'Etranger is to provide us with
that key. The killing, the trial, and the months in prison do not
exactly change Meursault's attitudes; neither can it be said with
certainty that they make him conscious of why he has lived as
he has lived; they do, however, make it dramatically plausible
that he should finally explain himself. The language used to
describe the hallucinated, sun-tormented state in which Meursault kills the Arab prepares us for a new and larger range of
expressive resources. As W. M. Frohock was the first to point
out, the style suddenly becomes densely metaphorical (there are,
according to Frohock's count, fifteen metaphors on the first
eighty-three pages and twenty-five on the last four pages of Part
One);[11] and the section ends with Meursault's explicit realization that the four shots fired into the Arab's already "inert body"
were like "four brief raps on the door of misfortune." "I understood that I had destroyed the balance of the day, the exceptional silence of a beach where I had been happy" (1168).
In contrast to the first part's progression from one "atom of

11. "Camus: Image, Influence, and Sensibility," Yale French Studies, II
(Fall 1949), 93–94.

time" to the next,[12] the second part of L'Etranger includes summaries of Meursault's feelings over a period of several months, discriminations among the different stages of his life as a prisoner. And in his outburst on the novel's last couple of pages, Meursault interprets and justifies everything which, beginning with the bizarre first paragraph of L'Etranger, may have led us to see in him an authentic stranger, that is, a man authentically ignorant of the responses by which he might have been recognized as belonging to a human community.

Meursault's indifference is the form taken by a passion for life when one realizes that death makes all human experience equally unimportant and yet equally precious.

> I had been right, I was still right, I was always right. I had lived in a certain way and I could have lived in some other way. I had done this and I hadn't done that. I hadn't done a particular thing but I had done something else. So what? It was as if I had waited my whole life for this moment and for that dawn when I would be executed and justified. Nothing, nothing at all was important and I knew why. He [the chaplain] knew why too. From the depths of my future, during all the absurd life I had led, a dark and mysterious wind had been blowing toward me, crossing over years that were yet to come, and that wind levelled out everything people proposed to me during the equally unreal years I was living through. What did I care about other people's deaths, a mother's love, what did I care about his God, the lives people choose, the fates they elect, since a single fate was to elect me and with me billions of privileged men who, like him, called themselves my brothers. (1210–11)

What can this possibly mean? I realize that L'Etranger is not reducible to a logical argument, but this final passage, for all its passion, is an argument, and is presented as crucial for an understanding of Meursault's life. His execution, as he clearly says, "justifies" his life, which also naturally means that Meursault's

12. Sartre, "Explication de L'Etranger," p. 118.

imminent death vindicates the way in which he has related his story to us. His logic is simple, and mystifying: since all men die, everything that men do is of equal value. The connection between these two clauses escapes me. From the fact of a common destiny, Meursault—and Camus—jump to the impossibility of preferring anything *in* life to anything else. It is as if the proposition were being put to us that if two plays had similar endings, everything that goes on in both plays would therefore have to be equally uninteresting.

Does Meursault really believe this? "Salamano's dog," he goes on to say, "was as good as his wife," but Céleste "was better than Raymond." And swimming in Algeria is apparently better than working in Paris (a "dirty" city where "people have white skins" [1156]), just as certain convictions appear to be valid enough to justify the stranger's stubbornly resisting the religious bullying of the examining magistrate and of the prison chaplain. To the extent that death really has "levelled out everything people proposed to" Meursault, we get a hint of the missing logical connection I referred to a moment ago when he speaks of his angry outburst as having "purged" him of evil and "emptied" him of hope. Indeed, death makes *hope* absurd. It is not simply a question of Meursault's hope for a reprieve, or at least not in a limited sense. The point of the book is that we live, all the time, under a death sentence, and (*Le Mythe de Sisyphe* confirms this) to be fully aware of that implies an ability and a willingness altogether to abolish hope from life. But since it seems to me very theoretical indeed to argue that since I may die at any time it is absurd for me to hope intensely for something I want to happen next week or next year, we can only say that death has had such a devastating effect on the stranger's life because the only thing he can conceive worth hoping for is immortality. Without a belief in God, death does of course make *that* hope absurd. That is, Salamano's dog is worth as much as Salamano's wife for a man interested neither in the dog nor in the wife, but only in his own life everlasting.

A metaphysically disappointed, bitter man adopts a pose of defiant indifference toward the world. The indifference seems all the more theatrical and defiant if we try to reconcile it to the concluding, somewhat wilfully optimistic affirmation of life as happy after all in *L'Etranger*. "As if my fit of anger had purged me of evil, emptied me of hope, in front of this night heavy with signs and with stars, I opened up for the first time to the tender indifference of the world. In feeling the world so similar to myself, in short so fraternal, I felt that I had been happy, and that I was still happy" (1211). Certainly there is in Camus, from *Noces* to *L'Homme révolté*, a kind of felt accord with the world (expressed best as the pleasure of swimming under the Mediterranean sun) which he writes about with a moving if occasionally stilted eloquence. The problem is that he is also so determined to be a thinker, and in spite of his constant polemic against dehumanizing systemizations of life, Camus himself never ceases to offer some philosophical account for both an invincible need to detach himself from human affairs and an innocent, lazy sensuality which of course needs no justification at all.

The end of *L'Etranger* illustrates some of the resulting confusions. We could probably go along with the assertion, implied in *L'Etranger* and explicitly made in *Le Mythe de Sisyphe*, that the passion for beauty and the capacity for enjoyment can be intensified if we cure ourselves of the temptation to penetrate the surfaces of things in the hope of finding a universe sympathetic to man's condition, a universe of reassuring transcendental significances. The final ambition of "une pensée absurde," Camus writes in *Sisyphe*, is simply "to describe"; and the work of art— as well as the joy of life—is born of a willingness to give up attempting to find meanings and depths in the concrete. ("L'œuvre d'art naît du renoncement de l'intelligence à raisonner le concret.")[13] But is a night "heavy with signs" a description of something concrete? Is a "fraternal" world whose indifference

13. *Le Mythe de Sisyphe*, in *Essais*, ed. R. Quilliot and L. Faucon (Paris, 1965), pp. 174 and 176.

is "tender" one that has genuinely lost the transcendence we wishfully project on it? And, finally, we come back, in another form, to the first and major difficulty I have indicated. The indifference of the universe to our desires may, logically, inspire either suicidal despair or a passion—cleansed of the need for transcendental reassurances—for the strictly natural and the strictly human. But how can that renewed passion for life not be full of explicit discriminations? With nothing more to know and to hope for than what we can know and hope for *here*, the necessity for an art of exclusions and commitments becomes all the more immediate and urgent. It is precisely the disappearance of transcendence in the universe which makes indifference spiritually obsolete, and its persistence in Camus suggests an unconfessed nostalgia for the comforts of transcendence, for the comforts of an absolute.

I do not want to judge *L'Etranger* by the philosophical deficiencies of *Le Mythe de Sisyphe,* and the objections I have raised seem to me justified by a reading of the novel, which, perverse as it may now seem to say it, is far more interesting than the essay. The weaknesses in Camus's more or less philosophical writings have been competently spelled out by John Cruickshank, an admirer of Camus; he has, in *Albert Camus and the Literature of Revolt,* some very good things to say about the different meanings of the word "absurd" in *Le Mythe de Sisyphe,* the confusion about how "logic" is to be interpreted at the beginning of the essay, and the ambiguities in Camus's use of the word "revolt" in *L'Homme révolté.*[14] I would simply add that the entire argument in *Le Mythe de Sisyphe* depends on the nostalgia I just mentioned for the securities of religious faith. The absurd in Camus presupposes a *need* for cosmic unities and ultimate meanings which Camus presents as an unarguable fact of human nature. "The absurd is born of this confrontation between what men call out for and the irrational silence of the

14. See especially Chapter 3 and p. 118.

world." And Camus sets out to examine whether life's absurdity demands that we escape from life by either suicide or hope, both of which he will judge to be unsatisfactory solutions. But these unacceptable consequences are really premises without which the argument would never have gotten started in the first place. It is precisely the "meeting" of hope and suicidal despair which *creates* the sense of the absurd, and the silence of the world is neither rational nor irrational unless we take for granted the "desire for happiness and reason," the need for unity and transcendental order which Camus would present as independent of his description of the world.[15] That is, there is no "confrontation" between "l'appel humain" and the world's "irrational silence," but rather a single, emotionally prejudiced description of the world. The absurd man, Camus announces, does not believe in the profound or hidden meanings of things.[16] But of course—and it is impossible to break out of the circle—there would not be any absurdity unless man thought it inconceivable that the world should be *without* profound and hidden meanings. Absurdity, as Robbe-Grillet has seen, is "a form of tragic humanism"; it is a metaphysical romance between man and the universe, "a lover's quarrel, which leads to a crime of passion." [17]

Camus, less reticent in his essays than his heroes are in his novels and stories, reveals a schematic, abstract mind which, finally, it is impossible to penetrate. Meursault's and Rieux's temperamental reticence is paralleled by an undoubtedly unconscious philosophical obfuscation in Camus the *moraliste*. Perhaps his most admirable sentence is a plea for verbal directness and honesty: "Every ambiguous expression, every misunderstanding gives rise to death; only a clear language, the use of simple words, can save us from that death." [18] It is extraordinary that this warning should be made in *L'Homme révolté*, a book in

15. *Le Mythe de Sisyphe*, pp. 117–18.
16. *Le Mythe de Sisyphe*, pp. 142–43.
17. "Nature, humanisme, tragédie," p. 71.
18. *L'Homme révolté*, in *Essais*, p. 687.

which experience is so desiccated by abstract dualisms—revolt
versus revolution, totality versus unity, nature versus history,
"German dreams" versus "the Mediterranean tradition"—that
it makes no sense at all except as a bizarre and unsuccessful
stylistic exercise in the lyricism of abstract antinomies. Camus
is an ideal example of the writer unable or unwilling, to use
Proust's phrase, to express the "fundamental notes" of his personality. His writing is, on the surface, a marvel of discipline:
so much rigor would seem to be necessary to maintain the equi-
librium of sentences structured by contrapuntal abstractions. But
these balances easily become a habit, a tic, and we find a stylistic
version of Meursault's apathy in the torpor with which Camus
seems to float on the surfaces of his linguistic vaguenesses and
confusions.

The Proustian criterion for judging literature—according to
the depths of self "sounded" by style—is not, as we can see in
Roussel, Robbe-Grillet, Pinget, and Beckett, the only imaginable
basis for critical appreciation. And Proust himself, as I have
shown, subverts his own theoretical notion of a monotonously
profound self-expressiveness as the sign of genius in art by his
avid exploitation of local narrative occasions in *A la Recherche*
for unexpected and unpredictable self-renewals. But with Camus
we don't have the impression of a fundamental revision of the
very notion of self-expression in art. He in no way contests the
assumptions about personality in traditional fiction, and he even
complained about the fact that modern novelists had lost the
secret of portraying characters in depth.[19] Camus is not moving
away from a center of psychological pressures or fixed patterns
toward either the liberatingly evasive ironies of Stendhal, or the
self-multiplications of Proust, or the attempted *écriture blanche*
of psychological neutrality in Robbe-Grillet and in Blanchot. He
is, on the contrary, a classical writer, that is, a writer whose sentences tend to be portentous understatements of implied depths

19. See the *Nouvelles littéraires* interview, and Roger Quilliot's report
of a conversation with Camus, in *Théâtre, Récits, Nouvelles*, p. 1918.

in the self and in the world. The classical style refers us to unexpressed and perhaps inexpressible realities beyond language; it closes in on those realities and, as it were, picks up their echoes without ever claiming to embody adequately the realities themselves. "Mon mal vient de plus loin," Phèdre suggestively says. The subjects in Racine and in Madame de La Fayette are, in effect, at a certain remove from the works which treat them, at a distance never crossed by the language which ceremoniously points at them. But whereas Racinian verse picks up the echoes, Camus's language merely seals off the accesses to opinions and feelings easily articulated, or it creates a smoke screen of systematic thought which smothers all psychological resonance. It is, in other words, a kind of parody of classical *pudeur* and of the classical *litote*. With Meursault, we have a mystifying character who is finally revealed to us as having no mystery at all, but only a logically dubious philosophical position.

He is, alas, also the occasion for a shallow social polemic.[20] A crude attack on supposedly conventional habits of thought allows Camus to exaggerate his own imaginative capacity for the psychologically unexpected. Superficially, *L'Etranger* seems to expose the emptiness of psychological and moral fictions by which society attempts to control and make coherent an individual's behavior. The novel appears to attack the very activity of novelizing, even to subvert its own existence by demonstrating the irrelevance of any stories one might invent about Meursault's life. We could think of the trial as a novelistic competition between the prosecuting and the defense attorneys. The raw material is provided by what Meursault does in the first half of the book; using that material, each of the lawyers tries his hand at spinning a yarn about Meursault's "soul." *We* know that they

20. For more favorable views of Meursault as a rebel against society, see Philip Thody's discussion of *L'Etranger* in *Albert Camus/A Study of His Novels* (London, 1957), and Louis Hudon, "The Stranger and the Critics," *Yale French Studies*, No. 25 (Spring 1960), 59–64.

are both wrong: Meursault is neither the insensitive monster described by the prosecutor nor the tireless, faithful employee and compassionate spirit sketched by the defense. But the satire against such simplifications turns against itself. For Camus takes the risk of making the prosecutor's version of Meursault's behavior an immensely probable one. It is not the *true* story, but, for anyone who, unlike the reader, is living outside Meursault's mind, it certainly represents an intelligent and wholly plausible deduction. Meursault's behavior at his mother's funeral, the affair he begins with Marie just two days later, his testifying for Raymond, and his returning to the beach with a gun: it takes very little ingenuity to interpret so many coincidences as fitting into a consistent pattern of heartless, deliberately criminal behavior. When Meursault tells the judge that he killed the Arab "because of the sun," people in the courtroom laugh (1198) —but why shouldn't they laugh? The fact that Meursault pulled the trigger probably in order to shake off an unbearable physical discomfort in no way detracts from his being a man about whom a fairly intelligible and definitive story can be told —a story to which his remark about the sun hardly does justice. If the people at Meursault's trial are ridiculous, it is just because they have the disadvantage of being outsiders, and not because anything in the novel has convincingly shown us that human experience can be lived fragmentarily, without unifying intentions, conceptions, and feelings.

It is not the storytelling process which is being satirized in *L'Etranger,* but rather a *certain class* of fictions, and they are of course the easiest fictions in the world to make fun of. Camus has a very crude view of the taboos, expectations, and ideals which organize life in society. The examining magistrate and the prosecutor are parodies of religious fervor and social morality, and Camus's failure to imagine any better alternatives to Meursault suggests the kind of cynical simplifications about human behavior which will occupy almost the entire field in *La Chute.*

Now Camus is, at his best and at his worst, profoundly mistrustful of speech. I say at his best because, whatever function verbal reticence may serve for Camus, it works, in his fiction, to create his most moving scenes, such as the communion in silence or near silence between Tarrou and Rieux as they swim, and between Daru and the Arab in "L'Hôte." But these dramatic successes are too infrequent, and in contexts too ambiguous, to make us forget the imprecise nature of the critique of language which they presuppose. Camus's distrust of speech often seems to serve as an excuse for not being clear and explicit when we feel that he needs most to be clear and explicit. In *La Peste*, what does Tarrou mean by "peace"? What does Rieux mean by "sympathy"? What is the exact personal meaning of that "hope" which makes Rieux different from Tarrou? Does anything in *La Peste* satisfactorily refute Cottard's contention that " 'the only way to bring people together is to send them the plague' " ? [21] Perhaps the saddest thing in Camus's fiction is the *end* of the plague, that is, the end of a fraternity which Camus clearly has difficulty imagining except in the midst of crisis.

With a language frequently sentimental, evasive, and abstract, Camus controls and masks what seems to be a desperately cynical view of human possibilities. His reticence keeps him from developing, and overexposing, a tritely disabused strain in his work which we catch a glimpse of when Caligula (and Camus?) stupidly thinks it "clear" and "logical" to say that human life cannot be important if money is important;[22] a strain of bitterness which explains the obscure but crucial role of Cottard in *La Peste*, and which is supported by an intellectual mediocrity most embarrassingly evident in Clamence's facile exposure of human egotism in *La Chute*. Camus is explicitly suspicious of language as a source of misunderstandings, and misunderstandings, as he writes in *L'Homme révolté*, can lead to death; to this admirable

21. *Théâtre, Récits, Nouvelles*, pp. 1427, 1459, and 1378.
22. *Caligula*, in *Théâtre, Récits, Nouvelles*, p. 22.

caution, however, we should perhaps also add a suspicion of self in the light of which Camus's cryptic style may appear to apply the brake to a spontaneous flow of cynical mockery.

The trick which I see *L'Etranger* attempting to carry off consists in making us attribute the value of a fundamental critique of fictions to an easy satire of some official moral clichés. Meursault is as much an interpreter as the prosecuting attorney, but his quietness creates the illusion that he lives unreflectively, and his purely moral advantage over the other characters can be confused with the epistemological superiority of being able to live a naturally insignificant life, of being able to resist the impulse to fictionalize which conveniently simplifies and unifies experience. In part, *L'Etranger* is Camus's attempt not to give in to what he calls in *L'Homme révolté* the novelist's "unreasonable"—but admirable—desire to "correct" life, to transform its meaningless fragments into a significant "destiny." [23] But Camus tended to confuse the particular form of traditional French fiction with form itself. The art of that fiction, he wrote in an essay of 1943, is a "revenge" on life, "a way of rising above a difficult fate by imposing a form on it." [24] The trite and questionable distinction which this implies between formless experience and the forms of art undoubtedly made it all the more difficult for Camus to conceive of ways of organizing life radically incommensurable with the prosecutor's third-rate novelizing. It is possible to dismiss certain widespread fictions about personality without posing as an alternative the myth of experience as naturally unstructured. Fictions of subjective depth, of complex motivation, of affective entities such as love or hatred, for example, can be viewed as historically and ideologically significant rather than as accurate descriptions of reality; and this critical attitude toward a particular order of fictions can make us more imaginative about other, equally useful types of linguistic and mental structures. The danger, of course, is that we may take our new fictions for scien-

23. *L'Homme révolté*, p. 666.
24. "L'Intelligence et l'échafaud," in *Théâtre, Récits, Nouvelles*, p. 1901.

tific discoveries about the objective nature of reality. The sterile scientism of the review *Tel Quel* involves just such a failure to apply a criticism of ideologies to a new programming of experience, or at least to have that tentative approach to the analysis of forms which is the best sign of a nontotalitarian approach to the myth of truth.

This is not, of course, the danger in Camus; with him we have, instead—at least in *L'Etranger*—an attack on fictionalized experience in the name of supposedly formless experience. Meursault's experience, however, is far from being formless. And because Camus had little imagination for behavioral structures other than those proposed by the classical French novel, he makes of Meursault simply an undeveloped classical character. He cannot carry through what appears to be the project of creating an insignificant character (which he probably confused with an effort to portray formless experience), and, on the other hand, his only idea of significance is a conventional one. Consequently, nothing is more artificial in *L'Etranger* than the passages meant to be most natural. Meursault's willful refusal to make causal connections explicit, his pose as a man without feeling or thought, are manifestations of a merely queer personality. There is indolence in his reticence, there is perversity in his indolence, and a frustrated desire for immortality explains his perversity. In short, he is a character of several layers, and the easily dissipated strangeness of the novel consists in the hero's tactical postponement of the information which finally allows us, unlike the prosecutor, to detect and read his soul.

Where, then, is the residual originality of *L'Etranger*? In the psychological margin created by their proud reticence, Camus and Meursault divert themselves in appealingly eccentric ways. The latter pastes an ad for Kruschen salts in an old notebook where he keeps things from newspapers which amuse him. Like Tarrou in *La Peste*, Meursault is attracted by mildly odd behavior. Tarrou is the chronicler of the old man who delightedly spits on cats from his balcony, and Meursault follows into the street the "strange little woman" who, while having dinner in Céleste's restaurant, checks off a dozen or so pages of radio programs in a magazine with rapid, machine-like precision (1157). In prison, Meursault reads "thousands of times" the story, which he finds both "improbable" and "natural," of the Czech who returns to his native village after an absence of twenty-five years and is killed for his money by his mother and sister. He had stopped at their inn and, with the idea of surprising them, had failed to reveal his identity. Now this bizarre story "means" nothing, although, interestingly enough, Meursault manages to find a moral in it: ". . . it seemed to me that the traveler had partially deserved [what had happened to him] and that one should never play games" (1182). The failure of *Le Malentendu,* the play inspired by the Czech's story, is due largely to Camus's own inability to leave the story alone. Its weirdness is diluted by the banal message that "when one wants to be recognized, one gives one's name . . . ," [25] and the incident serves as a pretext for some absurdist philosophizing on the part of the mother and a hymn to the sea on the part of Martha, who seems to kill because she can't stand living in a country without a coastline. Camus's attraction to the subject of *Le Malentendu* is the most interesting thing about the play. The work itself, on the other hand, illustrates how unprepared he is to treat such an anecdote without offering a moral and intellectual justification for it. The incident is much more successfully taken up in *L'Etranger,* where, except for Meursault's final remark about it, it is simply a gratuitous, unilluminating, and inexplicable bit of narrative.

But, from a certain point of view, that is exactly what *L'Etranger* itself is. For the people who attend Meursault's trial, there is nothing at all strange about his story: his crime is the premeditated act of a cold-blooded gangster. For the reader too, although in a different sense, there is nothing strange about Meursault: his apparent insensitivity is understandable as a refusal to

25. *Théâtre, Récits, Nouvelles,* p. 123.

pay lip service to the pious clichés of official morality, and his indifference expresses his sense of the meaninglessness of choice and of hope in a life always threatened by death. But there *is* something strange, for us, simply in the events of his life. Knowing as we do that he is not a criminal, what could be more bizarre than the accumulation of circumstances which makes it inevitable that he be judged as a criminal? *L'Etranger,* like the Czech's story, is an anecdote of freakish coincidence. It says nothing at all about the absurdity of life, as Camus defines that in *Le Mythe de Sisyphe*; rather, the novel is such an ingenious concoction of chance events that we can hardly not feel how *exceptional* Meursault's destiny is. René Girard has acutely spoken of "the accident theory" which *L'Etranger* illustrates and which "reduces Meursault's case to the proportions of a pathetic but rather insignificant *fait-divers.*" [26]

We can go even further: instead of dramatizing a confrontation between the human need for unity and significance and the "unreasonable silence" of the world, *L'Etranger* studies one of those rare occasions in life in which there does seem to be a perverse, nonhuman intention which deprives us of our freedom by making each of our gestures fit into a rigorously significant pattern. *Le Malentendu* and *L'Etranger* are dreams of coherence, or rather nightmares of coherence. They satisfy, in a cruel parody, the nostalgia for unity; their horror is not the horror of insignificance, but rather of an inescapable significance which organizes separate gestures into an unintended and tragic unity. Indeed, *L'Etranger* is, like *Oedipus Rex*, a tragedy of chance; but whereas Oedipus's unintentional crimes are written in the book of a more than human fate, there is nothing to account for Meursault's imprisonment in *his* chain of coincidences. Nothing, that is, except Camus's intention, and this unhappily atheistic author plays the role, in *L'Etranger* and *Le Malentendu,* of a demonic unifier of experience. The random is perversely transformed into the sig-

26. "Camus's Stranger Retried," *PMLA*, LXXIX (December 1964), 522.

nificant, and our interest in such stories could be explained by the temporary guarantee they offer, their catastrophic content notwithstanding, of a kind of order and logic in the universe.

The order, however, is a mock one, and the elaboration of such stories as Meursault's and Jan's is of course meant to draw our attention to the lack of a *sensible* order in life. But the stories are too peculiar to lend themselves to generalization; their very improbability undercuts the ingenious but deceptive coherence they unconvincingly celebrate. What we are left with is a test of the frankly bizarre as a legitimate inspiration for literary fictions. The watertight case which coincidence builds against Meursault is coherent but meaningless, and the very writing of *L'Etranger* suggests an interest in literature as an exercise in the improbable and the irrelevant. As I have shown, Camus was undoubtedly also interested in what he took to be serious social and philosophical issues in writing *L'Etranger*. But the novel is original and liberating, I think, to the extent that we can neglect those issues and respond to the provocative amount of space given to the trivial and to the bizarre. In its veiled ambition to be a "profound" novel, *L'Etranger* is mediocre. But the curiously meticulous descriptions of gestures and appearances; the partially successful displacement of emphasis from psychological probing to such novelistically "light" details as Meursault's wondering if his mother died today or yesterday, or his telling us why he prefers to wash his hands at noon rather than in the evening (the office towels are drier at noon); the narrative allowance made for the little mechanical woman and for the story of the Czech; and, more generally, the weirdness of the plot itself—we can easily see how all this might stimulate fiction into new directions. At its best moments, *L'Etranger* illustrates the appeal and the workability of the irresponsible. A Balzacian digression, as I have said, is always illustratively responsible to the story which it only appears to interrupt; and Marcel's analytical and descriptive wandering in *A la Recherche du temps perdu* is after all part of the experiment in self-expansion which is the novel's subject. *L'Etranger*, on the other hand, hints at what a literature of psychologically inexpressive ingenuities would be like.

Camus would certainly not have been satisfied with being remembered for that. He saw *L'Etranger* as the first stage in "a kind of difficult progression toward a saintliness of negation—a heroism without God—in short, toward human purity." Meursault is the *point zéro* "on the road of a perfection without any reward." [27] In 1955, Camus again spoke of Meursault as an image of "a truth which is still negative, the truth of being and of feeling, but without which no conquest over the self and over the world will ever be possible." [28] Nothing, however, prevents us from ignoring such morally precious pretentions, and from seeing in *L'Etranger* an interesting illustration of both the persistence and the subversion of personality in modern literature. Even in the much more radical experiments of Robbe-Grillet and of Beckett, the psychological neutralizing of language (in the former) and the desperate mockery of language's expressiveness (in the latter) are somewhat undermined by the transparent and ironically reassuring presence of psychological continuities. On the other hand, to the extent that the thrust of contemporary fiction is away from secure and limiting centers of self-definition, Camus deserves to be mentioned for those strategies of psychological dislocation which *L'Etranger* imperfectly exploits.

Les Gommes, Robbe-Grillet's first published novel, is an exquisitely programmed exploitation of the literary possibilities of extravagant coincidence—possibilities which, as we have seen, *L'Etranger* already plots. But whereas Camus's narrative originality appears to be almost the accidental virtue of an attempt to obscure a conventional metaphysical protest, techniques similar to Camus's will be used by later writers in an effort to escape from the assumptions about reality implicit in that protest. The artificial, the arbitrary, and the psychologically inexpressive in con-

27. *Théâtre, Récits, Nouvelles*, p. 1932 (from Camus's *Carnets*, 1942).
28. *Avant-propos* to the American edition of *L'Etranger*, ed. Germaine Brée and Carlos Lynes, Jr. (New York, 1955), p. viii.

temporary art are ambitious wagers in the name of a range of being even more unconstrained by the given or by the past than the continuous self-re-creation of *A la Recherche du temps perdu.* The very bareness of the French New Novel, its apparently limited, even specialized vision of the real, is first of all a dismissal of any predefined range of being, and, most excitingly, it is the sign of a literary—and more than literary—availability to the possible and to the new.

2

NARRATIVE MURDER

[Robbe-Grillet's *La Jalousie*]

In the final essay of *Pour un nouveau roman,* Robbe-Grillet makes a remark which in itself might well redeem the more familiar confusions and polemical simplifications which have attracted attention to both his criticism and his novels. He has been arguing against the "probable" and the "typical" as criteria for judging contemporary literature: "It is even as if the *false*— that is, at once the possible, the impossible, lies, hypotheses, etc. —had become one of the privileged themes of modern fiction; a new kind of narrator has been born: he is no longer merely a man who describes the things he sees, but also one who invents the things around him and who sees the things he invents. As soon as these hero-narrators begin ever so little to resemble characters, they are immediately liars, schizophrenics or victims of hallucination (or even writers, who create their own story)." [29]

29. Alain Robbe-Grillet, "Du réalisme à la réalité" (1955 and 1963), *Pour un nouveau roman,* in Collection Idées (Paris, 1963), p. 177. Subsequent references to Robbe-Grillet's critical essays will be to this French edition. All translations in this section, except those of *La Jalousie,* are my own. There is, however, an excellent translation of *Pour un nouveau roman* by Richard Howard, published by Grove Press (*For A New Novel: Essays on Fiction* [New York, 1965]).

The passage provides a refreshingly peculiar way to discuss the question of whether or not "there is psychology" in Robbe-Grillet's fiction. It has been the apparent triumph of a criticism hostile to Robbe-Grillet's theoretical intentions to point out how little his novels realize the project of describing an emotionally neutral world of things, a world of mere objective *presences* uncontaminated by human interference. Gaëtan Picon, for example, has been able to show, quite convincingly, that the unrelenting catalog of physical surfaces in *Le Voyeur* is actually an airtight system of psychological significance. Everything in the novel is a sign, and the phenomenological exercise of pure description is defeated by an existential document which charts definite intentions, a calculatedly biased point of view *on* the world.[30] In the sentences I began by quoting, Robbe-Grillet disarmingly dissolves the terms of the dispute by defining the kinds of significance Picon discovers in *Le Voyeur* (specifically, the compulsive sadism which determines what objects are described as well as the manner in which they are described) as the inevitable but somewhat negligible by-product of a wholly different, and more original novelistic ambition. Pathology is the accident of a total psychological freedom. Instead of being determined by psychology, the Robbe-Grilletian hero-narrator discovers it at the outer limits of an inventive process which, at the start, had been psychologically empty.

Such formulations, as we shall see, do not exactly solve the problems raised by Robbe-Grillet's novelistic experiments. They do, however, suggest the terms in which I think those problems can best be discussed, and the terms are different from those originally used by Robbe-Grillet himself and taken up by critics both sympathetic and hostile to him. Robbe-Grillet first saw himself as practicing and promoting a literature at last freed from the "fringes of culture (psychology, ethics, metaphysics, etc.)" which "are added to things, giving them a less alien, more comprehensi-

30. "Le Probleme du Voyeur," *Mercure de France,* No. 1106 (October 1955), 306–7.

ble and more reassuring aspect." To see the world at all is to see it nonanthropomorphically, for ". . . the world is neither significant nor absurd. It *is*, quite simply." The reality of the world resides mainly in its presence; thus, in the novel of the future, ". . . gestures and objects will be *there* before being *something*. . . ." [31] To illustrate man's absence from nature, and to show up the notion of psychological depth as a dispensable myth of classical psychology, Robbe-Grillet recommended a rigorously superficial presentation of people and of things. A geometrical, nonmetaphorical description of the world would correct the humanistic mistakes of seeing man everywhere. Metaphor is the writer's chief enemy. Any analogy is potentially dangerous: if I compare a wave to a horse's mane, my image implies a common quality (of power or wildness) between the two, therefore a "superior nature," therefore a transcendent unity in which, as Robbe-Grillet writes, "the universe and I now have a single soul, a single secret." [32]

Olga Bernal, who sympathizes with Robbe-Grillet's attempt "to replace meanings with forms," has competently spelled out the analogies between the novelist's program and the preoccupations of philosophical thought since Husserl and Heidegger.[33] Indeed, Robbe-Grillet's essays do seem to point to a novel of phenomenological description, but while the philosophical quality of his particular commitment to such descriptions can obviously be made to profit from these *rapprochements,* in themselves Robbe-Grillet's statements strike me as more suggestive of an awkward intellectual transition from agronomy to literature. Robbe-Grillet's scientific, or, more exactly, technological background was perhaps responsible for what I see as his early distrust of the kinds of truth proposed by art. Now the engineer, his instruments of physical measurement notwithstanding, can hardly

31. "Une Voie pour le roman futur" (1956), pp. 21–25.
32. "Nature, humanisme, tragédie" (1958), pp. 59–65.
33. *Alain Robbe-Grillet: le roman de l'absence,* in Collection Le Chemin (Paris, 1964). The quote comes from p. 22.

be said to possess a blueprint of the *être-là* of the physical world. The most we can say for him is that he has a technique of description which facilitates his manipulation of our physical environment. The epistemological value of his descriptions is, in fact, irrelevant to the success of his efforts to impose changes on nature. And the changes are originally imaginative constructs, although, once having imagined how a mountain will look covered with roads or dynamited with tunnels, it would of course obstruct the engineer's ambitious vision were he to substitute for the image of tunnels analogies celebrating the mountain's "majesty." Engineering and poetry, it could be said, are different modes of imaginative activity; the differences between the objects of reorganization require the use of different reorganizing processes.

But, from the greater visibility of technological restructuring of the world, it is tempting to deduce the epistemological validity of procedures which have actually been shown to be no more than *manipulatively* valid. Science, Robbe-Grillet writes in "Nature, humanisme, tragédie," "is justified only by the establishment, sooner or later, of utilitarian techniques. Literature has other aims." But this appropriate distinction between different goals leads Robbe-Grillet to a more questionable distinction between the nature of scientific and poetic statements about the world. "Only science . . . can claim to know the *inside* of things," by which Robbe-Grillet means "the *knowledge* of textures (internal as well as external), of their organization, their functioning and their genesis." [34] But the precise degree of correlation between my description of chlorophyll transformations in plant life and the "plantness" of plants is something I will never know. A useful nomenclature is not a *"knowledge* of textures." What we call scientific knowledge has to be defined in terms of a process blending observation and hypothesis, experiments in control, and the imaginative forging of a language which makes experimentation and hypothesis possible and intelligible.

34. "Nature, humanisme, tragédie," pp. 79–80.

76 BALZAC TO BECKETT

But, for the Robbe-Grillet of "Nature, humanisme, tragédie,"
science speaks to us accurately of things themselves; his epistemological skepticism is reserved for the too human images of things
in the poetry of Francis Ponge. Robbe-Grillet's condemnation of
metaphor presupposes this unexamined confidence in another,
a scientific language of description. The function he assigns to
literature—although this was certainly not intended—sounds like
a *pis aller:* unable to penetrate the "real" interiority of things, the
writer should content himself with describing their surfaces. But
is it possible, especially if the instrument of description is a language whose nature is to be significant, to describe gestures and
objects as *"there* before being *something"?* The "before" assumes
a priority of presence over identity within an activity of consciousness which cannot help but be, at every moment, an activity of
identification. And the effort to hide this inevitable projection of
meanings on the world can easily result in a literature of mystification, or a literature of the unnatural. Robbe-Grillet's nonmetaphorical descriptions, far from making us aware of the mere presence of objects, make us extremely uneasy about the hidden projects of the person describing them. Indeed, in *Le Voyeur* this
person seems to be a sadistic murderer, and in *La Jalousie* he is
an obsessively jealous husband. Both novels show the neutral, disinterested point of view as a diseased point of view, one in which
repressed interest and self-projection may finally explode as violence. Meaningless space, as Bernard Dort has said, is the alibi by
which characters try to mask their guilt; what starts as a novel of
surfaces becomes a novel of depths, and the depths are all the
more active for having been held in abeyance for a certain time.[35]
Seen from this point of view, psychology in Robbe-Grillet's novels
is the determining pressure, the magnetic center of attraction
from whose orbit description vainly tries to escape. *Le Voyeur*
and *La Jalousie* would therefore illustrate the classicism of sur-
veyors, and the art of the *litote* reappears in the modern guise
of ominously bland geometric measurements.

35. "Sur l'espace'," *Esprit*, XXVI (July–August 1958), 80–81.

Robbe-Grillet's refinement of his theoretical stand seems, understandably, to have been a difficult undertaking, involving both thinly disguised self-repudiations and tortuous efforts to reconcile contradictory positions. In 1961, he announced that "the New Novel aims only at a total subjectivity." Objectivity, he then wrote, "taken in its usual sense—neutral, cold, impartial— . . . became [as used by certain critics] an absurdity." Robbe-Grillet recognizes that the man who describes things in his own novels is "the least neutral, the least impartial of men: *always* engaged, on the contrary, in the most obsessive emotional adventure, obsessive to the point of often distorting his vision and producing fantasies close to delirium." [36]

A few years earlier, Robbe-Grillet had conceded that the novelistic character he was attempting to create might use objects as "the prop of his passions." But he was careful to insist that this excluded "any suspect understanding, any complicity" with things. Such a character "asks nothing" of objects, is neither in nor out of harmony with them; ". . . his passion . . . rests on their surface, without wishing to penetrate them since there is nothing on the inside, without feigning the least appeal, for they would not answer." [37] But how can a distorted vision, an almost delirious imagination remain so disciplined, so judicious? In the midst of his "obsessive emotional adventure," does the Robbe-Grilletian character really "ask nothing" of objects? Can he have the philosophical wisdom of not wishing to penetrate objects, the emotional stability and leisure necessary to recognize that they would not answer his appeal? If Robbe-Grillet's characters have passions to begin with, his later remarks are a much more accurate description of the images of reality produced by these passions. A delirious view of objects is not the same thing as a disinterested use of objects as a mere "prop" for feelings (although I confess being unable to imagine what the latter might be). Above all, Robbe-Grillet has rid himself of the arbitrary, purely abstract

36. "Nouveau roman, homme nouveau" (1961), pp. 148–49.
37. "Nature, humanisme, tragédie," p. 59.

distinction between two "moments" of human description, one when objects would simply be *there* and another when they would, as it were, agree to be *something*. The affectless *être-là* of objects has been repudiated, and the "prop" of passion has, at least implicitly, been recognized for what it always was: a metaphor for passions. Anthropomorphic adjectives are not necessary, as Robbe-Grillet's novels amply demonstrate, to "violate" the surfaces of things with our intentions.

Is that, then, the interest of Robbe-Grillet's theory and fiction: the recourse to geometry as a metaphor for feelings? If so, the later essays are simply retreats in the face of assaults from a psychologizing criticism. The fatal blow seems to have come from Bruce Morrissette's sympathetic, convincing, unfortunate discovery of myth and psychology in Robbe-Grillet's novels.[38] To admire Morrissette, whose admiration of Robbe-Grillet might have been taken as a promise of academic consecration, required some fast backtracking from the lines along which the shock produced by Robbe-Grillt's fiction had been felt most strongly. The principal backtracker was Roland Barthes, who had also been principally responsible for defining the original shock. In reviews of *Les Gommes* and *Le Voyeur* called "Littérature objective" (1954) and "Littérature littérale" (1955), Barthes had unambiguously said that Robbe-Grillet's experiment was interesting "only if it is radical, if it postulates a novel without content." [39] In both novels Barthes saw and praised nonexpressive objects, objects deprived of all attributes except that of their superficial, meaningless existence. The sensationalist story of *Le Voyeur* tends "toward zero"; here, happily and at last, was the "absolute exercise of negation" needed to knock down the assumptions of "bourgeois psychologism." [40] But in his polite preface to Morris-

38. *Les Romans de Robbe-Grillet*, preface by Roland Barthes (Paris, 1963).
39. "Littérature littérale," *Essais critiques*, in Collection Tel Quel (Paris, 1964), p. 69.
40. "Littérature littérale," pp. 64 and 69.

sette's study, Barthes surprisingly, if with some reluctance, announces the "return" of meaning to Robbe-Grillet's work. The meanings have apparently been created by the public's demand for meaning, since "we are all part of Robbe-Grillet," and the evolution of his work cannot be separated from what so many people have persisted in demanding from it.[41] The work has thus capitulated to the demands of a meaning-hungry society, and the symbolism and psychology not there at the time of Barthes's reviews have been installed in time for a preface which nicely—humbly—illustrates the historical relativism of literature and of literary criticism.

It has been one of the virtues of recent French criticism to subvert the notion of the literary work as an object having definite, analyzable, and final meanings. Raymond Picard justifies his fury at Barthes's brilliant, psychoanalytically oriented reading of Racine by appealing to this inviolable objective truth in art: "There is a truth about Racine on which we can all agree." [42] But this deceptive submissiveness to the text masks, as Barthes has shown,[43] the tyranny of a *particular* "truth"—Picard's—about Racine. No one has argued more convincingly than Barthes for the open-endedness of literary activity, for the constant, vitalizing re-creation of significance through diversified critical re-enactments of the writer's performance. The meanings of literature are in the responses to literature; a work's significance is exhausted only when it is no longer read. Unfortunately, Barthes's preface to Morrissette is an inferior, suspect version of this approach to art. The glibness of "we are all part of Robbe-Grillet" can be explained by the disappointment evident in the preface: Morrissette's installation of psychological meanings is so much less interesting—can Barthes help but recognize it?—than Barthes's extravagant denials of psychology in Le Voyeur and Les Gommes.

41. *Les Romans de Robbe-Grillet*, p. 15.
42. *Nouvelle critique ou nouvelle imposture*, in Collection Libertés (Paris, 1965), p. 69.
43. In *Critique et vérité* (Paris, 1966).

Robbe-Grillet's own reaction to Morrissette's investigation only added to the critical confusion and sidestepping. Besieged by all the hostile psychologizing about his work, he thanked Morrissette for having "saved" him "from symbolism by inventing the 'objective correlation' [sic]." [44] But the notion of the objective correlative doesn't save Robbe-Grillet from anything except perhaps from a certain kind of confessional literature in which there is a minimal mediating of feelings through objects, characters, and situations not directly traceable to autobiographical sources. Furthermore, Morrissette did not "invent" the objective correlative, and Eliot did not propose it *for* Robbe-Grillet. It describes a relation between literary images and the self which is as characteristic of Homer and Sophocles as of the New Novelists, and to propose it as a key to Robbe-Grillet's technique is to make short work of his claim that contemporary literature is producing "a more total revolution than those from which, in the past, romanticism or naturalism was born." [45] In short, however we look at it—from the point of view of a "return" of meaning to Robbe-Grillet's work or from the theoretical perspective of objective correlatives—the concession to psychological significance in Robbe-Grillet's fiction has been made in ways that limit his originality and expose his descriptive technique as little more than a mildly novel mask for a fundamentally conventional art. [46]

Must we be satisfied with this? I think not, and the best way to avoid this watering down of Robbe-Grillet's originality is to try out an approach which takes for granted the presence of psychological meanings in his work, and concentrate on the processes which create those meanings. What Robbe-Grillet most radically questions—and this brings us back to my first quotation from "Du réalisme à la réalité"—is not the necessity

44. Morrissette, *Les Romans de Robbe-Grillet*, p. 29.
45. "Une Voie pour le roman futur," p. 18.
46. The preceding pages develop and modify my expressions of uneasiness about Robbe-Grillet's critical positions in a review of *Les Gommes* for *Partisan Review*, XXXII (Spring 1965), 305–10, and in a review of *Pour un nouveau roman* for *Book Week*, March 20, 1966.

of psychology in the novel, but its dependence on extranovelistic sources for its inspiration. Barthes, while confusing issues by applying to *Le Voyeur* such striking but senseless formulas as "une littérature du constat," [47] gets close to the real literary adventure in the work by speaking of its creative rather than expressive constellations of objects. Far from providing a model for a literature of objective statement, of the mere recording of facts, *Le Voyeur* creates a psychology *from* its "blinding literality." [48] The question, as Barthes suggests in certain passages of his essay, is not whether or not there is a crime, but how the crime is made. His most brilliant insight into what I think Robbe-Grillet has almost done is his remark that the murder in *Le Voyeur* does not proceed from, or refer us to, a pathology; our mistake in reading the novel would be to induce a hidden content from the form. The epistemological lesson of *Le Voyeur* is a critique of our tendency to see the imaginary as a symbol of the real, as a *litote* of nature.[49] The exemplary value of Robbe-Grillet's work would therefore be in its demonstration of the imaginary as nonderivative. And while Barthes seems to feel that a crime which does not allude to a preexistent pathology thereby excludes any pathology, or psychology, at all, it is possible to say that Mathias *is* a sadist, but that his sadism is the consequence of visual play rather than the pressure determining, at every moment, the course of his vision.

Robbe-Grillet himself has defined his ambition most simply and directly in speaking of the novelist's strength as his ability to invent freely, "without a model." [50] "Before the work, there is nothing, no certainty, no thesis, no message." [51] Instead of "having something to say" and then looking for a way in which to express it, the writer uses style in order to constitute reality: his

47. "Littérature littérale," p. 63.
48. "Littérature littérale," pp. 66–7.
49. "Littérature littérale," p. 67.
50. "Sur quelques notions périmées" (1957), p. 36.
51. "Nouveau roman, homme nouveau," p. 153.

282   BALZAC TO BECKETT

style "never knows what it is seeking, it is ignorant of what it has
to say; it is invention, invention of the world and of man, constant invention and perpetual self-contestation." [52] To read this
kind of self-improvising work is to participate in the improvisation. There are no settled meanings to receive or to decipher;
critical appreciation becomes a creative exercise, and Robbe-
Grillet's ambitious extraliterary design involves nothing less than
the desire to train us in self-creation, to teach the reader "to invent his own life." [53] To read freely is to live freely, for—and we
see how completely an esthetic of art as imitation or distillation
of life's essences is dismissed in this simple but nonetheless radical formula—"art is life." [54]

The substance and workability of this formula depend on
where we "place" psychology in Robbe-Grillet's fiction. When I
attempt to participate as fully as he invites us to in the creation
of his work, to what extent do I find my freedom constrained by
those pathological obsessions which, to judge from the richly
vague and provocative passage quoted at the beginning of this
chapter, Robbe-Grillet wants to prevent from settling into a
given character? To remove this constraint means taking risks
greater than we might at first imagine with the definiteness of
human figures in fiction. Thus, in La Jalousie, Robbe-Grillet's
most difficult enterprise, as we shall see, is not to avoid telling
us any supposed truth about the relation between Franck and
A. . . , but rather to keep the narrative from being consistently
oriented by an emotion as specific and purposeful as jealousy.
Now it is of course impossible to say if this is Robbe-Grillet's
major intention in the work. Remembering his remark about
the "obsessive emotional adventure" in which his narrative centers
are "always" engaged, we could easily read La Jalousie as a diagram of such an adventure. On the other hand, remembering
other remarks, we might focus on the priority of emotionally non-

52. "De réalisme à la réalité," p. 175.
53. "Temps et description dans le récit d'aujourd'hui" (1963), p. 169.
54. "Du réalisme à la réalité," p. 173.

contaminated objects over feelings in the novel. In fact, the work is a fascinating drama of confrontations among different kinds of novelistic choices—choices which, in the essays of *Pour un nouveau roman*, appear in the less interesting guise of shifting, even contradictory theoretical positions. But the very confusions of the essays are useful, I feel, in helping us to separate and identify the often conflicting impressions which the novel gives us as a single, undifferentiated shock. For Robbe-Grillet, theory has generally been reflection after the fact of fictional creation. If I have reversed the terms, it has not been to show up the dissonances between the two, but rather to preface my own reading of *La Jalousie* with the novelist's sense of what is at stake, for fiction in general, in his work. Thus, theory will hopefully not be the foil which adorns, by contrast, a secure, fixed reading of the novel, but will rather help in providing the terms of co-existence for different ways of participating in the novel's sense.

La Jalousie consists almost entirely in a few conversations and in descriptions of the external world. A woman referred to only as A . . . lives on a banana plantation in what is probably a non-African French colony. Franck, who lives on a nearby plantation, often comes to lunch or dinner at A . . .'s home; he is almost never accompanied by his wife Christine, who suffers from the tropical climate. One day Franck and A . . . take a trip to town. Franck says he wants to buy a new truck; A . . . perhaps has some shopping to do. They say they will return the same evening, but they come back the next morning, explaining that Franck's car broke down and that they were forced to spend the night in a hotel.

It *could* be argued that there is no one else in the novel. But, when Franck and Christine are expected for dinner, there are four chairs instead of three on the terrace. At lunch the day she comes back from town, A . . . asks someone what has happened on the plantation during the time she has been away. And, in a few passages of dialogue, parts of the conversation, reported in

the *style indirect libre,* are attributed to neither Franck nor
A. . . . While it is not said once in *La Jalousie* that A . . . is
married, it would require a heroically literal reading of the novel
not to feel that she has a husband. And since many of the scenes
described are scenes from which A . . . and Franck are absent,
the reader would have to be only slightly less remarkably passive
not to conclude that the story is being told from the husband's
point of view. Finally, since that point of view comes back so
often to images of A . . . , to conjectures about what one of her
smiles or remarks might mean, and, especially, to the night she
spends with Franck in town, we are compelled to infer that the
husband is obsessed by the idea that A . . . and Franck are having an affair. But the husband has no name, he is never referred
to directly, there is not a single analytical passage on his jealousy,
and the question of whether A . . . and Franck are lovers is
never explicitly asked. Why, then, if the novel's subject is the
husband's jealousy, has so much care been taken to avoid mentioning both the husband and jealousy?

This question can be answered in conventionally realistic terms.
The anonymity at the center of Robbe-Grillet's novel corresponds,
in part, to the anxiously investigative nature of jealousy. It is as
if the world, described objectively enough, would *reveal* the
truth about A . . . and Franck. The danger for the husband is
to let himself be tempted by interpretation. Any single reading
of his wife's words or gestures is apt to trap him in the wrong
version of her behavior. Dramatic tension in *La Jalousie* is created less by the relations among the characters than by this anti-
interpretive will, this effort to achieve a kind of epistemological
austerity. Furthermore, in his passionate pursuit of the truth
about A . . . and Franck, nothing—and this is plausible
enough—interests the husband less than himself. The particular
character of jealousy is revealed to us by the husband's visual
itinerary. It is the way he sections off the world around him, the
time he spends looking at certain things, the transitions from
one scene to another, the repetitions and associations, which de-

fine the external world circumscribed in the novel as exactly equivalent to the mental universe of a jealous man. Robbe-Grillet describes jealousy by allowing jealousy to describe the world.

Jealousy in Robbe-Grillet is, then, not an analyzable mental reality, but rather the medium (mental blinds or shutters, as the title suggests) through which the world is seen. When the husband, for example, leaves A . . . and Franck alone on the terrace and goes into the house to get some ice for their drinks, his anxiety and curiosity are presented entirely in terms of the way he charts his course from the terrace to the pantry. They are revealed, created for us by his detour into the office and the time he spends looking at the dining room table. Jealousy is what is being surveyed and the time taken to survey it:

> To get to the pantry, the easiest way is to cross the house. Once across the threshold, a sensation of coolness accompanies the half darkness. To the right, the office door is ajar.
>
> The light, rubber-soled shoes make no sound on the hallway tiles. The door turns on its hinges without squeaking. The office floor is tiled too. The three windows are closed and their blinds are only half-open, to keep the noonday heat out of the room.
>
> Two of the windows overlook the central section of the veranda. The first, to the right, shows through its lowest chink, between the last two slats of wood, the black head of hair—at least the top part of it.
>
> A . . . is sitting upright and motionless in her armchair. She is looking out over the valley in front of them. She is not speaking. Franck, invisible on her left, is also silent, or else speaking in a very low voice.
>
> Although the office—like the bedrooms and the bathroom— opens onto the hallway, the hallway itself ends at the dining room, with no door between. The table is set for three. A . . . has probably just had the boy add Franck's place, since she was not supposed to be expecting any guest for lunch today.
>
> The three plates are arranged as usual, each in the center of one of the sides of the square table. The fourth side, where there is no place set, is the one next to about six feet of the bare

partition where the light paint still shows the traces of the
squashed centipede.

In the pantry the boy is already taking the ice cubes out of
their trays. A pitcher full of water, set on the floor, has been
used to heat the back of the metal trays. He looks up and
smiles broadly.[55]

The absence of "I" in this passage—and throughout the novel
—completely subjectivizes the world. Whereas Proust maintains
a duality between the self and the world simply by having the
narrator point out the peculiarity of his recognizing his love for
Albertine through pictures of the Gare d'Orsay or of Saint-Loup
writing a telegram, Robbe-Grillet abolishes that duality by a total
identification of the self with its pictures. And the result is not
the disappearance of the self, but rather the denial of any objective existence to the world. The important fact that the husband
is not the narrator of La Jalousie guarantees his omnipresence: a
single "I" would have allowed the world to assert its status as an
independent *object of* consciousness. Robbe-Grillet's confusing
theoretical statements about nonanthropomorphic descriptions of
objects and "total subjectivity" can be reconciled only if we see
the former as a strategy for achieving the latter. Far from eliminating man from the world, the absence of all reference to a human
point of view so thoroughly humanizes the world that it is no
longer necessary to speak of point of view. Instead of being looked
at, external reality embodies the glance which determines its nature. As Robbe-Grillet himself puts it in a much more satisfactory
formula than the ones about the world's être-là, objects in his
novels are both "alien to man and constantly being invented by
man's mind." [56] The alien quality of things in La Jalousie lies
precisely in their failure to reveal any pattern or sense other than

55. *Two Novels by Robbe-Grillet/Jealousy and In the Labyrinth*, tr.
Richard Howard (New York, 1965), pp. 58–59. La Jalousie (Paris,
1957), pp. 48–50. All other page references to *La Jalousie* will be given
in the text. The page numbers from the English translation precede the
page numbers from the Editions de Minuit edition in French.
56. "Temps et description dans le récit d'aujourd'hui," p. 161.

that invented by the husband's jealousy. Their inaccessibility is pointed to by the very docility with which they become his jealousy. Totally subjective, they leave no space across which the husband might at least have the illusion of looking at something different from himself—that is, at the relation between A . . . and Franck. At the furthest limits of his nonmetaphorical style, Robbe-Grillet thus reaches a subjectivity which, as he says in "Nouveau roman, homme nouveau," helps us to see, by contrast, the ambition behind Balzac's constant plunges into the heart of things as that of knowing, and possessing, the world with a god-like objectivity.[57]

Robbe-Grillet's experiment in "total subjectivity" makes the problem of A . . .'s conduct much more excruciating for the reader than it may be for the husband. We suffer, for example, from the apparent disadvantage of having to reconstruct scenes as they "really" happened. Several crucial incidents—Franck's killing of the centipede, conversations before and after the trip to town, the husband's going to the pantry for ice—are told more than once in the novel, and no two accounts are exactly the same. It is tempting, but impossible, to figure out which is the most accurate version of a particular scene. It is obviously arbitrary to say that a fuller account is truer than a scantier one: how do we know that the extra information is not being invented rather than remembered by the husband? For that matter, how can we tell whether or not all the versions—and the incident itself—are purely imaginary? Any distinction between what is seen and what is imagined is subverted by the husband's silence. We may of course guess that the husband is inventing certain scenes and actually seeing others: the meals with A . . . and Franck could be thought of as really taking place, while the images of them together in the hotel room or of Franck's car in flames seem to be fantasies. But the scene in the hotel room is presented in exactly the same way as the more probable incident of the hus-

57. "Nouveau roman, homme nouveau," p. 149.

band going into the house for ice. Furthermore, what may at first seem like another account of an already related event may be an account of another event, or both accounts may be mixtures of two or even several events. And since everything is given to us in the present tense, how can we establish any chronology for the story? Even more important, how can we establish the time at which the incident is being told? Is it at the time of the incident itself, or afterwards? And if it is the latter, how much time has elapsed between the action and the memory of it, and how can we be sure that certain scenes do not belong to the past and that others (which ones?) are not contemporaneous with the narration itself? I shall presently consider how we can convert all this confusion into profit, how we may find in it a freedom difficult to imagine for the husband. But it is important, first of all, to see how lost we are. Everything in *La Jalousie* may be true, and everything may not be true; all this pseudo-evidence (so unlike the real if temporarily obscure evidence of the detective story) is equally valid and equally uncertain.

   La Jalousie is like the native song the narrator describes about halfway through the book. The song begins again just when one thinks it is over, and when the listener imagines he is in the middle of the poem it abruptly stops. It starts again "on notes which hardly seem to constitute a beginning, or a reprise." The narrator decides, however, in favor of some hidden continuity, development, and unity: "It is doubtless the same poem continuing. If the themes sometimes blur, they only recur somewhat later, all the more clearly, virtually identical. Yet these repetitions, these tiny variations, halts, regressions, can give rise to modifications—though barely perceptible—eventually moving quite far from the point of departure" (83–84; 100–101). Of course, this is a tantalizing nonexplanation if we try to apply it—as we surely do—to *La Jalousie* itself. The implied analogy between theme and event is a confusing one. It is clear that various scenes in the novel are thematically similar, but that is scarcely a guarantee that they refer to the same incident, or, if they do, that the incident is real rather than imaginary. And where, exactly, is that place "quite far from the point of departure"? Applied to *La Jalousie,* this remark could mean either that we get closer to the truth as the novel proceeds or that we get further away from it, that the real situation is slowly filled in for us or that we get more and more entangled in the husband's distorting fantasies— or (to make the phrasing of these alternatives as Robbe-Grilletian as possible) the remark could mean nothing at all.

The only conclusion—and it is a startling one—that we can draw from this tactic of bewilderment is that Robbe-Grillet wants to make us more insane than the husband. We don't know, after all, if *he* is insane. We would be in a position to say that he is if this narrative of discontinuous events and of apparently hallucinatory associations were being presented as a *monologue intérieur,* directly from the husband's point of view. But, since we never hear the husband speak, we could imagine that he has a rational sense of chronology, that he knows when he is remembering and when he is fantasizing, and perhaps even that he has a critical view of his own jealousy . . . The reader, on the other hand, unable to organize and judge what he sees, merely wanders, in a continuous present, through a world contaminated by jealousy. The questions I have just asked about the husband and about the novel's action could be thought of as our attempt to escape form the dizzying whirlpool of fantasy into the sanity of secure interpretations. But this sanity is an illusion, a false hope: we simply substitute a perhaps interminable series of unanswerable questions for the obsessive pictorial themes of jealousy. The narrator excites our curiosity while imprisoning us in our ignorance. If it is possible to think that the husband is torturing an innocent A . . . with his suspicions and his spying, an even more cunningly sadistic *narrator* can be inferred from the frantic helplessness which we recognize as our own "ideal" response to the floating pseudo-point of view of *La Jalousie.*

Now the interpretative trap in *La Jalousie* is not only a potential threat to our sanity; it is also a test of our literary sophistica-

tion. With brilliant perversity, Robbe-Grillet has written a work
which plunges us into chaos and stifles criticism by the very
strategy used to lure us into trying to make critical sense of the
work. He invites us to be nostalgic for the kind of novel being
read by A . . . and Franck. Although we hear about this novel
only from the point of view of someone who apparently has not
read it, it seems to have analogies with the situation of the characters in *La Jalousie*. It is, however, probably a more traditional
piece of fiction. To judge from A . . . and Franck's talk about
it, we imagine a book which leaves no doubt about "what is happening," a book which checks the reader's imagination for *other*
stories by having such a definite story of its own. With great good
sense—which, in the context of *La Jalousie*, can mean only the
subtlest bad faith—the narrator suggests a criticism of the way
A . . . and Franck react to the novel. Instead of judging its
"value," or speaking of "the verisimilitude, the coherence, or the
quality of the narrative," they discuss "the scenes, events, and
characters as if they were real: a place they might remember (lo-
cated in Africa, moreover), people they might have known, or
whose adventures someone might have told them." As they would
do for mutual friends, ". . . they frequently blame the heroes
for certain acts or characteristics . . . ," and they deplore the
coincidences of the plot, going so far as to construct "a different
probable outcome starting from a new supposition, 'if it weren't
for that.' Other possibilities are offered, during the course of the
book, which lead to different endings. The variations are extremely numerous; the variations of these, still more so. They
seem to enjoy multiplying these choices, exchanging smiles, carried away by their enthusiasm, probably a little intoxicated by
this proliferation . . ." (74–75; 82–83).

A . . . and Franck are bad readers—or rather, they are bad
readers of a particular type of novel. They respond to the work
they are reading as if it were *La Jalousie*—that is, a novel in
which the facts are (insidiously) left to the imagination of the
reader. They violate their more conventional novel by making

it richer than it is; free of all critical scruples, they indulge in an interpretive promiscuity from which other, competing versions of the work emerge. They are, in short, making the novel indefinite, opening it up, participating in its creation. One might almost say that they would be ideal readers of Robbe-Grillet: they invent the novel as they go along, and they make no distinction between art and life. The work they are reading, however, finally discourages them, and Franck, suddenly a prudent critic respectful of his text, remarks on the futility of all their hypotheses, "since things are the way they are: reality stays the same" (75; 82). But wasn't he right to ignore that "reality"? In their uncomplicated and healthy confusions between art and life, A . . . and Franck were rejecting a view of art which Robbe-Grillet himself, in his criticism and in his fiction, constantly attacks: a view of art as final and definitive, as gathering and distilling ready-made meanings from life and passing them on to a passive public. Franck's submissiveness only reveals the ridiculous nature of the claims implicitly made in the novel he is reading. With its fixed plot and complete characters, the African story disguises an inventive process as a scientific document; it tyrannizes the reader into an impoverished view of the possible by denying its own status (the status of all art) as a tentative, ultimately dismissable version of the real.

But can A . . . and Franck's promiscuous reading really be trusted as a key to the reading of La Jalousie? A . . . and Franck, so to speak, are moving ahead in literary history—toward a Robbe-Grillet novel—with their multiple versions of a story. We, on the other hand, may be longing to regress to the clear and trustworthy plot and characters of the fiction they treat with so little respect. But we are of course punished for giving in to this temptation. A . . . and Franck can perhaps enjoy their imaginary adventures because they can always return to the unchangeable "reality" of their novel. But our relation to whatever story there may be in La Jalousie is not the same as theirs to the novel they are reading; rather, it is similar to the husband's relation to

that novel. He apparently would like to know what is in the
novel in the hope that it will tell him something about A . . .
and Franck; but, instead of ending up with an unattackable version of the story, he tries out contradictory versions of the story
which lead nowhere and which could go on endlessly:

> The main character of the book is a customs official. This
> character is not an official but a high-ranking employee of an old
> commercial company. This company's business is going badly,
> rapidly turning shady. This company's business is going ex-
> tremely well. The chief character—one learns—is dishonest.
> He is honest, he is trying to re-establish a situation compromised
> by his predecessor, who died in an automobile accident. But
> he had no predecessor, for the company was only recently
> formed; and it was not an accident. Besides, it happens to be a
> ship (a big white ship) and not a car at all. (137; 216)

There is our danger, and it is by asking the questions I raised
earlier about La Jalousie's story that Robbe-Grillet's reader
espouses the husband's routed imagination. Security, even sanity,
lie in the conventional novel Robbe-Grillet has not written. But
as soon as we begin to imagine that novel, we are lost in a
labyrinth of conjecture even more anguishing than the "con-
vulsed question mark" made by the centipede on the dining room
wall with which each page of La Jalousie is stamped (62; 56).

Our only solution is to suppose nothing—and the condition
for this is to seize the opportunity Robbe-Grillet has given us to
do away with the husband. The very device by which Robbe-
Grillet allows the husband to invade every corner of the world—
his absence as a character capable of thinking "I"—increases our
chances of successfully getting rid of him. Robbe-Grillet's narrative method subverts the psychology of jealousy which it appears
to express so ingeniously, and it therefore may free his work
from the sentiment of jealousy itself as the psychological de-
terminant of the novel's development. The husband has to be inferred, and everything changes once we choose *not* to infer the

husband's existence and character. The trap represented by the husband in *La Jalousie* is the trap of realistic reference. To work out his presence "behind" the narrative surface is to open the way for inferences about everything else in the book, and the implied "real story" of *La Jalousie* is an analogue for a determining, enslaving reality behind all art, a reality which makes of art a tautological expression of life.

To read the novel in the light of the husband's jealousy is to allow for the questions raised by this jealousy, and therefore to be terrorized by the answers hidden from our view. Jealousy chains the novel to a single path of significance; but this significance, happily, is impossible to reconstruct. And we are helped in our effort not to attempt a reconstruction by the thinness of what can be inferred about the husband's personality. He is reduced to his jealousy. He lacks the physical reality which makes of A . . . , however distorted our image of her may be, such a powerfully erotic presence in the work. Of the three principal figures in *La Jalousie,* the husband is physically, psychologically, and socially the least rounded, the most abstract. But what might be felt as a fault in Balzac or even in Proust serves Robbe-Grillet's most original purpose. From the psychological point of view of realistic fiction, the husband really has no personality, and the very fact that he is almost entirely just a jealous vision helps us to take the crucial step of trying out the vision without the jealousy.

How does this change our reading of the novel? Unable to distinguish between what the husband sees and what he imagines, deprived of any view of A . . . and Franck distinct from a jealous curiosity, and, finally, suspicious of the jealousy itself as an obsession detached from a personality, we can consider the various scenes in the novel as purely projective rather than derivative. Each new version of an incident could be seen not as an effort to get back to the truth, but rather as an invention compositionally inspired by an earlier version or indeed by anything preceding it *in the text.* Our interest would then no longer

lie in the objects of description, but, as Robbe-Grillet says in one
of his essays, "in the very movement of the description." And
the movement is not toward a full and definitive picture, toward
a single story finally elaborated in all its detail; instead, description tends to contest the things described at the same time that
it brings them into being, thus instituting "a double movement
of creation and destruction [gommage], which one also finds,
moreover, on all levels in the book and in particular in its total
structure—whence the *disappointment* inherent in contemporary
works." [58] Each section in *La Jalousie*—ideally, each paragraph,
each sentence, each word—is a new beginning. Its relation to
what precedes it is ambivalent: it picks up and develops an inspiration in order to destroy the source of inspiration, to reinvent
the world in a form which, in turn, will suicidally inspire further
inventions.

If we can experience *La Jalousie* in this way, its anecdotal and
psychological components must be dissolved. Or, more precisely,
the psychology that may emerge from this constantly retouched,
renewed, self-destroying vision will be constrained neither by the
"real" facts about A . . . and Franck nor by the obsessive emotional adventure of jealousy. The banana trees, the house, the
hotel bedroom, the photograph of the port, A . . . and Franck
would all be elements in an exercise of *free* association, that is,
an exercise that would both generate and discard meanings as it
proceeds ceaselessly to remake the self and the world. The enormous difficulty of this enterprise can be guessed from the fact
that we are unable to say exactly what *kinds* of new definitions
of experience are being proposed in *La Jalousie*. It is comparatively easy to see what type of psychology and what type of art
are being subverted, to define the techniques of subversion and
the disposition in which the reader can best collaborate with a
daringly open-ended art. But the old systems of coherence, the
old images of psychological complexity and of the richness of
experience, are replaced by a singularly impoverished range of

58. "Temps et description dans le récit d'aujourd'hui," pp. 160–61.

possibilities. Imaginative freedom in Robbe-Grillet seems to work principally as an act of denudation. The world is washed, meanings are erased; but what are the experiences born from all this cleaning up?

The destruction itself is sharply characterized: Robbe-Grillet's negations are extraordinarily precise, elegant, methodical, and brutal. They almost compose a character in themselves . . . Apart from this movement of pure negativity, we have, so far, a gallery of quite haunting and curiously frozen images: A . . . staring at herself in the mirror, the boy disappearing into the snow in *Dans le labyrinthe*, the sculpture in Lady Ava's garden in *La Maison de rendez-vous*, and A's poses in *L'Année dernière à Marienbad*. The technique of disappointment—the destruction of images before they can develop and combine into conclusive patterns of significance—leaves us with an album of discontinuous photographs, pictures of half-completed gestures. The very movement of contestation in Robbe-Grillet has an effect which paralyzes all movement. Things are freed from meaning what we might expect them to mean, but this is done by immobilizing them before they reach their meanings rather than by finding other movements and other choices which might create a new dynamics of significance. I don't mean simply that Robbe-Grillet's achievement is an incomplete one; we have seen in Proust that incompleteness can be compatible with, can even be the consequence of an intensely agitated drama of self-renewals. In contrast to the multiplication of tones and the metamorphoses of characters in *A la Recherche du temps perdu*, Robbe-Grillet's universe is fixed—*figé*—in a state of suspense.

It could be argued that it is up to *us* to complete those frozen gestures in whatever ways we like. If this is true, then it makes our creative responsibility immense. But then it must also be said that art is not at all like life: it freezes, and life puts things back into motion. This essentially conventional definition, however, does an injustice to Robbe-Grillet's ambition of making us recognize the analogy of invention between art and the rest of life. The fixed interrogation is not the same as the more liberal questions asked in a risky experiment of trying out answers (styles of being) which re-create the self while dissipating its energy, which become new questions because of the unpredictable shapes they assume while being lived. If *La Jalousie* destroys a conventional psychological causality, it does so with a regrettable asceticism. For the sake of its freedom, it mutilates itself. This, I think, is the profound sense of the "neutral" description. It is an even more extreme sense-depriving strategy than the sculptural poses of Robbe-Grillet's films. Description in *La Jalousie* (and in *Le Voyeur*) seems designed to smother plot and psychological characterization by its very mass. Measurements compete with obsessions, and Robbe-Grillet struggles to rid his novels of the latter by filling them with what he seems willing to accept as the benumbingly undramatic detail of the former. A description of indiscernible psychological interest might make the world new again, at least prepare it for lives unconstrained by all the human intentions which history has inscribed on our environment. To bore us into a liberating blankness of intention: this is the radical plan and austere discipline of Robbe-Grillet from the writing exercises of *Instantanés* to the counting of banana trees in *La Jalousie*.

But because the dismissal of jealousy creates a void in the novel, it is finally impossible to keep jealousy out of the novel. The movement of description is one of psychological desertion rather than psychological invention, and the world emptied of significance is not only once again invaded with significance but it is vulnerable to just those meanings which the narrative unceasingly contests. In the passage quoted at the beginning of this essay, Robbe-Grillet suggests that it is their freedom of invention which makes his hero-narrators become "liars, schizophrenics or victims of hallucination" once they begin to resemble "characters." [59] But it is of course impossible to locate in a

59. Ludovic Janvier also makes an interesting case for the liberation of Robbe-Grillet's hero-narrators from a crippling pathology. The psycho-

Robbe-Grillet novel the point where freedom, as he says, "immediately" becomes schizophrenia. More important, why should an advanced stage of self-invention be so easily recognizable as a familiar case of psychopathology? If the contemporary writer is inviting the reader "to learn to invent his own life," the model which Robbe-Grillet offers might well make us hesitate to accept the invitation. One could argue that we should never allow our self-creations to settle into a definable character. But what are some of the forms—since completely formless experience is unimaginable—which could replace the traditional notions of character and personality?

Robbe-Grillet's vision of psychological revolution is a promise of greater freedom, but the most disturbing peculiarity of his work is that the introduction of meaning into the surfaces of objects and the frozen poses is almost always a restriction rather than an enlargement of the field of possibility. And this is not simply because of the obvious truth that *any* meaning destroys the infinite range of pure possibility. Rather, the specific psychological identities which Robbe-Grillet himself recognizes in his work are of a sort which, instead of inspiring an opening out into other identities, merely repeat themselves in more and more aggravated forms. We jump from no meanings at all to the monotonous fantasies of "liars, schizophrenics or victims of hallucination."

These very words of course belong to a particular system of definitions; they correspond to notions of truth, mental health, and reality which we are naturally not obliged to consider as necessary or eternal. But Robbe-Grillet has not yet subverted that system to the point where the sense-making activities of his hero-narrators would be sufficiently original or diversified to make the irrelevance of such categories as "liars" or "schizo-

---

logical victim becomes a "montreur d'images"; a character who is hopelessly "fascinated" by the world comes to "fascinate" *us* by the power of writing ("écriture"). See "Alain Robbe-Grillet et le couple fascination-liberté," *Une Parole exigeante/Le Nouveau roman* (Paris, 1964).

298   BALZAC TO BECKETT

phrenics" evident. As a result, we may feel that his narrator-heroes do not *finally* begin to resemble pathological characters, but that their being such characters determines all their activity from the very start. However much we may try to imagine pathology as the psychological accident at the circumference of Robbe-Grillet's creation, it is difficult to resist the feeling that it really belongs at the center of that creation, that it is the point of departure to which the work indirectly but constantly and faithfully returns.

The "dream" of art, Robbe-Grillet suggests, unlike the dreams of our "agitated nights," [60] perhaps carries no message except the one it creates from its own material. But if art can thus escape being the psychological heir of the artist, it is, of course, still more or less constrained by the way its own messages or signs are organized. Jealousy in Robbe-Grillet's novel provides the centripetal force which draws each new version of the real back into the orbit of an exclusive, limiting passion intolerant of any meanings with which it cannot "associate." The geometrical descriptions, the absence of the husband, and, above all, the projective nature of a narrative in which there is no "real" story to be uncovered but only a search to be conducted: these, on the other hand, create a centrifugal pull which dissolves plot and character and makes the novel's message equivalent to the range and quality of the reader's own self-inventive powers. To feel simultaneously the power of these antagonistic forces is to realize the extraordinary literary tension of *La Jalousie*, a tension far more interesting than the merely psychological one of the husband's tortured curiosity. The subversion of the novel's liberating superficiality by an obsession which assimilates all objects into a single symbolic family makes for a continuous *test* of freedom more moving than the ideal of freedom so ambitiously but perhaps somewhat glibly proposed in *Pour un nouveau roman*.

The recurrent spot—*la tache*—in Robbe-Grillet's fiction has

60. "Joë Bousquet le rêveur" (1953), p. 111.

obvious psychological meanings. It is the crime in *Le Voyeur*, and in *La Jalousie* the outlines of the centipede's crushed body on the wall evoke Franck's sexual power and finally even A . . .'s existence. In their guilt, panic, and anger, the Robbe-Grilletian heroes seek to erase the source of their guilt, or to blot out the object of their sadistic desires. More generally, we might think of the spot in Robbe-Grillet's work as the very allowance he makes for such extreme psychological adventures. In a sense, the obsessional content of these fantasies is less important than the literary safety which they guarantee. Similar to the myths uncovered by Morrissette, pathology in Robbe-Grillet undermines the ideally floating story and makes for novels of perfectly controlled and definable psychological meaning. Like the detective-murderer Wallas in *Les Gommes*, who dreams of "an inevitable and perfect future," one toward which he could move in a straight line, with mechanical, precise, always necessary gestures,[61] Robbe-Grillet's narrators attempt to describe a world of sharply delineated forms, a world "sans faille," "sans bavures." Psychologically, the "fault" or "smudge" may be a crime. Esthetically, it suggests, on the contrary, the open-ended, nonpurposeful proliferation of fantasy which the criminal imagination transforms into an elaborate but predictable and decipherable system of psychological symbolism. The fantasies of the obsessively jealous man or of the sadistic murderer, while they may appear chaotic, apt to go off in any direction, are all controlled and directed by a relentlessly single-minded psychological purpose. Such fantasies, we may hope, are not psychologically significant information about Robbe-Grillet. They do, however, provide him with a reliable discipline to check his ambitions; and they therefore suggest, in this important and original writer, a reluctance to take too many risks, a longing for certain novelistic securities at the expense of as yet untried novelistic freedoms.

61. *Les Gommes*, suivi de "Clefs pour les Gommes," by Bruce Morrissette (Paris, 1953), p. 52.

3

BECKETT AND THE END OF LITERATURE

[The Trilogy: *Molloy, Malone meurt,* and *L'Innommable*]

Pour un nouveau roman: the very title for Robbe-Grillet's essays suggests a promotional aim which the essays themselves both realize and explain. Robbe-Grillet's decision to make explicit (even to simplify) his artistic goals in the frequently polemical formulas of his theoretical writing can be justified by the nature of the goals themselves. For the "New Novel," as Robbe-Grillet envisages it, will be nothing less than a model for human freedom; and if the model appears obscure or impenetrable, the novelist himself, it could be argued, has the duty of providing a kind of explanatory guide to help us to use his work—ultimately, to dismiss it—in the general enterprise of improvising a perhaps unprecedentedly free humanity.

Thus Robbe-Grillet, in *Pour un nouveau roman*, proselytizes for modern fiction as it has been practiced from Proust and Joyce to Beckett and Pinget in the hope that our "conversion" to modern art will coincide with radical transformations of the self and the world. In restating, often in oversimplified fashion, long-acknowledged achievements of the most interesting twentieth-century writers, Robbe-Grillet seems inspired by an urgently felt need to make those achievements available to the largest possible audience. From a man whose own work has been intelligently and generously praised, almost from the beginning, by such critics as Barthes, Blanchot, and Bernard Pingaud, Robbe-Grillet's complaints of all the hostile misunderstandings he has come up against may at first strike us as the sign of a petulant, insatiable appetite for praise. But we can also think of Robbe-Grillet's pursuit of popularity as proceeding from his conviction that unless art is popular and reaches minds less adventurous than those of Barthes and Blanchot, it can hardly be said to contribute to that revolution in consciousness which it is Robbe-Grillet's most ambitious desire to promote. The popularizer is the revolutionary. If Robbe-Grillet's program for fiction does an injustice to the richness of his own fiction, it may at least expand the audience ready to confront that ambiguous richness. The novelist turned filmmaker has found an even more effective way of making himself felt outside literary circles. *L'Année dernière à Marienbad* is as interesting a performance of Robbe-Grillet's profound intentions as any of his novels. And not only do films reach a public far larger than the audience of *Pour un nouveau roman*; *Marienbad* never trumpets forth any of those tendentious summaries of literary history which, however necessary they may be in a program of literary proselytization, may make some of us inclined to come back to Robbe-Grillet's novels in a mood of distrust rather than in the disposition to recognize the novelist's freedom and to exercise our own.

Compared to Beckett, the Robbe-Grillet of *Pour un nouveau roman* is the innocent child of a new Enlightenment—one as naïvely confident and enthusiastic about human freedom as the old. Far from proselytizing for new novels or new men, Beckett has been austerely reticent about both his own intentions and his views on the art of the future. The nearest thing we have to an explicit statement of esthetic tastes or program is the cryptic, self-mocking *Three Dialogues* with Georges Duthuit, written and published for the first time in 1949 in *Transition*, toward the end of that period of extraordinary production (of about three years) when Beckett wrote the trilogy and *En attendant Godot*. The essay on Proust (1931) is a longer critical discussion, but it is much less useful than the ten pages or so of the Duthuit dialogues for an understanding of what Beckett has been trying to do (or trying not to do) in his most interesting work.

Like Robbe-Grillet, Beckett has an image of what art might

become. Neither Masson nor Tal Coat lives up to what B. calls, in the dialogue on Masson, "my dream of an art unresentful of its insuperable indigence and too proud for the farce of giving and receiving." Since B. "exits weeping" when D. asks if we must really deplore the fact that Masson's painting admits " 'the things and creatures of Spring' . . . in order that what is tolerable and radiant in the world may continue," [62] we must wait for the third dialogue, on Bram van Velde, for an elaboration of B.'s ideal of indigent art. When D. asks if Bram van Velde's painting is inexpressive, B. waits a fortnight before answering yes. Having in this way either established the importance (or perhaps the silliness) of the question, or raised doubts about using Bram van Velde to illustrate his idea, or suggested that to formulate the idea is an agony, perhaps an impossibility, B. finally suggests an alternative to "the common anxiety to express as much as possible, or as truly as possible, or as finely as possible, to the best of one's ability." Bram van Velde is the first in whose painting that anxiety—common to all those "whom we call great artists"—is absent. His work is "bereft, rid if you prefer, of occasion in every shape and form, ideal as well as material." And at last, at the end of this intriguing blend of humor, pathos, and eloquent verbal obscurity, B. gives us something like a key—or at least the right lock to work on—for his dream of art when he praises Bram van Velde as "the first to submit wholly to the incoercible absence of relation, in the absence of terms or, if you like, in the presence of unavoidable terms, the first to admit that to be an artist is to fail, as no other dare fail, that failure is his world and the shrink from it desertion, art and craft, good housekeeping, living." [63]

The similarity between Robbe-Grillet and Beckett consists in

62. Samuel Beckett, *Proust* and *Three Dialogues/Samuel Beckett and Georges Duthuit* (London, 1965), pp. 112–13. Also in *Samuel Beckett/ A Collection of Critical Essays*, in Twentieth Century Views (Englewood Cliffs, New Jersey, 1965).
63. *Three Dialogues*, pp. 119–25.

little more than a rejection of certain traditional assumptions about the relation of art to the rest of life. And the rejection is such a widespread modern phenomenon that it hardly defines a particular affinity of talent or interest between these two writers. The common enemy (in theory, at least) is an esthetic of realistic reference: for both Robbe-Grillet and Beckett, the work of art is not dependent on, does not express anything that precedes it. It is against the notion of art's *derivation* from life that Robbe-Grillet argues when he writes that ". . . the duration of the modern work is in no way a summary, a condensation of a more extended and more 'real' duration which would be that of the anecdote, of the story being told." [64] The work of art constitutes its own reality, and for Robbe-Grillet this is equivalent to saying that it helps to constitute, to create reality itself.[65] "The common anxiety to express"—which Beckett allows Bram van Velde to have the extraordinary privilege of abruptly ending in the history of modern art—can exist only as long as artists believe there are prior "occasions" to be expressed. Early nineteenth-century French society is the "material" occasion which Balzac aims to transpose, "as truly as possible," in *La Comédie humaine*. Proustian "essences" and Flaubert's "nature telle qu'elle est" could be thought of as the "ideal" occasions which *A la Recherche* and *Madame Bovary* seek to make visible in language. If, Beckett seems to be saying, we could realize "the absence of terms," admit the impossibility of relating art *to* something else, we might finally have an art expressive of nothing but the resources it discovers in its own poverty-stricken, autonomous existence.

But the elusive complexities of Beckett's position become evident as soon as we examine how he connects the refusal of expressiveness in art to the praise of failure in art. For Robbe-Grillet, the dismissal of "real events" which art would merely

64. "Temps et description dans le récit d'aujourd'hui," *Pour un nouveau roman*, in Collection Idées (Paris, 1963), p. 165.
65. "Du réalisme à la réalité," *Pour un nouveau roman*, p. 175.

summarize and condense is an immensely optimistic act of faith
in art's ability to shape realities constrained, ideally, by nothing more than the number of combinations available to the
imagination at its moments of greatest leisure. Robbe-Grillet's
argument with the old ways of defining the artist's activity is
based on a premise which, at least superficially, could hardly
be thought of as disturbing: the work of art creates *more life*.
A good deal of what might trouble us in the New Novel disappears once we realize, first, that the artist is not trying to separate himself from life, and, even more, that he wants to help
us to be free men. There are no such "healthily" reassuring
aspects in Beckett's thought. "Living," like "desertion, art and
craft, good housekeeping," has nothing to do with being an
artist. And in its independence from life, art creates *nothing
at all*. For the artist Beckett has in mind, unlike Tal Coat and
Matisse (who only disturb "a certain order on the plane of the
feasible"), ". . . there is nothing to express, nothing with which
to express, nothing from which to express, no power to express,
no desire to express, together with the obligation to express." [66]
    The dependence of Beckett's advocacy of failure on the oppo-
sition between expressive and inexpressive art is what I find most
troubling in the *Dialogues*. The opposition itself suggests a hidden agreement with that view of art's derivative nature which, as
I said a moment ago, Beckett seems to be rejecting as firmly as
Robbe-Grillet. The assertion that expression is impossible is not
the basis of a new definition of art; rather, it merely restates an
old definition pessimistically. Since nothing is opposed to expression but the *absence* of expression, we may suspect that
Beckett, instead of imagining some sort of authentic independence for art, has merely experienced the anguishing impossibility of deriving art from life and, as a result, has concluded
that art can only be failure.
    I do not mean the "merely" as a dismissal of this experience

66. *Three Dialogues*, p. 103.

in Beckett, since his "fidelity to failure" has produced what I take to be the most impressive fiction in the West since Faulkner. But the *Dialogues* suggest something which I will develop in my discussion of Beckett's novels, and which provides us with a basis for some badly needed distinctions in our discussions of modern art. Beckett is disturbing without, in a sense, being radical; Robbe-Grillet, for all his reassuring rhetoric about freedom, is proposing the use of art for a revolution in human psychology. The *Dialogues*, even taken alone, suggest how alien such ambitions are to Beckett's temperament. Whereas Robbe-Grillet, in discarding an esthetic of expressiveness, attempts to find a new way to formulate what the artist does, Beckett seems to see being *in*expressive as the only alternative to the expressive. And yet how can we know that the artist is being inexpressive if he doesn't try—however reluctantly—to express? Indeed, B. insists that Bram van Velde cannot paint, but he is obliged to, and when D. asks why, B. must answer, "I don't know." [67] Why this peculiar "obligation to express" when there is nothing to express and no desire or power to express? Even more fundamentally, what makes expression impossible?

The logic of failure is the subject of Beckett's work, but the "argument" would be uninteresting—for his readers, at any rate—if the will to fail, to say nothing, did not meet so many resistances. Beckett's predicament has been the opposite of Robbe-Grillet's. The open-ended novel, ready to receive a rich variety of unpredictable extensions both from the author and his public, tends, as we have seen, to be narrowed into the predictable, excessively determined structures of pathological compulsions in Robbe-Grillet's work. Beckett's struggle toward unrelieved monotony and total inexpressiveness, on the other hand, has taken on a kind of bizarre heroism given his fantastic talent for stylistic and dramatic diversity. Robert Garis has rightly

67. *Three Dialogues*, p. 119.

emphasized the foolishness of complaints, from hostile critics, that Beckett simply "repeats himself" in each new work.[68] Certainly, there is a kind of artistic variety, of which Picasso is the most spectacular modern example, which is simply alien to Beckett. But in the history of art, such variety is the exception rather than the rule, and Beckett's detractors are probably not bothered by what is at least an equally transparent "repetitiveness" in, say, Vermeer or Racine. As in Racine's tragedies from *Andromaque* through *Phèdre*, or, to choose a contemporary example, in Antonioni's films from *L'Avventura* to *Blow-up*, Beckett's work tries out various representations of what are easily recognizable as the persistent themes of Beckett's imagination. But in how many writers do such "fundamental notes" (to use Proust's expression) *not* exist, and could it not be argued that, except for Shakespeare and perhaps Picasso, a certain kind of "variety-without-identity" in art is the sign of an imagination which has never sounded its own most intense, and intensely particularizing interests? We have said almost nothing when we say that certain themes recur throughout an artist's work. Appreciation and criticism begin only when we discuss the quality of their treatment and the ways in which an artist exploits particular occasions in his art either for the reduction of his work to its most limited obsession (or inspiration), or for the expansion of the work to the point where it entertains more possibilities than its mere theme would, superficially, seem capable of accommodating.

Beckett's theatre offers the most striking proof of his ability to undermine a potentially monotonous vision of human desolation by dramatic images so richly differentiated that they defy any attempt to settle on a single definition of the vision. Estragon and Vladimir, for example, are touchingly tender, simple, and bungling clowns compared to the more sophisticated, frantically self-centered, and continuously bitter Hamm and Clov. The

68. See "Journalist and Critic," *Hudson Review*, XIX (Spring 1966), 178–86.

central relationship in *En attendant Godot* includes a moving
if irritated tenderness, and Didi and Gogo play together—with
words and with things—like a couple of shabby burlesque-house
comedians resigned to the poverty of their material and the obligation to go on. Hamm's appeals to Clov's sentiments in *Fin de
partie* are, in comparison to Didi and Gogo's conjugal tolerance
of each other, an unsettlingly potent blend of cynicism, sadistic
taunting, and uncontrolled panic at the prospect of not being
attended to. A series of highly diversified attachments characterize Beckett's theatrical couples. The naggingly protective way
in which Vladimir takes care of Estragon is far from the sulky
servitude that ties Clov to Hamm, or from the ambiguous need
and gallantry with which Willie approaches Winnie at the end
of *Happy Days*. And in *La Dernière bande*, the couple becomes
the Krapp we see on the stage and the Krapp from the past
whom we hear on the tape; what might have been an autobiographical monologue is a brilliantly executed confrontation between a passive Krapp on tape and the puzzled, curious, ironic
Krapp of the present.

Furthermore, from the kind of grammatical exercise in suicidal longing which opens *Fin de partie* ("Fini, c'est fini, ça va
finir, ça va peut-être finir")[69] to Winnie's distinguished exclama-
tion of joy at the beginning of *Happy Days* ("Another heavenly
day"),[70] Beckett has made an extraordinary leap from an almost
unrelieved curse on life to an overwhelmingly touching image
of dignified if desperate optimism. On the one hand, Estragon
and Vladimir, and even Clov and Hamm, enjoy (so to speak)
some freedom of movement compared to the near buried Winnie.
But physical imprisonment and the possibility of suffocation in
Happy Days are brilliantly set against all the reasons Winnie
finds, in her startlingly inventive optimism, not to complain.
The Beckett motifs do not disappear: everywhere in his work
we find imprisonment, the horror of life, the wish for death or

69. *Fin de partie*, suivi de *Acte sans paroles I* (Paris, 1957), p. 15.
70. *Happy Days* (New York, 1961), p. 8.

at least total and silent immobility, a crippled sense of time, and an exasperation with both the appearances of meaning in language and the problematic relations of thought and language to both significance and reality. But, given the diversified embodiments of these themes, any underlying structure of self we might define in his work would be no more than a mere skeleton of general attitudes. Not only do we have this variety of dramatic images; each work also emphasizes different aspects of the fundamental concerns. The theme of an inconceivable past, for example, takes various forms: Estragon's funny puzzlement about what happened yesterday in Act 2 of *Godot*, and, in *Fin de partie*, the ash-can romanticism of Nagg and Nell's evocation of their engagement at Lake Como. References to what we are seeing as a play which the characters somehow feel obliged to accept the agony of participating in are more frequent in *Fin de partie* than elsewhere in Beckett's theatre, and the truth of the story Hamm tells from his past is put into doubt by his frequent shifting from a "narrative tone" to a "normal tone" in order to judge the quality and effectiveness of his performance.

Psychological diversity, changes of emphasis and tone, unfailingly original and surprising images of entrapment—and, of course, the astounding stylistic virtuosity of Beckett. The shift, for example, from a condensed, epigrammatic style (the vicious metaphysical punches at life) to the somber eloquence of Clov's last speeches or Hamm's "narrative tone" when he tells his story constitutes a range of expression impressively different from Estragon and Vladimir's "duets" and their more sustained colloquial speech. A comparable range can be found even in single passages. Lucky's famous exercise in "thinking" in *Godot* is certainly the most sense-devastating monologue in theatrical history. A basic structure of philosophical argumentation gives to the speech a mock coherence. Nonsense rhymes, mechanical repetitions, fractured syntax, the digressions and unexpected transitions within a more than three-page single sentence continuously threaten a fragile but stubbornly asserted order of thought with total chaos and unintelligibility. Despair about man and God is juxtaposed with the meaningless *quaquaquaqua* and the farcical references to scholarly investigations by Testew and Cunard (investigations "crowned by the Acacacacademy of Anthropopopometry of Essy-in-Possy"), and yet we somehow do move toward the almost buried, anticlimactic conclusion that man "wastes and pines" and is "fading" "in spite of the strides of physical culture the practice of sports such as tennis football running cycling swimming flying gloating riding gliding conating camogie skating tennis of all kinds dying flying sports of all sorts autumn summer winter winter tennis of all kinds hockey of all sorts penicilline and succedanea." [71] Lucky's complicated and significantly insignificant chatter parodies the resources of language and of logic with a power that makes Ionesco's demonstrations of the absurd flexibility of words and logical structures in *La Cantatrice chauve* seem like facile if clever horseplay. Finally, would it be possible to confuse the styles of Molloy, Malone, and the Unnamable? The sardonic density of Molloy's speech, Malone's tired eloquence, and the Unnamable's breathless accumulation of brief, meaningless phrases within often monstrously long sentences make for a linguistic diversity which both parallels and mocks the movement toward total meaninglessness and impoverishment which gives to the trilogy its obvious unity.

That movement is, of course, the principal action of the trilogy; *Molloy, Malone meurt*, and *L'Innommable* record the most stupefying enterprise of mutilation in contemporary literature. In Balzac, Stendhal, Proust, and Robbe-Grillet, we have seen what might be called the "normal" or at least traditional relation between self-repetitions and self-diversification in fiction. In all these writers, and in spite of the important differences among them, the novel seems to be a testing-ground for uncover-

71. *Waiting for Godot*, tr. by the author (New York, 1954), pp. 28–29. *En attendant Godot* (Paris, 1952), pp. 71–75.

ing and at the same time devising some means of escape from the self's most limiting (if fundamental) formulations of experience. In Beckett, this centrifugal aspiration is reversed, and in place of an effort to diffuse the self so that its liberty will not be crippled by a center of easily recognizable pressures and designs, we have an attempt to block all inventiveness and freedom and to return to the most extreme monotony of being. Now this experiment would have little dramatic interest if it were not for the almost incredible inventiveness I have just been discussing. The principal tensions of Beckett's work are generated by a strange, even ludicrous struggle against an imagination too rich to be successfully drugged into the uninteresting and meaningless monotony which it bizarrely yearns for. The trilogy gives us different forms of that struggle, and it concludes with the Unnamable's happy and unhappy failure to succeed in failing. What are the images and the logic of this exemplary experiment in self-stultification and in the stultification of literature?

L'Innommable is the most difficult work in the trilogy, but, novelistically, it is also the most impoverished. The philosophical issues implicit in the early sections of the trilogy become progressively more explicit, at the same time that the situations which embody them grow barer and barer. Beckett seems finally to make a desperate (and, as we shall see, impossible) effort to resolve certain questions without mediating them through dramatic imagery—as if the subject of his fiction existed in some pure version with which the fiction constantly interferes. Molloy, for all its peculiarity, has vestiges of a traditional novel with plot and character. Moran, who tells his story in the second half of the book, has more realistic attributes than any other figure in the trilogy. He has a house, a maid, and a son; he works as an agent for some secret society about which he himself knows very little; he is instructed at the beginning of the section to leave home and search for Molloy. This is the closest Beckett comes in the trilogy to a conventional richness of anecdote. But any conventional sort of interest we might take in the anecdote is dissolved from the very start. The mystery story is made absurd by an excess of mystery (Moran is told nothing at all about Molloy), and Moran's feeble attempts to formulate and carry out some lucid plan of action—and thereby to construct a tightly knit mystery story—are defeated by his brooding about the identity of Molloy, his nightmarish journey, and his gradual transformation into the crippled Molloy we already know from the first part of the novel.

But the Moran story does have suspense, comedy (especially in Moran's acidly witty account of how he is bringing up his dimwitted son), and pathos; and Moran has the most active project of any character in the trilogy. What the Beckett characters *have to do* becomes more and more meager. Molloy simply wants to visit his mother; Malone is just waiting to die; and the Unnamable's only wish and effort is to stop talking. Although Beckett is hardly trying to make the Moran adventure into a realistically serious detective story, there is more novelistic *matter* here than anywhere else. And Moran takes longer than any of the other narrator-protagonists to transform plot and character into nightmarishly comic fantasy and to invite the reader's disbelief and disinterest by making what he says as unbelievable, as confusing, and as insignificant as possible.

Molloy could be thought of as a crippled Moran, a Moran who has lost all illusions about being methodical and efficient, and who can tell us on the first page of his story: "The truth is I haven't much will left." [72] (Although the Moran section obviously belongs, in the movement I'm speaking of, before

72. *Three Novels by Samuel Beckett/Molloy, Malone Dies*, and *The Unnamable*, tr. by the author and, for *Molloy*, by Patrick Bowles in collaboration with the author (New York, 1955, 1956, 1958), p. 7. In French, the trilogy is in three separate volumes: *Molloy* (Paris, 1951), *Malone meurt* (Paris, 1951), *L'Innommable* (Paris, 1953). The passage quoted is on p. 7 of the French edition of *Molloy*. Subsequent page references to the trilogy will be to these editions, and will be given in the text, with the pages from the English version preceding those from the French version.

the chronicle of Molloy, our acquaintance with Molloy adds an element of sinister recognition and presentiment to our reading of Moran's account of his gradual physical and moral paralysis.) Molloy is probably the most "appealing" of Beckett's characters. As an intermediate stage in the progression (or regression) from an active, self-confident Moran to the bedridden Malone and to the armless, legless thing planted in a jar in *L'Innommable*, the still mobile Molloy has a recognizable humanness and a range of adventure and response which the Unnamable would treat with impatient scorn. Molloy is continuously interesting and unpredictable. He is the occasion for Beckett's most impressive novelistic display of talents the trilogy will relentlessly work to destroy: a brilliantly comic use of colloquial speech, an extraordinary ability to create suspense over events or questions as trivial as possible, the knack of making humorous an uncompromising sourness and crankiness, and a gift for casual, persistent, and astonishingly inventive obscenity.

But the poverty of Molloy's projects and resources creates a dramatic vacuum in which he can develop the logic of a more radical poverty and thus prefigure his later incarnations in the trilogy. The crippled derelict is an ideal image for a philosophical apprenticeship. In his remarkable book on Beckett, Hugh Kenner has said that the trilogy carries the Cartesian process backwards, starting with a bodily *je suis* and ending with a pure *cogito*.[73] In *Molloy*, the physical world is being prepared for that alien and autonomous *cogito*. Molloy's infirmities give him more time for reflection. Unable to move and to think at the same time, Molloy can enjoy, or suffer, an absolute mental concentration during the pauses between his painful movements. Even his lack of memory is an aid to pure thought: his incapacity to remember his mother's name or the name of the town she lives in diminishes the possibility of any effective action which might divert him from pursuing speculations to their use-

73. *Samuel Beckett: A Critical Study* (Berkeley and Los Angeles, 1968), p. 128.

less or pseudo-conclusions. The difficulty of translating thought into action—of actually finding his mother, or simply of making his body obey his will—gives Molloy an opportunity to wander and get lost in the universe of words and ideas. Precisely because he has to face such elementary problems of locomotion, for example, the enigma of how immaterial thought can produce changes in the material world (an enigma raised by Descartes's dualism between mind and matter and to which Malebranche proposed the rather desperate solution of a Providential intervention for every physical event) becomes a dramatically concrete issue for Molloy. His thought rarely "reaches" matter, and this provides a grotesquely comic confirmation of that autonomy of mind which Descartes experienced as the strength and dignity of mind.

Beckett had already satirized the Cartesian optimism about ratiocination in *Watt*. Watt's futile probing into the "fixity of mystery" at Mr. Knott's house,[74] and especially his breaking down of problems into interminable combinations and solutions, burlesque the easy confidence in analytic separations expressed in Descartes's second law for the infallible pursuit of truth: ". . . divide each of the difficulties that I would be examining into as many elements as possible and as might be necessary to solve the difficulties more effectively."[75] But Watt pursues these analytic proliferations with dogged seriousness, whereas Molloy engages in rational investigation with sarcastic thrusts at the process itself. Thought is mocked not just by the nature of the problems it attaches itself to (could Molloy's great love—Edith or Ruth?—have been really a man? how can he arrange his sixteen stones in his four pockets so that he won't suck any of them twice before sucking all the others?), but also by Molloy's comments about his own thinking. The diarrhetic flow of Molloy's prose includes a kind of parenthetical

74. *Watt* (New York, 1959), p. 199.
75. René Descartes, *Œuvres et lettres*, ed. André Bridoux (Paris, 1953), p. 138.

irony absent from *Watt*. The essentially aimless and uncon-
vinced nature of his chatter is emphasized by all the sentences
beginning with "And" (as if words could do nothing but accu-
mulate), and, most effectively, by his casual but sharp sarcasm.
Molloy handles words he happens to say like some comically
disgusting foreign matter he watches passing through his mind.
From a window in Lousse's house, Molloy sees a full moon;
but he thinks he remembers that just "the night before, or the
night before that, yes, more likely," the moon had been a mere
"shaving," and that a little while after its appearance to him, he
had decided to visit his mother.

> And if I failed to mention this detail in its proper place, it is
> because you cannot mention everything in its proper place, you
> must choose, between the things not worth mentioning and
> those even less so. For if you set out to mention everything you
> would never be done, and that's what counts, to be done, to
> have done. Oh I know, even when you mention only a few of
> the things there are, you do not get done either, I know, I know.
> But it's a change of muck. And if all muck is the same muck that
> doesn't matter, it's good to have a change of muck, to move from
> one heap to another a little further on, from time to time, flut-
> tering you might say, like a butterfly, as if you were ephemeral.
> And if you are wrong, and you are wrong, I mean when you
> record circumstances better left unspoken, and leave unspoken
> others, rightly, if you like, but how shall I say, for no good
> reason, yes, rightly, but for no good reason, as for example that
> new moon, it is often in good faith, excellent faith. (41; 61)

This distance which Molloy mockingly keeps from his own
speech raises the possibility of a Molloy distinct from his speech.
First of all, what connection is there between the account of
Molloy's adventures which we are reading and those adventures
as they really happened? Molloy warns us that the "limpid
language" he now uses expresses nothing more than his

> merely complying with the convention that demands that you
> either lie or hold your peace. For what really happened was

quite different. And I did not say, Yet a little while, at the rate things are going, etc., but that resembled perhaps what I would have said, if I had been able. In reality I said nothing at all, but I heard a murmur, something gone wrong with the silence [quelque chose de changé dans le silence] and I pricked up my ears, like an animal I imagine, which gives a start and pretends to be dead. And then sometimes there arose within me, confusedly, a kind of consciousness, which I express by saying, I said, etc., or, Don't do it Molloy, or, Is that your mother's name? said the sergeant, I quote from memory. (87-88; 134-35)

What "kind of consciousness," exactly? The trilogy and *Comment c'est* are Beckett's efforts to approach that reality of consciousness about which language lies, to torture words out of their "limpidity" and significance so that they may let us hear just "how it was" in the silence. The furiously conscientious chroniclers who are Beckett's narrators all insist that they live "far from words," as Molloy says (31; 45). Ignorant of "the meaning of being," Molloy can only walk among the "ruins" of his self, "a place with neither plans nor bounds and of which I understand nothing, not even of what it is made, still less into what. And the thing in ruins. I don't know what it is, what is was, nor whether it is not less a question of ruins than the indestructible chaos of timeless things, if that is the right expression" (39-40; 58).

Molloy tells the stories he doesn't believe in and uses a language which doesn't express anything with comparative nonchalance. Anxious only to "finish dying" (7; 7), he nonetheless accepts, with docile if ironic obedience, the mysterious punishment of having to write about a past made of silence and an inexpressible self. Furthermore, he has just enough purposeful behavior, and just enough mobility, to be mainly preoccupied with telling a story; compared with *Malone meurt* and *L'Innommable, Molloy* is an action-packed narrative. "And truly it little matters," Molloy claims, "what I say, this, this or that or any other thing" (31–32; 46), but that doesn't prevent him from telling a fairly stable story about himself and the way things happened. The doubts about the very possibility of telling a story will be more fully dramatized by protagonists who either don't remember or don't believe in their pasts, and who are therefore more "free" to consider the distance between what they say and what they are.

This mysterious distance—unlocatable, unbridgeable—becomes a more explicit obsession in *Malone meurt*. Malone has nothing to do but wait in bed for the death whose imminence he announces in the novel's first sentence: "I shall soon be quite dead at last in spite of all." ("Je serai quand même bientôt tout à fait mort enfin.") He is finally being "repaid" for having lived by being allowed to die. The only important thing now is to stay quiet, to "be natural at last," to "die tepid, without enthusiasm." Malone decides to pass the time telling stories, "calm" stories with "no ugliness or beauty or fever," stories "almost lifeless, like the teller." But the confusions and discouragements to come—which will of course make the interest of the book—are prefigured by Malone's excessive and already useless caution on the first pages. He recognizes several dangers which threaten to break his calm: the tendency to ask questions, the temptation to think ("If I start trying to think again I shall make a mess of my decease"), his uncertainty about the number of stories to tell, his wondering whether he should begin or end with the inventory of his possessions. No matter; with the sense of "making a great mistake," Malone nonetheless decides to divide his time into five ("into five what?"): "Present state, three stories, inventory, there" (with "an occasional interlude"). This mixture of fear, fussiness, weak self-assurance, and unconvincing good faith gives to the beginning of *Malone meurt* its highly original comic tension. Beckett has managed to announce an investigation into the reality and possibility of literary play entirely in terms of Malone's anxious efforts to settle calmly on the right schedule for his last days or weeks. Something is already pulling Malone away from his stories. "It is playtime now. I find it hard to get used to that idea. The old fog calls" (179–82; 7–14). Will Malone be able to play? And what is the "fog" which draws speech back into silence, which turns all stories— all literature—into ruins?

"I never knew how to play, until now," Malone writes at the beginning. He often tried, "but it was not long before I found myself alone, in the dark. That is why I gave up trying to play and took to myself for ever shapelessness and speechlessness, incurious wondering, darkness, long stumbling with outstretched arms, hiding. Such is the earnestness [le sérieux] from which, for nearly a century now, I have never been able to depart" (180; 9–10). Malone's disease of "earnestness" (a weak word to designate his yearning for nothingness) will return to plague him as he attempts to tell calm stories clearly. He stops in the middle of anecdotes out of boredom and disgust, he abruptly changes the names and lives of the characters he invents, and he moves back and forth between his stories and thoughts about himself. In a sense, his failure is Beckett's success. The richness of this part of the trilogy consists in its multiple but continuously suspended points of interest. Our expectations of drama are teased and disappointed by the incompleteness and triviality of the anecdotes; even the barest sense of psychological consistency is destroyed by Sapo's sudden transformation into Macmann; and the frequent returns to Malone in bed add to our reading of the stories he tells a suspenseful curiosity about how close the narrator is to death. It is therefore obviously not enough to say that *Malone meurt* is a novel which carries out its own destruction. Beckett, the plotter of that destruction, has weaved so many self-negating processes into a single narrative web that the very interferences among them create a complexity of drama and suspense which, for the reader, works against the pull toward fog, disappearance, total failure, and the silence of death. It is nonetheless true that for Malone the pleasure of dying is almost spoiled by his inability to keep

out of the fog long enough for the night to come. What destroys
the resolution of the early pages is Malone's inability to talk
about anything but himself (to be able to do that would be
"to play"), at the same time that his stories lose their "calm"
by becoming mirrors for the agitated "fog" of his own being.

A curious vindication of storytelling takes place in *Malone
meurt*. It is as if Beckett were trapped into an implicit recognition of the *possibility* of storytelling. *L'Innommable* could be
imagined as a furious revenge against Malone's demonstration
of imagination as adequate to being. Malone begins with a half-
hearted attempt to tell the story of the young Sapo, remarking
that "nothing is less like me than this patient, reasonable child,
struggling all alone for years to shed a little light upon himself,
avid of the least gleam, a stranger to the joys of darkness" (193;
34). But Malone's storytelling will become both interesting and
urgently necessary only when Sapo is transformed into Macmann, a character much closer to Malone himself. The account
of Macmann's stay at the asylum at the end of the novel is one
of Beckett's most extraordinary performances. The range of invention is staggering: from Moll and Macmann's hilariously
disgusting love affair to Macmann's nightmarish hallucinations
when he tries to escape from the asylum, and to the inmates'
outing with the philanthropic Lady Pedal and Lemuel's casual
slaughter of the sailors and Lady Pedal at the end.

Most important, this imaginative virtuosity spectacularly confirms the self-expressiveness of verbal play. For the wildness of
the Macmann episode dramatizes the death agony of Malone.
The obscene blasphemies, the confused perceptions, the murders, and the final vision of the inmates' "grey bodies" on the
bay ("Silent, dim, perhaps clinging to one another, their heads
buried in their cloaks, they lie together in a heap, in the night")
trace Malone's last moments alive in bed. Sequestration and annihilation: the two main themes of Macmann's life at the asylum bring us back to the imprisoned Malone waiting for death.
The identification is explicit in the last lines Malone writes.

Lemuel "raises his hatchet" again, but ". . . he will not hit anyone any more . . . ," and the hatchet becomes the stick and the pencil with which Malone will never touch anything any more (287–88; 216–17). Lemuel's murderous violence suggests the drunken suicidal elation of Malone's last moments, and the connections between hatchet, stick, and pencil define this *pre-mortem* literature as the symbolic murder of symbolic selves. To tell stories is to draw things into the self, as Malone uses his stick to draw things close to his bed. For Malone, it is also the ambiguous act of creating and destroying figures who are never exactly the self but who represent it sufficiently to become the objects of self-destroying impulses. Unwilling to talk about himself and unable not to, having opposed the play of telling stories to the fog of being, Malone ends with an anecdote which embodies his profound antipathy to anecdote at the same time that it appears to give shape and speech to the shapeless and speechless fog.

Behind the intermittent eloquence of Malone's style lies a tolerance of language perhaps made possible by his certainty that he will soon die. "There is no use indicting words, they are no shoddier than what they peddle [Ils ne sont pas plus creux que ce qu'ils charrient]" (195; 37). The successful act of expression which is Macmann's story depends on a double failure: the inability to play calmly with stories alien to the self, and the failure to drop the story for the sake of a return to "the rapture of vertigo, the letting go, the fall, the gulf, the relapse to darkness, to nothingness, to earnestness, to home." Confident of dying, Malone lets himself be seduced into expression. But if the richness of what he says gives the lie to the impossibility of expression, the mad and murderous universe evoked does locate the inspiration for Malone's most sustained story in a wish to multilate and end what he invents. "Of myself I could never tell, any more than live or tell of others" (195; 37–38). However contested this proposition may be by the work in which it occurs, it is also somewhat confirmed by Malone's

half-hearted effort to tell boring stories at the beginning of the
novel, and by that promise of vertigo and finally annihilation
(both for himself and for his characters) which seems to support
Malone in the chronicle of Macmann. But *why* is Malone unable "to tell of himself" ("se raconter") and why, as a result,
does he take up his pencil only to plot movements toward the
moment when he will have to let it go?

The answer is suggested in the passage from which I have
been quoting in the last paragraph. There Malone speaks—with
an ambiguity made greater by the differences between the
French and English texts—of someone else, or perhaps of two
other "people." In his returns "home"—"to darkness, to nothingness"—he has been welcomed by someone "waiting for me
always, who needed me and whom I needed, who took me in
his arms and told me to stay with him always." What relation
exists between Malone and this inhabitant of darkness? The
next sentence in French is simply: "Voilà que je commence à
m'exalter," while the English version teases us with: "There I
am forgetting myself again." And is Malone still alluding to this
mysterious figure when he goes on to evoke "another, far beneath me and whom I try to envy, of whose crass adventures
[les plates aventures] I can now tell at last, I don't know how"?
The suggestion of a self "beneath" the self is absent in French,
where Malone says of this other presence only that he "ne me
vaut pas" (and who may be just Malone projected into inaccurate stories). Finally, after writing that he has never been
able to tell of himself or of others, Malone raises a possibility
he hardly dares to believe in. "To show myself now, on the
point of vanishing, at the same time as the stranger, and by
the same grace, that would be no ordinary last straw." The
"stranger" may be someone different from Malone, but he may
also be a Malone deeper than Malone, "beneath" him, to whom
he returns as to a familar home after his useless attempts to tell
of others and of a less essential self. "What an end," Malone

ambiguously writes when he thinks of a simultaneous death for all these personae, or for the "real" self and its personae: "Then live, long enough to feel, behind my closed eyes, other eyes close" (195; 38).

It is of course difficult to say to whom these other eyes belong. Are they those of a self beyond (or prior to) all definition and expression, or of an impersonal presence which nonetheless inhabits the depths of personality, or perhaps of some jealous, uncreated divinity "who can neither live nor suffer the sight of others living"? (195; 37) *Malone meurt* provides no answers to these questions, but in the tensions it sets up between Malone's will to play and his inability to play, and between his contention that he cannot talk of himself or of others and the proof he offers of finding himself—and his death—through talking of others, this second work in the trilogy plunges us into that "impenetrable tangle of relationships between the essential Self and the apparent self" which Richard D. Coe defines as the "central theme of Beckett's philosophy." [76] The distinctive feature of *L'Innommable* is that there is no "tangle" between the two, but only a continuously reiterated chasm. "I, say I. Unbelieving," mutters the Unnamable at the start of his anonymous monologue. "I seem to speak, it is not I, about me, it is not about me" (291; 7–8). *L'Innommable* is the Beckett protagonist's desperate attempt to stop talking, to "overcome . . . the fatal leaning toward expressiveness [surmonter . . . le funeste penchant à l'expression]" (390; 212), and to arrive at a silence different from the pauses between words, at "the real silence, . . . that of the drowned," where the self perhaps merely *is,* but where being seems equivalent to nonbeing (408; 248–49).

Malone in bed deliberately transforms Sapo into Macmann. The Unnamable doesn't know where he is, but he has always been there ("my appearances elsewhere having been put in by other parties" [293; 12]). And among the various names and images in the narrative (Mahood and Worm; the gigantic crea-

76. *Beckett* (Edinburgh and London, 1964), p. 102.

ture unrolled around the earth, the thing planted in a jar near
a city's slaughterhouses, the round ball that may "snowball" into
a man), there are not metamorphoses but rather the aimless wandering of a voice which occasionally evokes a shape or a name
but never associates the two long enough to establish an identity.
Macmann and Sapo have consistent, almost realistic personalities
compared to Mahood and Worm. The Unnamable even shifts
from "he" to "I" in the middle of a description, or from "I" to
"he." The designations of person and the distinction between
singular and plural are the farces of an arbitrary grammar:
". . . no sense in bickering about pronouns and other parts of
blather. The subject doesn't matter, there is none" (360; 150).
Other Beckett figures—Mercier and Camier, Murphy, Molloy,
and Malone—seem to be circulating around the Unnamable,
and the possibility that, like him, they have always been there
retrospectively reduces Molloy's search for his mother and Malone's death to the Unnamable's fictions. The long voyage from
Mercier and Camier to the Unnamable has been an effort to
end all voyages, to be finally in a place one cannot go to: "The
essential is never to arrive anywhere, never to be anywhere,
neither where Mahood is, nor where Worm is, nor where I am,
it little matters thanks to what dispensation" (338; 105).

In this process of "retrenchment," as Ruby Cohn has aptly
called it,[77] anecdote, character, movement, desire, and intelligence have been gradually reduced in the hope that they can at
last be dispensed with completely. The Unnamable throws off
all the personae which, he claims, have been foisted on him by
"masters" who want him to confuse himself with his roles. He
wonders if now he will be able to express only himself, "to be a
little as I always was and never could be" (396; 225). The setting
of L'Innommable may be "the place where one finishes vanishing" ["l'endroit où l'on finit de se dissiper"] (293; 11), and the
image of someone who is nothing more than a "big talking ball"

77. *Samuel Beckett: The Comic Gamut* (New Brunswick, New Jersey,
1962), p. 7.

expresses the anguished need of the Beckett hero to get rid of all the things that "stick out" ("tout ce qui dépasse est tombé . . . ," says the Unnamable [305; 36–37]), from some mysterious core of being—everything from bodily protuberances to fictional characters and stories and, finally, verbal inventiveness or expression itself.

The Unnamable thus "refers" us to a self with which we are not to confuse either his characters or even what he himself says. If we take the dream of this self seriously in Beckett, we should perhaps do no more than repeat that it is indeed unnamable, indescribable. But we can draw a circle around that invisible point by tracing the possible motivations and the consequences of the search itself. A writer's experience of the power and apparent expressiveness of language may lead him to an intuition of and an interest in a reality which language cannot express, from which language in fact isolates him. Novelistic invention could be thought of as self-dispersion rather than as self-expression, as a loss or waste of energy which writers may alternately refuse and consent to. The writer's answer to the optimism of Descartes's *cogito* might be imagined as: "I invent, therefore I am not." Beckett's novels dramatize this radical doubt about the relation between imaginative language and the self: where am I in the world I am creating? In spite of his call for an inexpressive, autonomous art, Beckett's work is perhaps motivated by a deeper fantasy of literature as the passive receptacle for a self entirely independent of literary inventiveness. For what the Unnamable hates in expression is that it is *not* expression, but, inevitably, invention. More exactly, every expression is an invention. It violates the purity of being with the accidents of personality, language, and time.[78]

To be *anything* is not to be. The Beckett "ideal" seems to me more mysteriously abstract than the comparatively intelligible

78. I first expressed the ideas in this paragraph and in the preceding one in "No Exit for Beckett," *Partisan Review*, XXXIII (Spring 1966), 261–67.

disappearance of the self into the universe which Molloy occasionally experiences.[79] If the ultimate Beckett "home" contains
the entire universe, it is only in the sense that the inhabitant of
that home has not yet lost the possibility of being everything and
everywhere by being born into a particular body and a particular place in the universe. The Beckett hero—the one we never
see—is unborn. Beckett's difficult progress toward that realization can be measured by the difference between the still rather
vague notion of a self merely "improved out of all knowledge"
in *Murphy*,[80] and the brilliantly simple device of making the
Unnamable the victim of a conspiracy to force him just to live.
His persecutors want him to be a man, to be born. They give him
roles to play (which nicely accounts for the Beckett *œuvre*), but
he has resisted being identified with them (which dismisses the
Beckett *œuvre*). *L'Innommable* is Beckett's allusion to the absence behind his personae and the voices which speak through
them. It is his most radical experiment—short of complete silence
—in drawing his creation back into its uncreated source. An
absurd, suicidal adventure, the very authenticity of which is undoubtedly guaranteed by Beckett's frank recognition that the
inviolate, essential self "lives" only in the refusal to be, is equivalent to the death of the self.

Maurice Blanchot, whose *Thomas l'Obscur* records an analogous retreat, has called the Unnamable "a being without being
. . . the empty place where the idleness of an empty speech
talks, a place more or less successfully covered over by a porous
and dying *I*." For Blanchot, that "place," which is the Beckett
hero's "home," is also the "home" of literature: *L'Innommable*
is "the pure approach to the moment from which all books come,
to that original point where the work probably loses itself." [81]

79. See *Molloy*, 49; 73. The Unnamable refers to a similar absorption
in things (386; 204).
80. (New York, 1957), p. 105. First published in 1938.
81. "'Où maintenant? Qui maintenant?'," *Le Livre à venir* (Paris,
1959), pp. 259–60.

Beckett's work thus moves toward a self without personality and a literature without books. It seems hardly necessary to say that the failure to reach such goals is what allows them to be pursued. The metaphysical pathos of Beckett's work is that it exists. It has, however, existed by tending more and more to destroy itself. The voice which speaks in *L'Innommable*, a voice "not listening to itself but to the silence that it breaks" (307; 40), moves toward a meaningless verbal flow in which the silence can perhaps be heard. But the Unnamable also knows that he will go on, that he has to go on, tortured by the distance between his words and "how it is," a distance which, incidentally, the resurgent structure and inventiveness of *Comment c'est* (1961) simply confirm as unbridgeable. Moran had already spoken of all language as an "écart de langage," which in English becomes "an excess of language" (116; 179). Language is always in excess of being, and the end (goal and disappearance) which is silence is perhaps best approximated by a stupefyingly excessive language, by the long sentences in the second half of *L'Innommable*, sentences filled with commas separating and isolating and equalizing inexhaustible verbal signs or gasps which finally reduce the story, the language, and the mind of the narrator to an insignificant, rambling murmur.

Now the Beckett protagonists constantly complain of being forced to write and to speak. Life and language are punishments —although life itself seems to be the crime, so that they are entrapped in a sadistically imposed penance which increases their guilt. All Beckett's commentators have responded to the anguished religious sensibility in his work. Beginning with the easy game of reading *Godot* in the light of the broad hint which the title gives us and which the play neither confirms nor denies, we can hardly miss the combination of angry, mocking blasphemy and need without hope which characterizes Beckett's Job-like relation to God and his mystified fascination with the Crucifixion. God comes into existence in Beckett's world very much as He comes to exist in Descartes's world. The Cartesian *cogito* is naturally analyzed in the *Discours de la méthode* as a process of rational deduction, but it appears to have been experienced as an intuition which simultaneously proves human existence and divine existence. The latter is contained in the certainty of the former, and one could condense the rational sequence of Part IV of the *Discours* into the equation: I doubt = God exists. The Beckett divinity is also contained in the existence of the Beckett protagonist, and the protagonist's existence is also confirmed by a kind of "doubt" or "thought." But the Cartesian intuition is of course parodied: "doubt" is hopeless misery, and, instead of a good and perfect God being guaranteed by the very imperfection of doubt from which man suffers, Beckett's characters invoke a sadistic demon also "guaranteed," but this time by the impenetrable enigma of man's continuing to live an unlivable life. "Imperfection," far from certifying a perfect God from Whom the notion of perfection must proceed, more convincingly implies a divinity whose malevolent existence is needed to explain an aberration as monstrous as life.

"I say it as I hear it," Bom reminds us over and over again in *Comment c'est*. Life and the novel are *dictated*. The Unnamable, whose only real speech would be silence, tells us that he has no voice but must speak, ". . . that is all I know, it's round that I must revolve, of that I must speak, with this voice that is not mine, but can only be mine, since there is no one but me, or if there are others, to whom it might belong, they have never come near me, I won't delay just now to make this clear [ils ne viennent pas jusqu'à moi, je n'en dirai pas davantage, je ne serai pas plus clair]" (307; 40). And a few pages further on: "Having nothing to say, no words but the words of others, I have to speak" (314; 55). He *is*, literally, *nothing* but words: ". . . I'm in words, made of words, others' words, what others . . ." (386; 204). The impossibility of any speech adequate to being is dramatically rendered in *L'Innommable* by the physical impossibility of speech. In *Molloy* and *Malone meurt*, Beckett makes almost realistic provisions for the plausibility of his narrative by making

Molloy, Moran, and Malone writers. But how can a round ball speak? How can an armless creature write? No attempt is made to answer these questions, just as no attempt is made to explain how the Beckett protagonist can complain of using the words of others when the complaint itself, has, presumably, to be made in the words of others.

These are perhaps mysteries of divine machination, but we could also formulate them in terms of the impossible relation Beckett has established between the writer and his creation. The voice forcing Molloy, Moran, Malone, and the Unnamable to speak is, of course, Beckett's voice. And he has brilliantly expressed the enigma of identity in fiction (where am I in the world I am creating?) by having his characters protest, for and against him, that their reality is not to be confused with his. All words are naturally the words of others, since others use the same language as we do, and since language itself obviously expresses or proceeds from no single human subject. To this general sense of the impersonality of language, Beckett adds the much more particular drama of alienation and hostility between himself and his fictional world. The Beckett heroes, by refusing to be identified with the imagination they must "carry" in their words, enact in reverse the writer's rebellion against being confused with the creatures of his imagination. The trilogy's protagonists are the vehicles not simply of language, but more especially of Beckett's language. Thus the words we read belong to someone outside the novel, but they tell the story of someone in the novel who claims that his story cannot be told. The impenetrable divinity is Beckett, who will only talk *about* Malone and the Unnamable; but Malone and the Unnamable will allow themselves to be made to talk about themselves only if they can duplicate, with respect to their own creations, their author's implicit disclaimer with respect to them.

A terror at being identified, a despair because identification is impossible: this is the profound motivation which subjects Beckett's extraordinary language to a violent rejection of language. Beckett and his characters will perhaps go on because, as they say, they have to go on, and they perhaps have to go on simply as an alternative to the ecstasy and horror of drawing in their lips, as Winnie says in *Happy Days*, and reaching the absolute expressiveness of nonexpression. But they have been going on less and less in recent years, and while it is both right and too easy to say that Beckett has already given us more than any other living writer, we must also take his suicidal literature seriously enough to be willing to define our own participation in its longings for annihilation.

CONCLUSION

If Beckett is a suitable conclusion to this study of fiction, it is in part because *L'Innommable* would in fact be the conclusion, the end of all fiction. Beckett is our most extreme example of what I have called a centripetal movement in novelistic invention. Whereas Balzac both struggles to move away from a paralyzing center of being and also dramatizes a coherent psychological definition of that center, Beckett's work is an attempt to approach a center of being which all definition violates. It does, of course, seem a very long way from the heavily populated, active, and confidently articulated worlds of Balzac and Dickens to the senseless "plof" and "quaqua" of *L'Innommable* and *Comment c'est*. But Beckett's Worm, as we have had occasion to see, has been in the apple for some time. We recognize in the Unnamable's exasperation with the inaccuracy of everything he says the ultimate consequence of Flaubert's chimerical realism. There is something before or behind language and the novel; and the novelist's torture is that it is his use of language in order to write novels which nurtures his dream of a reality from which the novel is, by definition, a departure. We have seen the threat of imaginative paralysis even in Stendhal, although there the terms in which the threat is posed are less specifically literary. Politics provides the drama without which there would be no story in Stendhal, but it interrupts a paradise of play (in Madame de Rênal's garden, in the Farnese tower) which language could never describe adequately. Stendhal saves the goal of his fiction by his own attention to what destroys his heroes' dream but creates the novelistic milieu in which The Happy Few can express their nostalgia for the absent happiness of love.

For Stendhal, language violates passion; for Flaubert, it never gives "the exact measure of [our] needs, [our] concepts, or [our] sorrows";[82] for Beckett, it is always the words of others, never those of the self. A sense of language as inexpressive of anything distinct from itself brings us to that promise of silence which threatens the printed pages of modern literature since Flaubert, *or* it can lead to an interest in the very phenomenon of an inexpressive system of communication. If language is not merely the translator of reality, what are the laws which determine its organization? There is, in contemporary thought, a curious enthusiasm about the impersonality and autonomy of language. A new scientism (inspired by trends in linguistics and anthropology) is seeking laws and objective structures in ordinary language, in literary forms, in the human unconscious, and the implication of this search seems to be that once we have found the laws, we will have a sufficient knowledge of the forces which govern us to dispense entirely with the obsolete notions of the individual and of his particular psychology. We never make choices; we are *chosen through.*

It would be useless and absurd to warn against such tendencies; if they continue to interest the most interesting minds, we will probably live in a culture whose fundamental assumptions have been shaped by this strange idolatry of the predictable, the mechanical, the nonhuman. We should, however, be willing

82. *Madame Bovary*, edited with a substantially new translation by Paul de Man, based on the version by Eleanor Marx Aveling (New York, 1965), p. 138. *Madame Bovary*, in *Œuvres*, ed. A. Thibaudet and R. Dumesnil, 2 vols. (Paris, 1951–52), I, 500.

to see the tensions and ambivalence in writers who have helped
to inspire the current thrill about impersonal structures. The
disappearance of the self in "the words of others" is, for Flaubert
and Beckett, the horror from which they would retreat into silence. They believe in a reality prior to the "traces" of reality
made by language, which is to say that they aspire to be guilty of
that mimetic art so ferociously criticized today. Unable to believe
that a viable existence can be successfully forged from words
which can obviously never correspond exactly to a preexistent
reality or inner essence, they would punish language for its inexpressiveness by beating it into insignificance. In his deep re-
sentment of language, Beckett has striven to entrust less and less
of what has been a powerfully individual talent and personality
to the care and accursed inventiveness of words. His illusion of
a self outside time has brought him to a willful ontological miser-
liness, to a retreat from life and literature, that is, from the uncertain futures to which time and language subject both the self
and books. Flaubert is now most fashionable for wanting to
write books about nothing, as Beckett is for bringing us close "to
that original point where the work probably loses itself." But *they*
at least are willing to accept the nihilistic implications of such
ambitions (or maledictions), and, without being sentimental
about their careers, we can say that, like B. at the end of the
dialogue on Masson, they "exit weeping" from a world in which
they can conceive of language as expressing nothing more than
its own capacity for going on unproductively. The extraordinary
achievement of our contemporary enthusiasts for impersonal
media, for impersonal mental and linguistic structures, is the
cheer with which they have set out to program a kind of intem-
poral future, one which would be merely the docile enactment
of the laws which inhabit us.

Because such enterprises scorn history, they are of course reactionary enterprises. The attempt to join the new scientism to
movements of social revolution—I am thinking especially of the

claims made by the self-confident, ultrafashionable group of the review *Tel Quel*—is, at best, the expression of an uneasy conscience about the consequences of an effort to diagram human impotence. Superficially, this may seem a very unjust way to describe the efforts of those who are today proclaiming the death of man, of philosophical dualisms, or of book-oriented cultures. Indeed, a kind of revolutionary disposition is a common denominator in, say, the works of Marshall McLuhan, Michel Foucault, and Jacques Derrida. But it seems to me that all these enterprises, insofar as they demonstrate the limitations which our instruments of expression impose on efforts of self-renewal and social renewal, are particularly congenial to political conservatism, as well as to arguments for the social irrelevance of literature.

We can already see this in Flaubert. Given his sense of the impersonal autonomy of language, it seems only natural that he should view political behavior with the cynicism we find in *L'Education sentimentale*. In Platonic fashion, Flaubert identified the (inaccessible) true or the real with the good. Unable, as a result, to conceive of fictions as producing anything worth living by, he took the logical step of emphasizing only what might be discredited in the intentions behind political rhetoric. In *L'Education sentimentale*, we see the events of 1848 only through the envy and bitterness of men who haven't made it. No one doctrine, given the nature of *all* expression, contains more truth than any other doctrine; therefore, what is left except to expose the shady motives which "explain" the espousal of all doctrines? If the human use of language is incapable of coercing language into the shapes of new, unpredictable human projects, then we can perhaps only use the immutable structures of language to obscure a permanent wish to deceive and to dominate. The contemporary emphasis on language's resources of indirection—for example, in Roland Barthes's study of all the hidden messages in advertisements,[83] in Gérard Genette's study of Proust

83. See *Système de la mode* (Paris, 1967).

entirely in terms of the opportunities for lying which the science of rhetoric classifies[84]—does indeed suggest not the disappearance of man, but a return to a theory of human nature more frankly exposed in the *Maximes* of La Rochefoucauld.

In his daily struggles with language, Flaubert faced the threat of paralysis and of silence which was the logic both of his demand for truth and of his sense that it could never be expressed. But to drop his mystique of an inexpressible reality, and simply to keep his lack of faith in the power of impersonal structures to change the self or society, provide a no less convenient support for a narrow traditionalism in both art and politics. It is one thing to free ourselves from debilitating fictions about realities which somehow precede expression and which language would do nothing more than obediently embody. But if we replace the hypothesis of unembodied realities with the notion of timeless laws of language and structures of thought, are we any less enslaved to *given* realities which precede all particular experience? How necessary are *any* systems of supposed truths and realities for the perception and profitable use of form in our experience? As an alternative to Flaubert's and Beckett's *anguish* about the impersonal, I find little to prefer in the cheerful nihilism of a wish to codify and live by the laws inherent to the impersonal structures of myth, of media, of language. We have long been aware of the important role these structures play in our lives; no life, in or out of literature, has yet been shown to be so impoverished, so denuded of particularity (that is, of personality) as to be entirely determined by them.

Impersonality is a writer's stock-in-trade; it provides his daily challenge, it can be an escape for him, it can be his defeat. To write is to test the possibility of self in materials alien to the self: in a language the writer has not invented, in imaginary lives which never exactly represent "how it is" in his own life, in a book which will "stand for" him far from his own body. And

84. In "Proust et le langage indirect," *Figures II,* in Collection Tel Quel (Paris, 1969).

even the self, as we have more especially seen, can be reduced to themes and images which, by their narrow, repetitious nature, can make of personality an almost lifeless structure of predictable fantasies. Those *given* forms which limit us can obviously come from an individual history (can perhaps even be born and nurtured in an individual work of art), as well as from the cultural myths we are steeped in or the language we more or less helplessly inherit. What I have been most anxious to consider is how writers we admire have experimented with ways of breaking away from such self-limiting and even self-denying structures. Among the novelists I have discussed, Proust, Stendhal, and Robbe-Grillet invite us most convincingly to try the risky but nonetheless exhilarating radicalism of a constant reinvention of the self and the world. There are no rules for the practice of that radicalism, and the model of Stendhal is not only different from that of Robbe-Grillet, it is also different, in *La Chartreuse de Parme*, from the model of Stendhal himself in *Armance* or *Le Rouge et le noir*. Such a radicalism could, of course, produce anything. But, unlike those revolutionary programs which appeal to supposed laws of language and of history to sanction their own biases, a never forgotten sense of the arbitrary might promote, instead of Flaubert's despair about never "reaching" the real, a continuous revision of fictions always acknowledged as tentative and experimental. A willingness both to entertain and to dismiss anything, based partly on Flaubert's and Beckett's sense of how easily all our inventions can be equalized and therefore trivialized, partly on the more positive experience of how much life each fiction is capable of producing: such a willingness would allow for the wildest creations, but the mixture of fantasy and epistemological skepticism on which it is based also provides a new and attractive argument for the faded, indispensable virtue of tolerance.

INDEX

The following names are mentioned in the text or in the notes. For Balzac, Stendhal, Flaubert, Proust, Camus, Robbe-Grillet, and Beckett, references are given only to sections in which each of these writers is not the principal object of discussion.